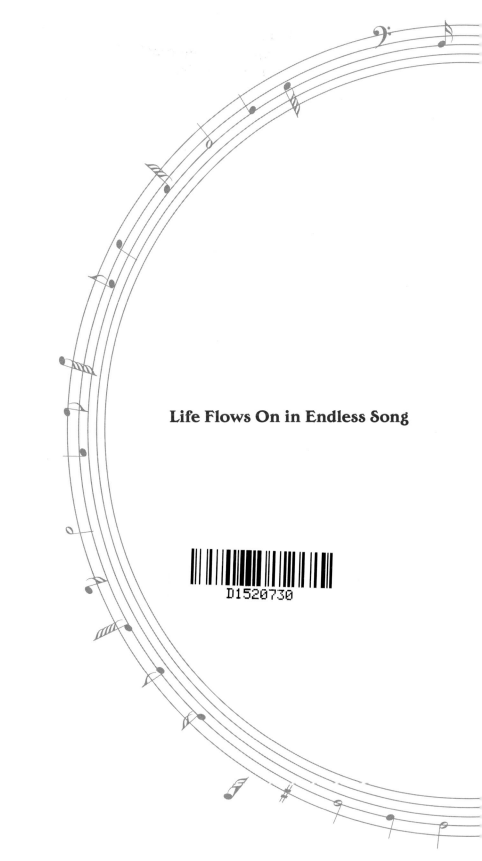

Life Flows On in Endless Song

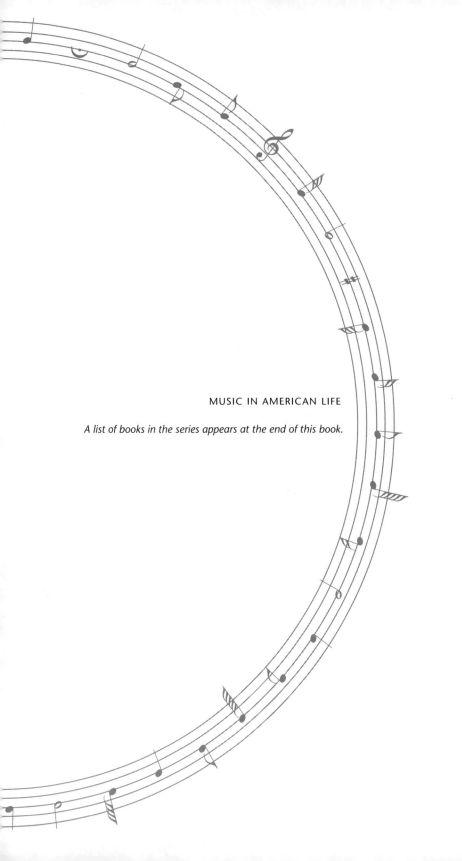

MUSIC IN AMERICAN LIFE

A list of books in the series appears at the end of this book.

Life Flows On
in Endless Song

Folk Songs and American History

Robert V. Wells

UNIVERSITY OF ILLINOIS PRESS

URBANA AND CHICAGO

© 2009 by the Board of Trustees
of the University of Illinois
Manufactured in the United States of America
I 2 3 4 5 C P 5 4 3 2 I
∞ This book is printed on acid-free paper.

Library of Congress Cataloging-in-Publication Data
Wells, Robert V.
Life flows on in endless song: folk songs and
American history / Robert V. Wells.
p.   cm. — (Music in American life)
Includes bibliographical references and index.
ISBN 978-0-252-03455-8 (cloth: alk. paper)
ISBN 978-0-252-07650-3 (pbk.: alk. paper)
1. Folk songs, English—United States—History and criticism.
2. United States—History.
I. Title.
ML3551.W46   2009
782.42162'13009—dc22   2008037939

To The Weavers:
who got me started,
and
To Cathie:
who fixes dinner while I sing.

Contents

Preface

Folk songs have been a conscious and important part of my life for almost half a century. Although I have dim, and possibly fanciful, memories of hearing songs like "Go Tell Aunt Abby" as a small child, my awareness of the genre came while I was in high school. At some point in the late 1950s, my brother, David, came home from college on vacation bearing records by the Weavers and Theodore Bikel, and a cheap guitar. The exact moments and sequence in which they arrived is beyond recall, but the impact has been permanent. A few simple songbooks and a subscription to *Sing Out*, inheriting the old guitar when my brother upgraded to a small-bodied Martin, and then acquiring my own better guitar, and I was on my way, though where I was headed with the music was uncertain. All I knew was that playing and singing, even if only for myself and family, was satisfying in ways I would have found difficult to express at the time. The songs spoke to me, even though the messages were often dimly heard by my young ears and unrecognized by my teenage psyche.

The awakening of my understanding of folk songs occurred on one memorable evening. Throughout high school and college, I acquired songs in an eclectic and unfocused fashion, gradually learning songs that appealed to me both musically and for their lyrics, and for which I could find the chords. While in graduate school, studying the complexities of social history applied to early America, I visited my parents' home one evening and sang "When I'm on My Journey, Don't You Weep after Me." A young woman who was boarding with them heard me and began to cry as I sang. A friend of hers had recently died, so the song spoke directly to her emotional state. It was at that moment that I realized the importance of song in the lives of people and began to pay close attention to the words. The songs mattered!

Not long after I started teaching at Union College in 1969, I was looking through my copy of Alan Lomax's *The Folk Songs of North America in the English Language.* As I read his brief accounts of the songs, I realized I could do a lecture in my course on early American history based on folk songs from before 1800. With forty class periods to fill in ten weeks, it seemed like a nice change of pace and fit well with my efforts to get students to think about sources in different ways. Since I am by training a specialist not only in early America but also in demographic history, the common references in folk songs to love, courtship, marriage, children, migration, and death formed natural, harmonious connections between my teaching and scholarly activities. Despite nervousness far in excess of my normal anxieties as a novice teacher, I managed to get through the class, both pleased and relieved that the students had liked it. Moreover, my colleagues were not only tolerant but actually supportive of this experiment. Soon a folk song class became a staple part of several of my courses, though never more than one per term. At that time, my family was young and growing, leaving little time for me to develop anything more than a single lecture on folk songs.

In 1997, with my children grown and out of the home, I was fortunate to be selected for a yearlong Fulbright professorship in Denmark at Odense University, now the University of Southern Denmark. I took a variety of songbooks along and bought a new and much better guitar there. For the first time in many years, I began to play regularly and learn new songs. Adding to my resources were several collections of folk songbooks the U.S. Embassy in Copenhagen had given the Center for American Studies at Odense University. As the fall term came to an end and my colleagues and I discussed what I would teach in the spring, I knew I would need a course that met once a week for two hours to complete my teaching load. Aware of the extensive resources on American folk songs available at the university and in the city's music library, I suggested, half in jest, a whole course in American folk songs and history. My colleagues welcomed the idea, at least in part because several of the permanent faculty were also interested in folk songs. The course was a great success for me and the class, an eclectic group of Danish students and others from Austria, France, Ireland, Spain, and the United Kingdom, present through European Union exchange programs. On returning to Union College in the fall of 1998, I decided I wanted to try a similar, though slightly expanded, version of the course. I have done so annually since then. This book is the result of both that course and several shorter versions of the course for groups of retirees. My approach has been tested and found effective on audiences of widely varying ages.

Of course, the corpus of folk songs is so great that any course or book linking songs to history is able to offer only a very small selection of songs. My choices here reflect the semi-random accumulation of fifty years of singing and playing, my own more systematic scholarship of folk songs since I started teaching the course, and interests that have grown out of a career-long study of social history as it relates to demographic patterns. One could no doubt write a book linking songs to history with an entirely different selection of songs (though some classics might carry over), organized by alternative themes. Indeed, the often unique categories used by many early song catchers in their publications in the first half of the twentieth century make this clear. But the points would, I trust, be the same: that folk songs must be understood via the context of the past from which they emerged, that they provide additional sources for understanding earlier times, and that songs themselves develop histories as they are transformed consciously and unconsciously by singers who find some merit in them.

My training is as an historian. I know a little about music and perhaps a little more of the techniques of folklore/folk song scholarship. My concern here has been to explore the historical side of the songs as their lyrics connect to wider themes of American social history. I do not trace out nor cite all the known versions of a song, though I do occasionally refer to alternative interpretations of a common topic or story. I have relied throughout on numerous, excellent studies of folk songs, both written and recorded. My intent here is not so much to add to these scholarly traditions but to explain how a social historian/folk singer has come to understand the songs and what they tell us about American history.

I have certainly come to understand the songs I sing and play in a far richer and more nuanced way than when I first struggled with the simple chord changes of "Skip to My Lou" and "Down in the Valley" so many years ago, and I may even play a bit better too. I want to share with any who find the old songs appealing some of what I have learned about what the songs meant in the past and, perhaps, even why they continue to appeal today.

♯ ♯ ♯

A few comments on citations and permissions are in order. Folk song scholarship has a tradition of extensive citations to numerous versions of a song. I have chosen to cite one or two easily accessible sources where a version of a song may be read or heard. I have known and sung many of the songs included here for a number of years. In keeping with the folk process, I have altered lyrics consciously and unconsciously, and combined verses from several sources; so I would be hard-pressed to trace where my particular version comes from. Thus the citations are intended to provide readers with a starting point for finding a full text, but not necessarily the exact one I have quoted. Nevertheless, the references should enable anyone who wants to examine full texts and variants to begin that process.

Many of the songs I have used are in the public domain, but some are still covered by copyright protection. I want to thank the various holders of copyrights who have granted their permission to include longer selections of the works than would be possible under the doctrine of fair use. Copyright recognitions have been included at the points in the text where the songs are mentioned. In some circumstances I was unable to obtain permissions I sought, so I reduced the length of those quotations to meet fair-use standards. I regret not being able to provide the full flavor of the songs as I had initially intended.

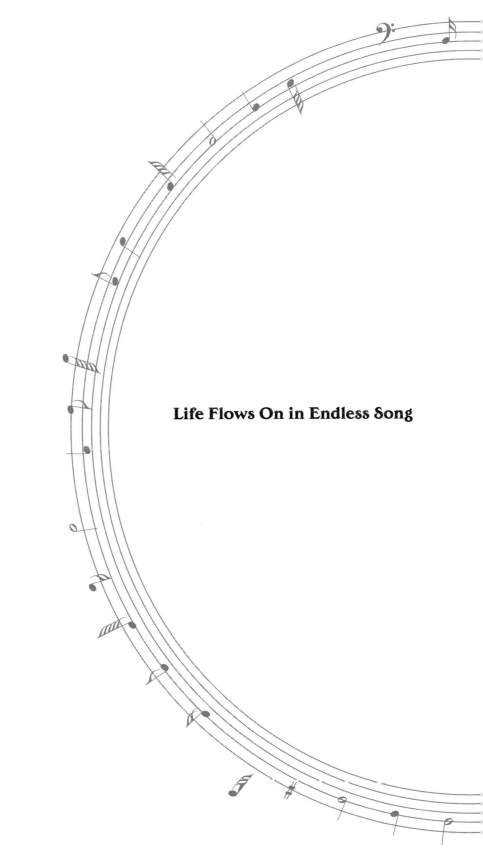

Life Flows On in Endless Song

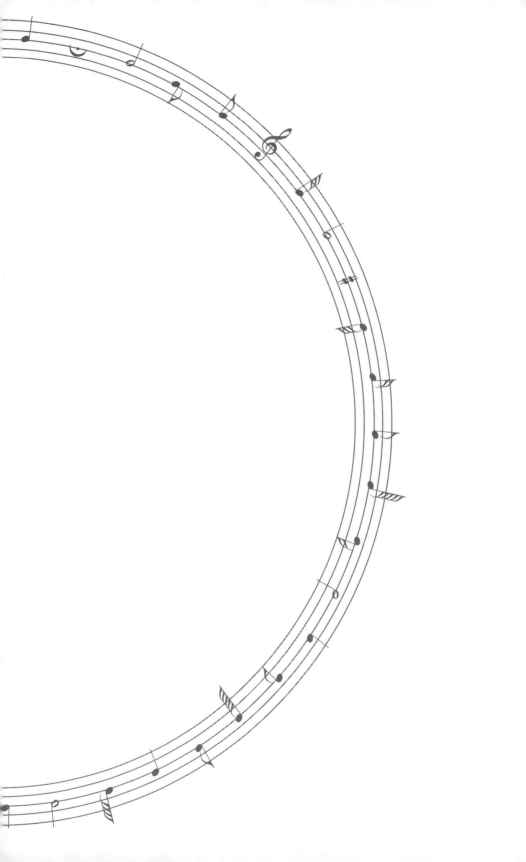

CHAPTER 1

Who Was Tom Dooley?

History and Folk Songs

In 1958 the Kingston Trio sold almost four million copies of "The Ballad of Tom Dooley," starting a revival of popular interest in folk music that lasted until the Beatles shifted attention to rock and roll. As sung by the Trio, "Tom Dooley" presents something of a mystery. In the verses, Tom Dooley admits to taking the life of an unnamed woman—sometime, on a mountain, somewhere. A Greek-like chorus tells him to "hang down" his head and cry because he is bound to die for his sin. Who the woman was and what she did to provoke Dooley's wrath is unexplained. Nor is it entirely clear whether Dooley has been brought to justice by due process or lynch law.

In fact, the history of Tom Dooley or, to be accurate, Tom Dula, is far more complex and engaging than the ballad suggests. It demonstrates the connections between history and folk songs on three levels. To begin, it is possible to learn the actual story and context behind the song—the history of its origins.[1] Tom Dula was a Confederate war veteran who, on returning home to North Carolina after the war, took up with three women, all cousins: Laura Foster, who ended up murdered, Pauline Foster, and the beautiful and dissolute Ann Foster Melton. At some point, Ann Melton discovered she had acquired a venereal disease from Dula, and she was not happy about having to explain this to Mr. Melton. Although a case could be made against Pauline, Tom and Ann decided that Laura was the source of the infection and deserved to die. No hard evidence ever connected Dula to the murder, though he suspiciously crossed the border into Tennessee in

1866, soon after Laura Foster disappeared. She had last been seen in Tom's company. He found work there on the farm of James Grayson; but when Grayson heard Dula was wanted, he arrested Dula, probably illegally, and brought him back to North Carolina. Dula was held in jail for two months before Laura's body was discovered, with knife wounds still visible. Tried and convicted on circumstantial evidence, Dula was hanged in 1868. Many suspected Ann Melton had instigated and aided in the crime, but Tom swore at the end that he did it himself, perhaps to protect her. Local opinion was divided thereafter as to whether Tom was a desperate villain or a lovesick fool.

The ballad also provides evidence for a number of historical trends. With the Civil War just over, many Northerners were willing to think the worst of their defeated foe. Thus it is not surprising that the *New York Herald* reported the crime, trial, and execution in a sensational manner, portraying the Southern hill folk who had sent their sons off to war as "ignorant, poor, and depraved," and Dula as "reckless, demoralized, and a desperado."[2] Although it is uncertain when the first ballad about the murder was composed, the newspaper made no mention of any songs, perhaps because all extant versions reported the story with little moralizing. "The Ballad of Tom Dooley" also belongs to a genre of songs collectively known as murdered-girl ballads. A change in courtship rituals and sexual mores at the end of the eighteenth century placed significant emphasis on young women protecting their virtue from predatory males. Omie (Naomi) Wise, whose fatal mistake was trusting John Lewis's lies in 1808, not far from where Tom killed Laura, may have been one of the first American victims to be used to warn young women via song to be careful, but she was not the last.

Besides the event and its context, the third way "Tom Dooley" connects with history is through the story of the song itself, its evolution and circulation. For years the ballad about Tom Dula was known locally among the mountain folk who were neighbors of Ann, Laura, and Tom. Although G. B. Grayson, a descendant of the Grayson who arrested Dula, recorded the ballad in the 1920s, the Kingston Trio version came from one collected by Frank Warner from Frank Proffitt in 1938. Proffitt's grandmother had known Tom and Laura, and he recalled that his earliest memory was hearing his father play "Tom Dooley" on a homemade banjo as meat was frying for breakfast.[3] Doc Watson, whose grandmother attended Ann Melton on her deathbed, also recorded the song, though his version reflects more of the complexities of the story, not only naming Laura as victim, but also accusing Dula of digging her grave and, after rolling her into it, "tromping the cold clay with

[his] feet." In Watson's version, Dula protests he would not harm a hair "on poor little Laurie's head," reflecting the speculation that Tom was covering up for Ann's murderous inclinations.

♯ ♯ ♯

Over the years, the value of folk songs in providing access to and a different perspective on the past has been recognized by scholars, collectors, and performers. Robert Cantwell argues that the appeal of "Tom Dooley" in the late 1950s was that "it carried the listener's imagination away from high school . . . into another world." That world was attractive because it was "conservative, or, more precisely, restorative . . . picking up the threads of a forgotten legacy to reweave them into history." According to Cantwell, the 1950s folk revival was "a moment of transformation . . . across normally impermeable social and cultural barriers" in which "the romantic claim of folk culture" was arrayed "against a centrist, specialist, impersonal technocratic culture."[4] Thus folk songs provided contact with a past, which helped deal with a present and future in which individuals did not matter much.

W. E. B. DuBois may have been one of the first Americans to recognize the value of old songs as windows on the past. In his chapter "The Sorrow Songs" in *The Souls of Black Folk*, DuBois calls the songs of the slaves not only "the sole American music" but also "the singular spiritual heritage of the nation and the greatest gift of the Negro people." DuBois identifies ten "master songs" by which "the slave spoke to the world," though the message was by necessity "veiled and half articulate," and, perhaps most importantly, "distinctly sorrowful," with "eloquent omissions and silences" reflecting "the limitations of allowable thought" and the pain of certain topics. To DuBois, these songs offered "the articulate message of the slave to the world," providing an "unhappy people" the means with which to tell the rest of the world of "death and suffering and unvoiced longing."[5]

Carl Sandburg—biographer, poet, and folk song collector and promoter—proclaimed the value of his 1927 collection of folk songs, *The American Songbag*, as historical sources. In the introduction Sandburg states his "song history of America . . . will accomplish two things. I will give the feel and atmosphere, the layout and lingo, of regions, of breeds of men, of customs and slogans, in a manner and air not given in regular history, to be read and not sung." Moreover, his collection will "help some on the point registered by a Yankee philosopher that there are persons born and reared in this country who culturally have not yet come over from Europe." Never modest about his material, Sandburg sees "a human stir throughout the book with heights and depths to be found in Shakespeare. A wide human procession marches through these pages." And, in a passage that can strike fear in the hearts of undergraduates, Sandburg urges use of the *Songbag* as "collateral material with the study of history and geography," where "students might sing their answers at examination time."[6]

Few have done more to collect and promote American folk songs as "worth preserving" than John Lomax and his son, Alan. To the Lomaxes, folk songs were not just relics of the past to be cherished and displayed like delicate museum pieces, but living, thriving, vital parts of the varied, contentious, dynamic American democracy. In introducing their first collection, *American Ballads and Folk Songs*, the Lomaxes observe, "For all their crudeness, traditional songs are interesting for breathing the mind of the ignorant, and as 'a voice from secret places, silent places and old times long dead.'" The Lomaxes were among the first to actively promote African-American songs, but they recognized that even among white Americans, "a life of isolation, without books or newspapers or telephone or radio, breeds songs and ballads. The gamut of human experience has been portrayed through this unrecorded (at least until recently) literature of the people. These people had no literary conventions to uphold. But they were lonely or sad or glad, and they sought diversion." In the Lomaxes' view, "folk songs, however fragile in thought and rough in phraseology, have won their way to recognition [as literature]," worthy of historical study.[7]

When Alan Lomax published his last great collection, *The Folk Songs of North America in the English Language*, in 1960, he stressed its importance to history. Although the younger Lomax understood American folk songs were "in one aspect, a museum of musical antiques from many lands," he also believed they should be seen as "the mixing and blending of various folk-strains to produce new forms." In a section of the introduction explicitly devoted to "Folk Songs and History," Lomax describes his intention as putting "a choice selection of our folk songs into their historical and social setting so that they tell the story of the people who made and sang them—to compose, in a word, a folk history, or a history of the folk of America." Lomax observes that few folk songs had much to say about national politics, except as they commented on deep-seated economic and social changes. Rather, folk songs, "even the seemingly factual ones, are expressions of feeling . . . outlets for all sorts of unconscious fantasies." Thus "an ideal folk-song study could be a history of popular feeling."[8]

In 1952 Harry Smith issued one of the great documentary collections of the American past with his *Anthology of American Folk Music*.[9] Unlike previous song catchers, who had either taken songs down by hand or recorded them in the field, Smith based his *Anthology* on records made and sold by commercial companies between 1927 and 1932. Smith selected eighty-four songs, ranging from old English ballads to recent blues, and arranged them under the rubrics of "Ballads," "Social Music," and "Songs." The *Anthology* was intended to document both "the rhythmically and verbally specialized musics of groups living in mutual social and cultural isolation," which were rapidly disappearing by the 1950s, and the "historic changes [produced] by making [recordings] easily available to each other." The accompanying booklet includes not only bibliographies and discographies of the songs but also historical context for understanding them. One of the most engaging parts of Smith's descriptions is his attempt to provide newspaper-like headlines for many of the songs. Thus the well-known song "Froggy Went a Courtin'" (number 8 in the *Anthology* as "King Kong Kitchie Kitchie Kime-o") was summarized as "Zoologic Miscegeny Achieved in Mouse Frog Nuptials, Relatives Approve."[10]

In his 1997 book, *Invisible Republic: Bob Dylan's Basement Tapes*, Greil Marcus reviews the uniqueness of the historical vision in Smith's *Anthology*. Although Marcus is primarily interested in Smith's influence on Bob Dylan and other contemporary musicians, he is also convinced that Smith's perspective offered Americans a version of their past they had never before encountered. According to Marcus, the men and women Smith helped speak provided "a national narrative that had never included their kind, they appeared like visitors from another world." Smith presented us with "a confrontation with another culture . . . here, in the United States," in which one could "feel the ground pulled right out from under your feet."[11]

According to Marcus, Bob Dylan understood the different view folk songs offer when he commented, "Folk music is the only music where it isn't simple. It's never been simple. It's weird." Likewise, Marcus quotes Peter van der Merwe's observations on Appalachian music, that "the biggest danger lies in *under*estimating the strangeness of these cultures. It takes an effort of imagination to realize the isolation of their lives, the lack of canned music, the scarcity of professional musicians, the grip of tradition."[12]

Marcus recognizes the value of folk songs as historical documents when he asks us to consider them not as "fragments . . . drawn from a floating pool of thousands of disconnected verses . . . [or] a singer's random assemblage of fragments . . . [but rather as] a heretic's way of saying what never could be said out loud, a mask over a boiling face." If there were to be "a master narrative," it would be constructed out of "hints and gestures," rather than bold assertions of might and right. The *Anthology* meant that "for the first time, people from isolated, scorned, forgotten, and disdained communities and cultures had a chance to speak to each other and to the nation at large. A great uproar of voices that were at once old and new was heard, as happens only occasionally in democratic cultures." This curiously harmonious cacophony of unfamiliar and disconnected voices demanded to be heard for their "pride of knowledge to pass on, which is also a fear for the disappearance of that knowledge and of its proper language, and a step past that fear, a looming up of an imagined America one never dared imagine before."[13]

At the end of his discussion of the *Anthology*, Marcus sums up Smith's view of our past as it is embodied in a mythical place called Smithville.

> What is Smithville? . . . a small town . . . not distinguishable by race . . . the prison population is large, and most are part of it at one time . . . some may escape justice . . . executions take place . . . a lot of murders here . . . both murder and suicide are rituals, acts instantly transformed into legend . . . humor abounds, most of it cruel . . . a constant war between the messengers of god and ghosts and demons, dancers and drinkers. . . . Here is a mystical body of the republic, a kind of public secret . . . a declaration of a weird but clearly recognizable America within the America of the exercise of institutional majoritarian power . . . here everyone calls upon the will and everyone believes in fate. It is a democracy of manners—a democracy, finally, of how people carry themselves, of how they appear in public. . . . The ruling question of public life is not that of the distribution of material goods or the governance of moral affairs, but that of how people plumb their souls and then present their discoveries, their true selves to others.[14]

The bulk of the historical record used to reconstruct our past was produced by and for wealthy and powerful people. In his recent exploration of the life and times of Landon Carter, one of the great planters of Revolutionary Virginia, historian Rhys Isaac laments that he could not balance the stories the master told in his diary with versions from the slaves via "the folksongs that have been the principle [*sic*] way of telling history for those who could write little or not at all."[15] Fortunately, many folk songs have survived to provide "an intimate personal articulation of history."[16] Thus it is possible to listen to the variety of voices that echo throughout the land and to construct our past at least partly from the small, daily successes and failures, joys and sorrows that bring us all to song.

♯ ♯ ♯

But what exactly is a folk song? Opinions on this differ. A useful definition should be broadly, though not mindlessly, inclusive, avoiding extremes of both rigidity and utter lack of standards. At one extreme, folk songs can be defined as anything the folk are singing, though that might include irritating advertising jingles that get stuck in our minds or the most ephemeral productions of Tin Pan Alley. At the other extreme is the insistence that true folk songs must be of anonymous origin, with no identifiable author of the lyrics or composer of the music, and for which a case can be made that the song was a social—that is, collective—production and a reflection of "the people."

For the purposes of this book, folk songs meet four criteria of differing specificity. The first, and simplest, is that the song has been transmitted aurally/orally, even though it may have an identifiable origin or been circulated in print at some time. Thus both the "Battle Hymn of the Republic" and "Amazing Grace" can be considered folk songs, even though we know Julia Ward Howe wrote the lyrics of the former and John Newton, the latter. A second, though somewhat more ambiguous, characteristic of folk songs that has proven useful in shaping this study includes a certain "forthright and unaffected style," as described by G. Malcolm Laws.[17] Norm Cohen offers a third criterion, namely that a song "must be performed for self-enjoyment in a non-commercial act."[18] Finally, although folk songs should have a traditional element to them, with roots in the past, both Sandburg and the Lomaxes were influential in insisting that folk songs should not be considered as frozen in time but instead be recognized as still alive, growing and changing in the hands of current performers. Thus, though there may be a foundational text, there is no one correct version of a folk song, only versions to be respected for what they meant to their singers and appreciated for what they mean to us.

Because this book focuses on the value of folk songs as historical sources and their connections to American history, recent compositions in the folk style have been excluded. Benjamin Filene has recently identified "vernacular music" as the music that is "current, familiar, and manipulable by ordinary people." He then distinguishes "popular" music—the creation of professionals for widespread public consumption—from "roots" music, which he defines as the "pure" sources that gave rise to popular forms like rock and roll.[19] Roots music, as indicative of traditional songs connected to the past, would be a more precise term to use here, especially as many contemporary performers/composers like to call themselves folk singers, but "folk song" is a comfortable and familiar way to encompass the genre.

An essential element of folk songs is that they should grow out of or resonate with the lives of common people. As such, they should address emotions and basic values, helping people get through life by expressing, enhancing, or altering a mood. Folk songs make work more endurable, put a child to sleep, and exhibit pain, sorrow, joy, or foolishness. A single singer may tell a long and complex story with little or no overt moralizing via an ancient European ballad, or a group may build a sense of community with the collaborative singing so common in parts of Africa. But all folk songs have meaning to their singers in terms of their immediate personal life, and the songs offer evidence about what common men and women thought about their past, present, and future. Ballads and folk songs have long provided a means of "transforming the prosaic concerns of everyday life into stark poetry."[20] Moreover, folk songs "[are] cultural messages that people [send] to themselves, . . . [which] provide insights into past lives and past mentalities."[21]

# # #

It is now time to turn to the rich array of folk songs that resonate with the American past, sometimes in a major key and sometimes in a minor, both up-tempo and slow. For those interested in the emergence of scholarly interest in folk songs and some reflections on how to think about the songs, a coda completes the text.

CHAPTER 2

Careless Love

Courtship, Marriage, and Children

Sex and death: without them what would be left of folk songs or popular music? Perhaps no song epitomizes the connection better than "Banks of the Ohio," an American classic. The song begins on a cheerful note, with a young man declaring:

> I asked my love to go with me,
> To take a walk a little way,
> And as we walked and as we talked,
> About our golden wedding day.

Nevertheless, a hint of danger is suggested in the chorus, where he expresses a certain possessiveness that has far too often led men to commit violence against women they cannot marry. He asks his love:

> Then only say that you'll be mine,
> In no other arms entwine,
> Down beside where the waters flow,
> Along the banks of the Ohio.

As the story continues, he is denied his love's hand in marriage by her mother, who doubts her daughter is old enough to marry a man the girl has only recently met. Enraged by this denial, the man decides if he cannot have her, no one will. He admits:

I held a knife unto her breast,
As in my arms she trembling pressed,
Crying Willy, oh Willy, don't you murder me,
I'm not prepared for eternity.

Unlike many men in similar songs, he soon regrets his passion and does not flee but returns home, presumably to pay for his crime. The song concludes:

I started home twixt twelve and one,
Crying, my God, what have I done,
I murdered the only woman I loved,
Because she could not be my bride.

♯ ♯ ♯

Perhaps no other aspect of life is more central to determining who we are and what our life will be like than our family. Families provide food, shelter, direction, and a start in life; families fit us into our community and teach us the rules of society. Most of us continue the process by marrying and raising the next generation. What demographers call the central life events of birth, death, marriage, and migration are intimately connected to families. Such physical actions can readily be observed and often counted. They also give rise to and are influenced by personal and communal values, subject to constant public articulation and frequent debate. Folk songs are one means by which values about getting married, having a child, losing a loved one to death, and leaving one family and forming another get expressed.

This chapter is devoted to examining the attitudes toward courtship, marriage, and child rearing evident in folk songs. Death is so common in folk songs that it can hardly be separated out for special treatment, though I comment briefly on mortality at the end of the chapter. Migration, touched on here with regard to abandoned lovers, receives much more attention later. A whole book could be dedicated to the family alone, so numerous are the relevant songs, but I have simply provided a selection of well-known, representative, and readily accessible examples, recognizing that another author might write a similar chapter with a wholly different set of songs. Many of the songs from later chapters could easily be included here, so pervasive are these themes, but I have reserved them to aid in future discussions.

♯ ♯ ♯

Between the eighteenth and twentieth centuries, Americans experienced profound revolutions in the most intimate aspects of their lives and the values they attached to their actions.[1] Folk songs comment on many of these changes, some more than others. Marriage has always been common and even necessary in American society. Although most people married, the average age at first marriage cycled several times from the early to late twenties, especially for women, and parents were vitally involved in the choice of a spouse. Other aspects of marriage, however, were of greater concern to the singers of folk songs. Until 1880, when divorce became more acceptable, marriage ended primarily through death, or occasionally abandonment, so the choice of a spouse required special care. "Careless Love" could lead to all kinds of problems. In the second half of the eighteenth century, about one-third of all brides were pregnant at the time they married, reflecting not only relatively loose attitudes toward sex but also a way to challenge parental control over marriage. As marriage came under the control of the courting couple after 1800, young women began to hear, and, it was hoped, attend to, musical warnings to grant their sexual favors carefully. After the Revolution, marriage for love slowly became more acceptable and expected. Apparently the advice of the songs was heeded, since fewer brides were pregnant when they married.

One of the earliest revolutions occurred in childbearing. From about the time of the American Revolution, parents increasingly chose to have fewer children. A colonial couple, which might have expected to have eight children, would have descendants who averaged about two. Women began to use various forms of birth control to reduce their childbearing, cutting the birth rate in half by the early twentieth century. Having fewer children coincided with other changes in women's status during the 1800s; women in the first half of the nineteenth century were expected to demonstrate greater independence as they achieved more property rights, received more formal education, and assumed greater control in the home, especially when their husbands went out to work. During the nineteenth century, as urban, middle-class families experienced the separation of work from the domestic setting, family life and the home came to be seen as a "haven in a heartless world."[2] After 1920 the combination of fewer children and longer lives shifted the focus of family life from child rearing to adult companionship because couples could expect significant years together without children around.

Along with the trends toward fewer children and freer courtships, attitudes regarding sex were transformed and expressed in numerous forms of print and oral culture. Richard Godbeer describes how the perception of women's sexuality changed in the last quarter of the eighteenth century, from seeing women as lustful and dangerous, capable of leading men astray, to portraying women as pure and innocent, in need of protection from men. He attributes the change—which he found in newspapers, magazines, and almanacs—to republican politics at the time of the Revolution, a politics in which virtue, both private and public, was vital to the success of the new nation.[3] Others have used novels and political cartoons to trace similar messages for women about guarding against the sexual and violent threats of men.[4] The same warnings are evident in the folk songs from about 1800. In the nineteenth century, sexuality was not often a topic of public discourse, though anxiety to protect women's virtue is apparent in writings on birth control, abortion, and prostitution. Despite this public stance, a significant number of erotic verses in folk songs can be traced to the nineteenth or early twentieth century, before the discussion of sex became commonplace in public arenas.[5]

Despite, or perhaps because major improvements in mortality only began in the late nineteenth century, folk songs have often commented on death and the need to be prepared for its unpredictable arrival. Until 1880, when the germ theory finally led to medical actions that could prevent and later cure disease, life expectancy remained low, varying more from accidental circumstances like environment and epidemics than from the ability of doctors to help anyone. A life expectancy of forty years at birth in the late eighteenth century was as good as might be found anywhere in the world, but it stands in sharp contrast to the eighty years we are closing in on today.

Death, ever present and uncertain as to time and cause before 1880, was ideally faced with resignation to God's will and the need to be prepared for judgment at all times. The victim in "Banks of the Ohio" pleads for her life on the grounds she is "not prepared for eternity." Such morbid but practical attention to reality is evident even in children's songs. Folk songs are full of violent deaths, which are often implicitly and occasionally explicitly depicted as the wages of sin. Although doctors could do little to delay death until after 1880, the latter part of the century saw a softening in the attitudes toward death, as heaven came to be portrayed not only as accessible to almost all but also as a family reunion.[6] So pervasive was this idyllic view of heaven that Mark Twain felt comfortable satirizing it in his 1907 short story, "Extract of Captain Stormfield's Visit to Heaven." Given the often bitter comments on family life in many folk songs, it is somewhat surprising that the Carter Family had such great success with asking, "Will the Circle Be Unbroken?" by death, when many spouses could hardly wait to be rid of an ill-matched partner, and no doubt many children were glad to be free of an abusive parent.

Over the course of several centuries, relationships and power within families changed noticeably. Folk songs often hint at these changes and occasionally comment directly on them. Before 1800 family life was patriarchal and complex. Families were composed not only of married couples and their children but also of other relatives, servants, and even slaves. Family roles and roles in society were defined and limited by age, sex, and degree of freedom. Only a few households had elderly people in them. Husbands were expected to control their wives, and both parents were to oversee children and servants. Church membership and religious attitudes followed from birth. Families educated children to fit into society and for work, and occasionally taught boys, and even more rarely girls, to read, write, and do arithmetic. Both production and consumption were located in the family, often in or around the home.

Property was important not only in the form of land to farm but also in choosing a spouse and defining family relations. When a woman married, she and the property she brought with her to the marriage commonly came under the complete control of her husband, under the legal doctrine known as coverture. A widow retained a right to use one third of the estate, but only until her death, when it went to her husband's designated heirs. Children were valuable economic assets, providing work while young and perhaps some security in old age, especially when a promise of the farm could be used to ensure cooperation. As a result, parents were often involved in courtship, trying to select a dependable mate and making sure that sufficient property was available to keep the young couple secure.

Aware of the changes that were occurring in their lives and the lives of their neighbors, Americans were often uncertain about what to make of them. Some actively sought and supported new relationships, others resisted mightily, and still others accepted the inevitable but tried to moderate the most unsettling effects. Debates about abortion, divorce, and the appropriate level of governmental interference in private matters that began in the nineteenth century still resonate today. Books were published, sermons were preached, and newspapers kept their readers informed.

Folk songs contributed to the chorus of opinion, albeit selectively, by reinforcing or challenging old and new attitudes. Folk songs commonly warned young women and men that marriage involved critical choices and was not to be entered into lightly. In keeping with the confusion and cacophony of voices heard elsewhere in the debate, folk songs offered mixed messages, since old ballads remained popular, even though their basic messages often differed significantly from those of the newer songs. In general, songs from the nineteenth century contain moral messages that are clear, though rarely stated explicitly, and tend to be more direct and simple in the values they express than older ballads.

♯ ♯ ♯

Complex stories of immoral actions, violence, and betrayal, all revolving around sex, marriage, and parent–child relationships, are often central to the 305 traditional English and Scottish ballads collected and made famous by Francis James Child.[7] Although the values and attitudes expressed in these texts are generally far more complicated and ambiguous than many folk songs of American origin, it is worth beginning with several of them, not only because they are among the oldest songs we have, but also because they have resonated so well with people as to endure long past the time of their origins. They have been found in most parts of the United States, even into the twentieth century, and among both white and black Americans.[8] Ballad singers Jean Ritchie and Joan Baez have recorded whole albums of Child's selections, but the songs are also present on recordings of Woody Guthrie ("Gypsy Davy" or "The Gypsy Laddie") and Huddie Ledbetter, also known as Leadbelly ("Gallis Pole" or "The Maid Freed from the Gallows").[9] I discuss three of the most famous ballads here, including "Lord Thomas and Fair Eleanor," recently covered by Jerry Garcia of the Grateful Dead and Dave Grisham; others are considered at appropriate places later.

Originating at a time when parents expected to control who their children married, it is not surprising that many of the Child ballads relate tales of friction and betrayal in courtship as children sought some say in the matter. One of the best known is "Lady Isabel and the Elf Knight," a story of multiple sins and ambiguous moral outcome.[10] The song clearly contains powerful cross-cultural messages, as it has been found across most of Europe. It was written down in Germany in 1560 and known in Poland, Portugal, and Italy; there are eleven Danish versions. Child thought the song might have remote links to the Old Testament story of Judith and Holfernes, as well as to the tale of Bluebeard. While the song clearly warns young women to take care in choosing a mate, it also celebrates the heroine's initiative in protecting herself from danger and, more ambiguously, in betraying and deceiving her parents.

The song begins with a young woman being persuaded to sneak off at night with a man, stealing both gold and horses from her father as they depart. There is no mention of a promise to marry, such as rationalizes similar actions in other songs. After riding awhile, they come to a cliff beside the sea, where the young woman discovers she has run off with what we would today call a serial killer when her young man announces, "It's six pretty maidens I have drowned here, and you the seventh shall be." Greed, however, will be his downfall; he asks her to take off her dress because it is too nice to "rot in the salt, salt sea" along with her, and he wants to sell it. In an improbable turn of events (recall that she is dealing with a serial killer), she convinces him to turn away while she takes off her dress, since it would be improper for him "a naked woman to see." Taking advantage of his willingness to accommodate her apparent modesty, she pushes him into the sea to drown and immediately starts for home. She arrives in time to put the horses and gold back, and she would have returned to her room without disturbing her parents, except her parrot squawks out, "Why do you travel . . . so long before it is day?" Her father hears the parrot and comes in to find out why it is awake. Instead of betraying his mistress, the bird makes up an excuse about a threatening cat and needing the girl to drive it away. After the father retires, reassured all is well, the girl promises to reward the parrot with a cage of gold and ivory.

While this is clearly a story about a young woman of independent spirit and quick wit, though with one horrible lapse of judgment, its moral core is uncertain. In meeting the same end as his previous victims, the murderer does receive his just reward, though not by due process. The young woman successfully flouts her parents' authority, steals from them, commits murder (albeit in self-defense), and rewards the parrot's lies. The parrot colludes in deceiving the parents after rousing the father, perhaps anticipating a reward for either its betrayal or its lie. And the parents are completely unaware of what their daughter has been doing. Since any sexual threat is diffused when the killer agrees to turn his back, the story seems to focus on property (horses, gold, a fancy dress, and a gilded cage) and its rewards. It also seems to value quick thinking, especially when those in apparent power are outwitted. Suffice it to say, no indigenous American ballad tells a story as complex and morally corrupt, with the possible exception of some versions of "Frankie and Johnny," to be discussed later.

"Lord Thomas and Fair Eleanor" relates a tale of how marrying for the wrong reason, and incredible stupidity, can lead to violence and death.[11] English versions date to the second half of the seventeenth century, when the American colonies were being established. The song begins with Lord Thomas dutifully asking his mother for advice on whether to marry fair

Eleanor or "bring the Brown Girl home." She responds, as many parents of the time would, by recommending the Brown Girl, for "she has houses and lands, Fair Eleanor she has none." Thus wealth and property are more important to a marriage than sexual attraction. Perhaps the story would have ended well if Lord Thomas had not made the mistake of asking Eleanor to come to the wedding as a guest, or if she had possessed the good sense not to go. But then we would have no ballad. When Eleanor arrives at the wedding and meets the bride, she rudely remarks, "She is wonderfully brown," a condition she contrasts to herself, who is "as fair . . . as ever the sun shone on." The comment on the bride's color may reflect class consciousness if the girl is brown from working in the sun or from dirt, as some versions suggest. It may also reflect racial awareness, since seventeenth-century Englishmen had recently come into contact with Africans and were beginning to enslave them in various parts of the Americas. Whatever the source of the insult, the Brown Girl responds angrily, seizing a penknife and stabbing her rival to death. Lord Thomas, who has also come to the wedding armed, takes out his sword and cuts off his bride's head, and, in a particularly violent image, "kicked it against the wall." Perhaps recognizing his own stupidity and series of wrong choices, the groom then kills himself. But before he dies, he leaves instructions to be buried with both women, with "Fair Eleanor in my arms, and the Brown Girl at my feet." In marrying for property rather than love, Lord Thomas was doing what many of his contemporaries would have done. His undoing was in inviting Eleanor to the wedding and not recognizing the depth of passion still felt by all three of them. Surely, few weddings have ended so badly.

From the time of Homer's *Odyssey*, authors have written about men fearing for their wives' chastity and faithfulness when the husbands are traveling.[12] The ballad known as "Little Musgrave" or "Matty Grove" is one such story, with one version taking twenty-seven verses and almost thirteen minutes to tell.[13] Texts exist from the early seventeenth century that refer to the ballad as ancient, but little is known of its origins, though they are clearly deep. The story begins on a holiday (holy day), when Matty Grove goes to church, along with many others in town, but he has "more mind for the fair women than . . . for Our Lady's grace." As he stands by the church door eyeing the women, who should return his gaze, and with passion, but the local lord's wife. After she makes so bold as to invite him home to sleep in her "arms all night," Matty rejects her offer, not on moral grounds, but because he fears the lord (variously named Arnol, Barnard, Dannel, Darnel, Donald, Thomas, etc.) will harm him.[14] She reassures Matty that the lord is away, sometimes reported as being at school learning a language, perhaps not a very manly thing for an aristocrat to do. Matty then joins her for the night. But a young page in the household overhears the arrangement and decides to tell his master, who is actually not that far from home. When the lord is awakened with the unhappy news of his wife's betrayal, he tells the servant that if he is telling the truth he will be rewarded with land and status, otherwise he will die. On the way home, someone in the lord's party blows a horn, possibly to warn Matty, or possibly in anticipation of the hunt. When Matty awakes with a start at the sound and thinks to flee, his lover reassures him and persuades him to stay. When they next awake, the lord is standing at the foot of the bed, whereupon he asks Matty how he likes his cover, his sheet, and his fair lady. With nothing to lose, Matty replies he likes them all, especially the lady. The lord then demands his foe rise and dress, for he will not slay a naked man. Matty refuses, saying he is unarmed while the lord has two swords. The lord offers Matty a sword, the lover strikes the first blow ineffectively, and the lord then lays Matty "dead in his gore." When his wife says she still prefers Matty, he "split[s] her head in twain."

Compared to the other two ballads, this one has obvious morals: the marriage bed is sacred and married women are the property of their husbands. The lady is lustful and passionate, easily leading Matty into sin for her own pleasure. Matty takes advantage of her sexual offer but is constantly frightened and in need of reassurance. He fails to defend his or his lover's life when given the chance; it may be fear that makes him unable to strike a fatal blow. The lord knows his rights and defends them, and he promises to reward a loyal liege. Presumably the seventeenth century would be more sympathetic to the lord's double murder than ours would be, though men continue to use violence to protect perceived property in women. The page demonstrates his loyalty to his master, despite being assigned to the lady's household. He clearly takes a risk, for if Matty had left before morning, the page might have lost his life.

In addition to the violence and moral ambiguity of such ballads, what also stands out are the women in them. All are dangerous to one degree or another, most are sexually aggressive, and none appear to need protection. Even though songs of more recent American origin portray women in a much different light, these European ballads remain popular in the United States, offering positive and negative models at the same time.

American folk songs about courtship and marriage tend to be much shorter, simpler, and morally certain. They range in tone from light to bitter humor, and in style from laments to blunt warnings. Only rarely do we hear songs of love and affection, or songs that celebrate the joys of marriage. It is worth keeping in mind that most Americans lived in rural areas until after 1920, where communities were small, the choice of potential spouses was limited, and life was often full of dull, repetitive work. Since men enjoyed both greater freedom to move about, before and after marrying, and more education, it is not surprising to hear discontent in the songs sung by or about women.

"The Wagoner's Lad" comments directly on not only the status of women but also on the frustrations of courtship, especially when parents intervene. There are a number of different versions, some overlapping with familiar courtship songs like "On Top of Old Smokey," but Buell Kazee begins his with the observation:

> The heart is the fortune of all woman kind,
> They're always controlled, they're always confined,
> Controlled by their families until they are wives,
> Then slaves to their husbands the rest of their lives.[15]

The song continues with a conversation between a courting couple. The woman complains about her lack of options:

> I've been a poor girl, my fortune is bad,
> I've always been courted by the wagoner's lad,
> He courted me daily, by night and by day,
> And now he is loaded and going away.

It is unclear how interested in a long-term commitment the wagon driver really is, but her parents oppose the courtship because the young man has limited financial prospects. He resents this attitude and believes himself to be an independent, hard-working person, worthy of respect, when he tells her:

> Your parents don't like me, they say I am poor,
> They say I'm not worthy of entering your door,
> I work for my wages, my money's my own,
> And if you don't like me you can leave me alone.

She is unhappy to see him go and tries to persuade him to linger, if only so he can get his horses and equipment in proper shape. But he is adamant about going, as their final exchange makes clear:

Your wagon needs greasing, your whip's for to mend,
So come sit here by me as long as you'll stand,
My wagon is greasy, my whip's in my hand,
So fare you well darling, no longer I'll stand.

If there is a recurring theme in songs about courting, it is to be careful
to choose the right partner, for the old saying "marry in haste, repent in
leisure" was surely endorsed by many. Despite this concern, songs frequently
laugh about young women's haste to marry, recognizing that for most girls,
the drudgery of domestic chores and close supervision must have been
stifling. Erotic songs, generally omitted from most scholarly publications
before World War II, though clearly present, also suggest that women were
eager to enjoy the sexual pleasure of marriage. "Lolly Too-Dum" tells the
tale of a young woman in conflict with her mother over whether she can
marry and thus escape her parents.[16] The mother tells her daughter she is
too young to marry and bids her, "Go wash them dishes, and hush your
fluttering tongue." The daughter replies by asking her mother, "Pity my
condition . . . for fourteen long years I've lived all alone." The mother is not
entirely unsympathetic; she too may want to have the girl out of the house,
because they then review the prospects. From "handsome Sam" to "men
of high degree," to "peddlers and tinkers, and boys that follow the plow,"
the young woman is confident that someone will marry her. Her optimism
is rewarded, and the song ends with her married and "well for to be." The
mother, with her six daughters now wed, is "on the market too."

"Where Are You Going?" is written in the same lighthearted vein, though
this time the conversation is between a courting couple.[17] The dialogue begins with the simple question of "where are you going my pretty little miss,"
to which she replies she is going crazy if she does not "get a young man
soon." When asked how old she is, the girl replies that, if she does not die of
a "broken heart, I'll be sixteen next Sunday." Soon the young man proposes
and she accepts, with the stipulation that she will not do his "washing or his
cooking." At this point the courtship ends, because the man clearly wants,
and perhaps needs, a helpmate and not a girl who simply wants to escape
from her parents.

Young men might well enjoy the advances of eager women like "Cindy,"
who is definitely attractive, causing her beau to "wish I was an apple a hanging on a tree, and every time that Cindy passed she take a bite of me." He
notes with pleasure that she "took me in her parlor and cooled me with her
fan, and said I was the prettiest thing in the shape of mortal man," and when

she put her arms around him, he "thought [his] time had come." Despite her evident appeal, the young man keeps telling her, "Get along home, I'll marry you some day," perhaps when she is older and more willing to do his washing and cooking.

However anxious young women may have been to marry, their choices were not always exciting, with most facing life as a farmer's wife. A common admonition in folk songs is for girls not to be swept away by the temporary and dangerous excitement offered by "roving gamblers" or railroad men, both transients who either had or promised more ready cash to lavish on a woman than a farm boy could or would.[18] According to "The Roving Gambler," the attraction can be explained by the fact that "a farmer's always in the rain," while gambling men "wear the big gold chain." In this song, gamblers are even preferable to railroad men, who regularly lie to their wives. As two girls compare the merits of "The Shanty-Boy [logger] and the Farmer's Son," one favors the former, not only because he has more money to spend, but also because he is more sophisticated and stays away for part of the year.[19] The other initially values her farm boy's presence, hard work, and essential stability, but she eventually decides the shanty-boy is a better catch.

Most, however, had to settle for the farm boy. As "Common Bill" suggests, the choice was not always thrilling but was perhaps more agreeable than might be admitted.[20] The opening verses depict Bill as bland and unappealing, even with regard to his name. Although he "wishes me to marry," she does "not think I will." Bill comes courting and, instead of kindling a flame of love, the "lunkhead" bores the girl by overstaying his welcome. In the end, she justifies her choice, perhaps less reluctantly than she makes out, by the Bible. Bill has told her if she refuses him "he cannot live another minute"; so, faced with the commandment not to kill, she decides to marry Bill.

What we know about marriage patterns in early America suggests few women actually wed before their late teens, and the average age was almost always in the early twenties. But we also know that almost all women who were healthy married, if only because few other options for single women were available until the middle of the nineteenth century. Thus the urge to marry may reflect worries about becoming an old maid. Jean Ritchie recalls she and her ten sisters sang "I Wonder When I Shall Be Married" so often the neighbors called it "the Ritchie old-maid song."[21] With good looks and a bit of property, the girls sang, "Won't I be a bargain . . . for someone to carry away?" Bob Carpenter's "Burglar Man" tells the "sniptious" story of a burglar who invades the bedroom of an old maid.[22] When she comes in, he dives under the bed and watches in horror as she takes out her teeth and a glass eye, and puts her wig on a table. Shocked by what he has seen, the burglar emerges only to be grabbed around the neck and threatened with being shot if he does not marry her. Faced with body parts lying around the room, he replies, "Woman, for God's sake shoot."

To the extent that young men worried about making the right choice, finding a proper helpmate who was willing and able to work was essential. "Billy Boy" lists a whole array of domestic skills a woman should have, including baking a cherry pie, before she could be considered ready to leave her mother.[23] Being unwilling to do the washing and the cooking, whether at sixteen or twenty-six, was certain disqualification for most prospective brides. Like Lord Thomas, young men also had to decide whether to wed for love or property and be able to know how to judge a woman's motives. The offer of a "Paper of Pins" begins one song. Such small tokens of affection, a young man assures the woman he is courting, is how "love begins."[24] She, however, is not impressed. Finally, after offering a series of ever more costly presents, the man suggests the keys to his chest so she "may have gold at your request." When she accepts this offer, he withdraws the proposal, remarking with evident disappointment that now he sees "that money is all, and a woman's love is nothing at all." The lovely and lonesome lament "Pretty Saro," whose melody echoes "The Wagoner's Lad," bides adieu to a girl who has rejected a suitor because he lacks "house and land" and cannot "buy all the fine things a big house can hold."[25]

But probably no set of songs became better known or provided a blunter message about the hazards of courting than the murdered-girl ballads. They are notable not only for the power and influence of their form but also for the stark contrast they offer to the powerful women of the old British ballads. The late-eighteenth-century change in attitude toward women's sexuality, and indeed competence, is apparent in these songs. The first of these cautionary songs in the American tradition is generally agreed to be "Omie Wise," from North Carolina in 1808. By 1896, when the body of a young woman named Pearl Bryan was found in Kentucky, headless and pregnant, and possibly the victim of a botched abortion, familiarity with the songs and the power of their images and basic format immediately shaped the newspaper coverage and later the construction of ballads associated with the case.[26]

The central message of these ballads is that young men will lead young women astray if given half a chance, and they will frequently commit murder to cover up their crimes. Courtship at the time of these ballads brought not only pleasure and love but hidden dangers as well. As with many of the songs, "Omie Wise" is based on an actual case, the 1808 murder of Naomi

Wise by Jonathan Lewis in Deep River, North Carolina.[27] The very first verse sets the tone of the ballad, asking us to listen to the story of how Omie was "deluded by John Lewis's lies." He "promised her marriage and many fine things" to persuade her to flee with him, only to discover that he intended to drown her. Omie begged for her life and that of their unborn child, to no avail. Lewis seems to have been a particularly cool killer, as some versions have him returning to the community and asking if anyone knows where Omie is. Eventually her body was found and he was arrested, but he escaped before the trial. Years later he was found and tried and then freed for lack of witnesses, though his guilt was an accepted fact among the ballad makers. This song, and the many that followed, warn young women not to trust young men, who might well get them pregnant and then kill them. Omie Wise was certainly not up to dealing with John Lewis as Lady Isabel had the Elf Knight.

At least a few of the murdered-girl ballads are based on English songs. "Pretty Polly," who is led to her death with the promise of "some pleasure to see," and "The Jealous Lover," which tells of "fair Florilla's" fatal mistake, both trace their roots to England.[28] But there are ample warnings with deep American roots, and once the form was established, it lasted over a century. "Tom Dooley" dates from 1866 and "Pearl Bryan" from 1896. "Lula Viers" from Kentucky loved John Coyer and was engaged to him, but he "ruined her reputation and later took her life."[29] This latter song was written about a murder in 1917, testifying to the enduring power of the warning ballad. Dolly Parton's recent heart-wrenching "Down from Dover" offers only a minor variation on the theme, ending with the baby's stillbirth providing evidence of the man's betrayal.[30]

Perhaps the one female character who most closely approximates the powerful women of the old British ballads is Frankie of "Frankie and Johnny" or "Albert" fame, even though the historical roots of the song may be traced to the African-American community in St. Louis in the late nineteenth century.[31] It is also a song with greater moral ambiguity than most murdered-girl ballads. The story is relatively straightforward. Frankie has been involved with Johnny, even buying him clothes. Upon discovering that he has been playing around with another woman, Frankie goes hunting for him and, finding him with the other woman, shoots him dead, because "he was her man, but he was doing her wrong." This is a much rougher world than that of Omie Wise. Frankie discovers Johnny's betrayal in a barroom (it is a truth well known in folk songs that nothing good ever happens in a tavern) and finally tracks him down in a hotel/dark alley/pool hall/coke joint. She variously gets her gun from a pawnshop or back at the crib house (brothel) where she works.

Even the conclusion is ambiguous, though more from one version to another than within any one example. In almost every case, Frankie regrets killing her man, most dramatically when she asks to be put in a dungeon where "the northeast wind blows from the southeast corner of hell." After being told she shot her lover in the third degree, Frankie takes a more aggressive stance in one version when she retorts that she shot him "in his trifling ass." The law also responds in wildly divergent ways. In some songs, Frankie is executed by hanging or the electric chair. In others, she is set free, either because the judge believes "a gambling man won't treat you right," or the jury concludes she should "go kill yourself another man if he does you wrong." One version has the judge instructing the jury that this was murder in the second degree, with the singer commenting it was neither second- nor third-degree murder but purely a case where a "woman simply dropped her man, like a hunter drops a bird, he was her man, but he done her wrong." Whatever the variations, this is a story in which no one is innocent, all are passionate, and justice is only occasionally related to the law. And any man with his wits about him would know not to mess with a woman like Frankie.

Warnings about trusting men too readily do not always involve murder, though they frequently end in death. "The Butcher Boy," an English ballad that is the parent of such songs as "Tarrytown," "Hard, Ain't it Hard," and "There Is a Tavern in the Town," relates the tale of a young woman who foolishly loved a railroad boy (in most American versions), only to be abandoned. She hangs herself with a note attached to her dress, asking that a turtle dove be carved on her gravestone "to signify I died of love."[32] In the beautifully plaintive ballad "Every Night When the Sun Goes In," discovered by Cecil Sharp in the Southern mountains, the singer laments her condition, wishing that her "babe was born, sitting on his daddy's knee" and that she "poor girl was dead and gone, for a Maid again I'll never be."[33] She instructs her true love not to weep, even though she is "going away to Marble Town." Abandonment by the one she "adored" led one young woman to proclaim, "I Never Will Marry," before drowning herself in the ocean. "Careless Love" could lead to apron strings no longer pinning as one's belly swelled, at which time the boy in question would "pass my door but won't come in," even though when she "wore her apron low, he courted me through ice and snow." On the other hand, at least one version of this latter song notes that the mother cannot speak too harshly to her daughter because she also "liked the boys when she was young."[34]

Even when both sides in a courtship had good intentions, things could go badly astray, as in "Barbara Allen." This old British ballad, which dates to at least the middle of the seventeenth century, has been found all over the United States, sung by both white and black Americans. The ballad was common in Mississippi when William Faulkner was growing up, and he may have used Barbara as the inspiration for one of his characters.[35] In this song, a young man is dying of a broken heart because Barbara Allen has rejected him. Over the course of the long ballad, it becomes evident that she is angry because she thinks he slighted her by "giving toasts to the ladies fair" while "drinking in the tavern," when, in fact, he did not include her because she is the one who has his heart. She is unable or unwilling to recognize this mistake and leaves, whereupon he dies. Versions differ as to how soon she repents her pride and anger, but she too "die[s] of sorrow" and is buried next to him. The rose and the briar that grow from their graves tie "a true lovers' knot" on the church spire, uniting the lovers in death, if not in life. In good Child ballad tradition, other versions suggest Sweet William should have realized there are "more pretty girls than one," so that Barbara is right to reject such a weak character. Some have her stopping the funeral procession to laugh at him one last time, which indecency may be the source of her death in more complex versions.

A similar Child ballad, known as "The Brown Girl," plays off of the theme of mistakes during courtship but in quite different ways on opposite sides of the Atlantic.[36] The mistakes in the song involve too hasty, and perhaps frivolous, decisions that cannot be later remedied. In the United States, the story serves as an antithesis to "Barbara Allen." Here, a rich woman, "fine Sally," rejects the love of a young doctor. She soon sickens and has to send for him to save her life, but he refuses, citing her rejection. In fact, he remains so angry that he promises never to forget or forgive but to dance on her grave. Thus a real rejection, in this instance with the gender roles reversed, can be dealt with harshly with no apparent punishment to the survivor. This is a curious case of editing, for the English original as published by Child has a man rejecting a wild and free woman because she is too brown (echoing Fair Eleanor). He too takes sick and calls her to him, regretting his earlier actions. Since there was no failure to communicate, as in "Barbara Allen," she finds no reason to accept him, reportedly laughing so hard at his condition as to be unable to stand. It is she who promises to dance on his grave. Unlike Barbara Allen, who suffers for her lack of compassion over an honest mistake, neither of these versions is at all sympathetic to the person who rejects love and later regrets having scorned a lover.

Marriage could bring unanticipated problems, as folk songs commonly reminded listeners. Spouses were not always as agreeable and reliable after the wedding as they appeared before. Several Child ballads reflecting on the old adage "marry in haste, repent in leisure" made it across the Atlantic. One of the central themes in "Matty Grove" is the concern men have that their wives will be faithful, especially while the husbands are away. At least three other Child ballads popular in the United States reiterate this anxiety. "The Gypsy Laddie" or "Gypsy Davy" tells the tale of a highborn husband coming home to discover that his wife has run off with a gypsy, attracted, at least in part, by his singing.[37] The husband eventually tracks her down, but after he reminds her of her fine clothes and child, she replies, "I wouldn't give a kiss from the gypsy's lips for all your land and money," suggesting a sexual attraction as well. In most of Child's versions, the lord then kills the gypsy and his henchmen (often described as dark) and takes his wife home and locks her up, reasserting control. But in American versions, the wife simply relinquishes her fine gloves and shoes, and she remains with her new lover, willingly exchanging her "feather bed" for a "cold straw bed with the calves a-bawling around" her. Perhaps material differences in the United States were not so great as to make sense of the conflict, since farm wives already lived close to bawling calves; or perhaps they related to the excitement of an exotic stranger coming and taking them away from a boring life, and so they did not want to have the husband reestablish his authority.

The story of "The House Carpenter" tells of a wife and young mother lured by a seaman away from her life as a carpenter's wife.[38] American versions agree with British in punishing her for her moral failure. One enticement to leaving her husband is material, the acquisition of fancy clothes and an easy life aboard ship. But she soon decides she has made a bad bargain and foolish choice. After several weeks, she begins to weep "most bitterly" for the child she carelessly left behind. Her conscience begins to bother her, and she tells her lover that dark clouds on the horizon remind her of "a place called hell . . . where I and you must go." In less than a month her fears are realized when the ship springs a leak and sinks "to rise no more." Farm wives may not have had to worry about being literally lost at sea, but they were clearly warned metaphorically about sinking in sin.

Even when couples stayed together, faithfulness was not assured. One of the most widespread and enduring songs on this topic is Child's "Our Goodman," often known in this country as "Four Nights Drunk." The song has many variants, from highly presentable to obscene, with versions updated to fit the modern urban scene. Legman suggests this may be the most popular of all the Child ballads in oral tradition, but collectors' reluctance to include obscene versions, at least in their published work, has given that honor to "Barbara Allen" by default.[39] The core of the song revolves around a man returning home to find what appear to be a horse, a hat, or pants, occupying space where his horse, hat, or pants "ought to be." His wife treats him like a fool, telling him that what he thinks he sees are really gifts from her mother in the form of a cow, a chamber pot, and a dishrag. He is either unwilling to provoke a fight, perhaps because he feels guilty about being out at night, is too stupid to know the difference, or is too drunk to recognize her deceit. But he does have enough sense of dignity and presence of mind to marvel that, though he has "traveled this wide world over," he has never seen "a saddle and a bridle on a milk cow, . . . a J. B. Stetson chamber pot, . . . [or] cuffs and buttons on a dishrag." A final verse often has a head in bed, which the wife insists is a melon, a baby, or even a servant girl, even though he clearly sees a mustache on the head. Left alone too often, the wife has found other ways to amuse herself, breaking her marriage vows. But the song is hardly an indictment of her actions, for it blames her husband for his slow wits, inattention, absence, and alcoholic stupor.

Songs that compare single and married life generally do not favor the latter. "Single Girl, Married Girl" offers a lament by a wife for better days before she married. According to the song, a single girl "goes to the store and buys," while the married girl "rocks the cradle and cries."[40] Likewise, the single girl goes "where she please[s]," while the married girl has a "baby on her knees." "The Single Girl," sung for Cecil Sharp by several mountain women, begins with the contrast between a girl being "dressed so fine" when single and appearing "ragged all the time" when married.[41] Shoes of new leather that once squeaked now leak. Too many children to feed and a drunken, abusive husband compound the misery. Too late the singer comments, "I'd never trust my happiness with no man again" before concluding in the chorus, "Lord, don't I wish I were a single girl again."

To this a man might respond, "When I was single my pockets did jingle," something they no longer do with a wife and children.[42] A woman might be "the plague of my life" to her husband, but marriage was so essential that even if death took one wife, it was critical to find another soon, especially if a man was left with children. Quickly remarrying was no better than marrying in haste the first time, because one might discover the new bride is "the Devil's stepmother," who will "beat," "bang," and threaten to "hang." One warning to young men was to "be good to the first, for the last is much worse."

Only rarely was a man lucky enough to escape such a terror. "The Farmer's Curst Wife" is a Child ballad in which the devil comes to take a member of a farmer's family.[43] The farmer fears the devil wants his son, only to find it is his wife the devil desires. He willingly consents, and the devil takes her off to hell. When they get there, the woman begins to abuse the little devils, kicking them and bashing out their brains until they beg their father to take her back before she ruins hell. Versions vary regarding the conclusion of this tale.[44] In some, she returns to make the farmer's life miserable again, having "conquer[ed] men and the devil too" and having "been to hell and come back worse." Another version has her worrying about what will happen when she dies, saying, "I ain't fit for heaven and they won't have me in hell." An ironic comment concludes one version by claiming to show women are "much better than men, when they go to hell they're sent back again."

Not all misfortune in marriage occurred because of moral failing by one of the partners. War could take a man away, leaving his wife with serious problems. "Shule Aroon," an eighteenth-century Irish lament on the fate of women whose men have gone to war, has survived in this country since the Revolution as "Johnny Has Gone for a Soldier."[45] Versions vary, but most have the woman supporting her husband's soldiering, which may or may not have been voluntary, selling household goods and even her "spinning wheel" to buy her love "a sword of steel" to enable him to return safely. Nonetheless, the singer also admits, "It broke my heart to see him go, and only time can heal my woe." In the eighteenth century, armies were notoriously slow in paying their men, and the logistics of getting any leftover pay sent home were formidable. Thus it comes as no surprise, but a definite sense of horror, when we hear the wife has had to buy or "dye myself a dress of red," and she tells us, "Through the streets I'll beg my bread," since "Johnny has gone for a soldier." To send her husband off to war and be reduced to prostitution by her ensuing poverty must have eroded this wife's sense of patriotism and the glory of war.

Upon reflection, it is surprising that anyone exposed to a significant number of folk songs would wed; at least they went into marriage with their eyes open. But for those who heeded the advice to choose carefully, marriage may have turned out to be a pleasant necessity.

♯ ♯ ♯

Children were and are a natural part of marriage, and folk songs aid in child rearing, from lullabies for babies, to play songs teaching physical skills to infants, to songs with deeper social messages for older children. Although most of the songs discussed here have roots in the agricultural world before the Industrial Revolution, much of what follows is still pertinent today. When children were raised in rural areas, references to animals came naturally and might even have served an educational function. Life expectancy was low, and animals had to be killed for food, making images of death common in the folk songs sung to children. Historians have debated how children were raised before 1800, but one need not think that all children were seen as sinners whose wills needed to be broken, in order to accept a gentler approach to child rearing in the nineteenth century. This new approach recognized childhood as a distinct stage of development that lasted a number of years, and it urged parents to nurture their children. Many European travelers were appalled at what they saw as excessive permissiveness leading to overly independent and undisciplined children in the new republic.

Lullabies are the first folk songs a child encounters, and while their main function is to put a child to sleep, they may also carry messages that both parents and older siblings could appreciate. Let me note here that I have used a number of these songs for my own children and grandchildren with mixed success. As a child becomes old enough to understand the words, any chance deviation may bring it suddenly wide awake, protesting that the song does not go that way. Moreover, parental weariness may be greater than that of the child's, making it a struggle to stay awake long enough to sing the child asleep. This may have been less of a problem in a dark cabin with few distractions.

One of the first folk songs I ever learned, sung to me by my grandmother and mother, was "Go Tell Aunt Abby/Nancy/Rhody/etc."[46] This song has been found all over the United States, and the tune is reported to have been used in an opera written by Jean-Jacques Rousseau in 1750.[47] Although its melody is soothing and the words somewhat repetitious and relaxing, the actual content of the song is morbid. It begins with instructions to go tell Aunt Abby that her "old gray goose is dead." The deaths of animals naturally and for food was common on farms, but we learn this death is noteworthy because the goose "died in the mill pond, standing on her head," thus thwarting the aunt's plans to use her "to make a feather bed." Counter to what might be expected from many folk songs, the goose apparently had a happy family life, for both the "old gander" and her "goslings" grieve her loss. At some point, a young child may have become aware enough of the lyrics to begin to comprehend the ever-present reality of death and the sorrow parting can bring. The subtext, that plans get thwarted, is also a valuable lesson.

Parents reassure their children of being loved and cared for with songs like "Hush Little Baby." This song actually is so short and requires sufficient attention on the part of its singer as to make it of doubtful use as a lullaby. The basic message, evident in the lyrics that follow, is, on the surface, material in that Poppa or Momma keeps buying things for baby. But, in fact, the song suggests the ephemeral quality of possessions that get broken or do not work properly. The only true and lasting gift the parent can give is love and care, and pride in "the sweetest little baby in town."

> Hush little baby and don't say a word,
> Poppa's going to buy you a mocking bird,
> And if that mocking bird don't sing,
> Poppa's going to buy you a golden ring,
> And if that golden ring is brass,
> Poppa's going to buy you a looking glass,
> And if that looking glass gets broke,
> Poppa's going to buy you a billy goat,
> And if that billy goat don't pull,
> Poppa's going to buy you a cart and bull,
> And if that cart and bull turn over,
> Poppa's going to buy you a dog named Rover,
> And if that dog named Rover don't bark,
> Poppa's going to buy you a horse and cart,
> And if that horse and cart fall down,
> You'll still be the sweetest little baby in town.

Now, if only the child will hush!

"The Riddle Song," one of the loveliest of lullabies, is the remnant of a raucous Child ballad known as "Captain Wedderburn's Courtship."[48] Captain Wedderburn has kidnapped a young woman, not entirely against her will, and wants to marry and bed her. She insists that he must answer some riddles, to make sure he has suitable wits to go with his force, before she will "lie at the wall." Fortunately, he proves smart enough, and after many verses they end up married and in bed. Such improper behavior apparently offended American sensibilities, so the whole abduction and seduction was stripped away, leaving only the riddles as a lullaby. Alan Lomax has argued that the "easy and natural acceptance of the pleasures of the flesh and the bed [in Britain, was] foreign to folk psychology in America."[49] He may have had this song in mind.

The essence of the song is simple. The young woman states:

> I gave my love a cherry that had no stone,
> I gave my love a chicken that had no bone,

> I told my love a story that had no end,
> I gave my love a baby that's no crying.

A second verse asks how these things can be, before the answers come:

> A cherry when it's blooming it has no stone,
> A chicken when it's peeping it has no bone,
> The story that I love you, it has no end,
> And a baby when it's sleeping, there's no crying.

Careful reading, however, suggests that the erotic tensions from "Captain Wedderburn's Courtship" have not been entirely eliminated. Barre Toelken has discussed in depth the sexual imagery implicit, and sometimes explicit, in folk songs, including this one.[50] He recalls the first time he heard the song it was sung by a young couple, alternating lines, with the sexual meaning made clear when they concluded the song, not with a sleeping child, but with "a baby when it's making, there's no crying." He also suggests that readers who have heard *cherry* used as a symbol of virginity must surely be able to give an alternate reading to the first line, which then affects the interpretation of the following verses. But for putting a child to sleep, the reminder that "the story that I love you, it has no end," is surely reassuring, along with the admonition that sleeping children are not crying. The erotic subtext of some lullabies is also apparent in the song "Go to Sleep Little Baby," used by the sirens in the film *O Brother, Where Art Thou?* to lure men into their clutches, when the originals were simple efforts to put children to sleep.[51]

As children grow older, songs can be used to educate and entertain, and to develop motor skills. Older songs continue to be sung by parents, while lyrics for children continue to be composed with the same goals in mind. "This Little Piggy," more chanted than sung, nevertheless offers a parent a chance to play with a child's toes. "The Itsy Bitsy Spider" not only teaches the value of perseverance but also coordination, with the fingers, hands, and arms all used to act out the story. This song is clearly still widely known and remembered with pleasure. I have had audiences spontaneously start the gestures when I have sung this song, and college students will sing it in class and act out the story, despite the imperative to be cool under all circumstances. Even though rural America is only history for most children now, "Old McDonald" continues to teach not only about the various animals on a farm but also the sounds they make, though encouraging young people to actually sound like a pig gets difficult after a certain age. "The Wheels on the Bus" is a recent song to educate and entertain urban residents as they go "all around the town."

The simple child's game of "Patty Cake," requiring the coordination and cooperation of clapping, gradually gives way to the more challenging and even competitive "Miss Mary Mack." The Lomaxes recorded some highly involved clapping songs among African-American girls in the South in 1934; not only are the hand actions more complex, but the messages are more sophisticated.[52] "Hopali" asserts, "When I marry, gonna move upstairs, gonna teach my children how to put on airs." Moreover, it "take[s] a man I love to soothe my mind." In a verse that suggests this song may have roots much earlier than 1934, the singer remarks, "Miss Bell promised me, before she died she'd set me free."

One favorite is "The Old Lady Who Swallowed a Fly," a mid-twentieth-century composition that teaches a sense of humor by way of a sense of the ridiculous.[53] This song is also good for memory and breath control. It begins with the most probable event of the whole song—that is, an old lady swallows a fly—but the singer can offer no explanation why. Then, in a series of ever more unlikely events, though always explained by what has gone before, she swallows a spider to catch the fly, a bird to catch the spider, a cat to catch the bird, and then other increasingly large animals, including a cow, before concluding suddenly after she swallows a horse, "She's dead, of course." Although the singer constantly asserts, "I don't know why she swallowed the fly" and warns, "perhaps she'll die," the accidental ingestion of the fly is the only action that makes any sense. With the exception of the spider, which is possible, if not probable, all of the other actions are wonderfully well explained, though impossible. In addition to being silly and fun, the song has much to say about not accepting "rational" explanations uncritically.

As children grow older, the messages in their songs become more sophisticated, conveying understanding of the world that is now more often taught in schools. One of the oldest folk songs still popular today is "Froggy Went a Courtin'," which can be traced back to a song copyrighted in England in 1580.[54] Queen Elizabeth apparently was fond of giving her courtiers nicknames, and the song may be a parody of that habit. Although I have seen no reference to this, it is possible that it also refers to the unsuccessful efforts by the French Duc d'Anjou to win the Queen's hand in marriage, for the English have long insulted the French by calling them frogs. On one level, the song is about cute, small animals having a party during the wedding ceremonies of a frog and a mouse. But the song carries far more serious messages as well. As might be expected from the time of its composition, the song makes clear that marriage without family consent runs counter to social norms when Miss Mouse says, "Without my Uncle Rat's consent, I could not marry the

President." Even though her parents have obviously died, Miss Mouse expects her uncle and guardian to look after her best interests by approving a suitable partner. The middle of the song consists of generally lighthearted comments on such wedding rituals as purchasing a gown, arranging the wedding supper, and inviting guests. But the end becomes serious with the arrival of two uninvited guests in the form of a big cat who devours the mouse, frog, and rat, and a snake who drives the rest of the party away.[55] Given the relative size of the animals involved, this can be seen as a reminder of the social hierarchy prevalent in the sixteenth century and a warning that small animals (the lower classes) had better not behave too freely and exuberantly, unless their betters approve. The cat may literally eat up the young couple in the song, but many aristocrats presumably devoured the wealth of their subjects through taxes and rents. We have already encountered one song from the period in which brown skin was portrayed negatively, raising the question of whether "Froggy" also warns against miscegenation. Even though Uncle Rat consented, and the wedding was well attended, society may not have approved of the union of two such different creatures.

Another song from about the same period is "The Fox," in which the basic message about authority runs counter to that of "Froggy." In this song, children learn that breaking the law is acceptable when it is necessary to feed one's children. It may also suggest that the force available to authority is no match for the quick wits of the common people. In England at the time, much land was under the control of the aristocracy, and hunting on the lord's property was considered poaching, punishable by death. Moreover, the criminal code was exceptionally severe, with many crimes judged to be felonies, including stealing a loaf of bread. In "The Fox," the hero of the song travels to town, where he liberates several geese and ducks from a pen and takes them back to his den to feed to his "little ones, eight, nine, ten." Ownership in the form of "old mother pitter, patter" alerts law enforcement. John "ran to the top of the hill, and blew his horn both loud and shrill," but the fox makes a successful escape. When the fox gets home, he and his wife serve up the goose, and the children conclude, "Daddy, Daddy go back again, 'cause it must be a mighty fine town-o." In the contest between property rights and preserving the family, the latter clearly wins out in this song.

Age and gender roles were taught through folk songs, helping to acquaint children with social expectations. The "Three Pigs" tells the tale of three young pigs who decide that saying "wee wee," as young pigs do, is childish and beneath them.[56] They resolve to adopt adult manners, saying "onk" instead. Unwilling to say "wee" and unable to manage the adult "onk," they soon grow thin and die of the strain and their inability to survive in the adult world. Such a song instructed children not to be in too great a haste to become adults, just as young adults were warned not to marry impetuously. "What Folks Are Made Of" combines age and gender roles.[57] From this song children would learn that early in the life cycle boys are made of "piggins and pails and little puppy tails," while girls are "sugar and spice and all things nice." As they grow older, young men are made of "thorns and briars, they're all bad liars," compared to the "rings and jings and all fine things" that comprise young women. This echoes courtship songs in cautioning against trusting men and worrying about the material demands of women. By the time old age sets in, grandfathers are "whisky and brandy and sugar and candy," while grandmothers are "moans and groans in their old aching bones." But babies are not distinguished by sex and are uniformly "sugar and crumbs and all sweet things."

We have already encountered numerous songs offering advice about the joys and perils of courtship, but a few remarks can be added here. Perhaps these lines from "On Top of Old Smokey" summarize this body of material best: "For courting is pleasure and parting is grief, and a false-hearted lover is worse than a thief." The song also warns that one can lose a lover "from courting too slow," though clearly undue haste is never recommended. Even young children could begin to learn about courtship via games like "Little Sally Walker," where a boy or girl in the middle of a ring is told to "rise . . . [and] fly to the one you love the best."[58] For older girls, the story of "Young Charlotte" or "The Frozen Girl" warned of the dangers of vanity. Seba Smith used a New York newspaper article from February 1840 to tell the story of a vain young woman who set off on a fifteen-mile sleigh ride to a party but refused her mother's advice to wrap warmly lest her silken cloak "never would be seen." By the time she got to the party she had frozen to death; her young man ruefully recalled her murmuring, "I'm getting warmer now," though he was complaining of the cold.[59]

One of the more curious of the Child ballads to have remained popular in the United States is "The Maid Freed from the Gallows," which offers an unusual critique of family.[60] This song was widely known all over Europe, from Sicily to Scandinavia, and from Great Britain to Russia, from at least the middle of the eighteenth century. It was common in this country, even spreading to African-American communities, where children were reported to have acted out the story as it was sung.[61] American versions tell of a young man or woman about to be hanged for some unnamed crime, unless a fine can be paid on time. In European versions, the victim is often held by pirates for ransom. The heart of the story is the failure of the parents and siblings to free the prisoner and save his or her life. One by one—father, mother, sisters, and brothers—show up, not with the hoped-for gold, but to see the hanging. Fortunately, the hangman is persuaded to slack his rope one last time, and the lover arrives to rescue the victim with the needed money. Despite all the warnings about hasty marriage and unhappy spouses, this song indicts the birth family as cruel and uncaring, while the chosen lover is the one who can be relied on at the most critical moment. Symbolically, the lover frees the prisoner both from the hangman and the family.

♯ ♯ ♯

Since death was a common and unpredictable part of life before 1900, and most marriages ended only with the demise of one spouse, it is to be expected that death features so prominently in folk songs about the family. Popular songs from the nineteenth century, including several that have crossed over into oral tradition, frequently deal with the topic, reflecting common attitudes of the time.[62] Having said that, it must be admitted that death is a common part of many other songs as well and appears in most of the following chapters. But a few words of generalization on death in folk songs about the family are in order.

Because death was an ever-present reality, it is not surprising that children should have been reminded of that fact even in lullabies. Death was often the result of immoral behavior, which would be expected in a world that taught the "wages of sin are death." Some sickened and died of natural causes, but most met their end through violence or misfortune. Death was inevitable, and while it might be resisted, individuals were well advised to be prepared for it, as we will see in later chapters. Despair occasionally drove the grief stricken to suicide at worst, or to lose the will to live after receiving a broken heart. Most suicides were women, such as those in "Butcher Boy" or "I Never Will Marry"; but this form of release or escape was not what religion had in mind when it taught of death as leading to a reward after a life of suffering. A song like "Will the Circle Be Unbroken?" might celebrate family and echo the late-nineteenth-century view of heaven as a family reunion, with some pioneers "not dead but gone before," until all would be gathered "never more to part."[63] But given the often blunt warnings about the dangers of courtship and the uncertainty of happiness after marriage, one can wonder how many husbands and wives, to say nothing of their children, relished the day when they would be separated, no longer enduring psychological or physical abuse, or restrictions of freedom.

CHAPTER 3

"Mine Eyes Have Seen the Glory"
Of God and Country

From its seventeenth-century colonial origins, America has repeatedly experienced both the violence of war and the enthusiasm of religious movements, sometimes together, and sometimes separately. Both have often
linked reform of society or the individual to a sense of mission. In 1630
John Winthrop, governor of the Massachusetts Bay Colony, reminded his
fellow Puritans "that we shall be as a city upon a hill. The eyes of all people
are upon us. So that if we shall deal falsely with our God in this work we
have undertaken . . . we shall be made a story and a by-word through the
world."[1] Although Winthrop did not call for war, he and his fellow colonists
soon confronted both indigenous people defending their homes and other
Europeans engaged in their own imperial ventures.

Winthrop's image of a city upon a hill has echoed throughout American
history with a repeated sense of mission to save the world, or at least a few
souls. As the conflict over the nature of the British Empire headed toward
war after 1763, the emphasis of American clergy on a righteous citizenry
reinforced similar calls for virtue by political reformers seeking to replace
corrupt monarchies with moral republics. Although Thomas Paine did not
rely on a religious vocabulary in his famous call for independence, *Common Sense*, his language recalled Winthrop. Paine reminded his readers that
the War for Independence was just, because "the cause of America is in a
great measure the cause of all mankind." Moreover, he warned and urged,
"Freedom hath been hunted round the globe. . . . O! receive the fugitive, and

prepare in time an asylum for mankind." Following the War of 1812, and in the midst of the major religious revival known as the Second Great Awakening, crusaders set out to reform souls and society via temperance, abolition, asylums, and even the end to Sunday mail delivery. But the link between God and national interest was still present. In 1845 newspaperman John L. O'Sullivan called for the annexation of Texas, itself the product of one war and the stimulus for another, by urging his fellow citizens to pursue "the fulfillment of our manifest destiny to overspread the continent allotted by Providence for the free development of our yearly multiplying millions."

Abraham Lincoln offered one of the most stirring concatenations of religion, war, and reform in his second inaugural address in 1865. After reminding his audience that both sides of the Civil War had claimed God's support, he admitted, "The Almighty has His own purposes." Raising the distinct possibility "that American slavery is one of those offenses which . . . He now wills to remove," Lincoln hoped that "this mighty scourge of war may speedily pass away. Yet, if God wills that it continue, until all the wealth piled by the bond-man's two hundred and fifty years of unrequited toil shall be sunk, and until every drop of blood drawn with the lash, shall be paid by another drawn with the sword, . . . so still it must be said the judgments of the Lord, are true and righteous altogether." By comparison, Woodrow Wilson's crusade to "make the world safe for democracy" in World War I seems quite tame.

Politicians still ask that "God bless America" when engaged in foreign wars. Indeed, the United States has been described as "a nation with the soul of a church," reflecting not only the powerful role religion plays in American public and communal life but also the civic religion that has grown around the people, places, and events Americans celebrate.[2] Religion and war are both collective activities that have profound effects on individuals. As a result, the folk songs that arise from both war and religion range from highly personal to broadly communal. It should be no surprise that collections of folk songs frequently devote significant sections to one, or both, of these topics.[3]

♯ ♯ ♯

No song better exemplifies the intersection of war and religion than "The Battle Hymn of the Republic," just as no war has seen more explicit use of religious themes in the folk songs arising from conflict than the Civil War. Julia Ward Howe's 1862 lyrics have been described as "the most symbolic song" of the nineteenth century, the "quintessence of the Evangelical consensus that dominated" American life at the time, and arising out of the

Second Great Awakening; the song "still lies close to the nation's ideological core."[4] Although Howe was inspired to compose the new lyrics after hearing "John Brown's Body," she may also have known William Steffe's hymn "Say, Brother Will You Meet Me?" which provided the tune for both.

The Second Great Awakening swept across much of the United States from 1800 to 1830. It emphasized personal faith and individual religious conversion over formalism. Free will allowed individuals to choose to follow God's teaching and win salvation, instead of being predestined to heaven or hell. The new hymns that emerged from this revival stressed God as "gentle shepherd and guide," quite a change from the "angry father" of Puritan days.[5] The Second Great Awakening also overlapped with several other musical developments, including shape-note, or sacred-harp, music; the use of camp meetings and hymn singing in mission activity; and the conversion of significant numbers of African Americans to Christianity. The revival touched all parts of the country but lasted longest in the South. Moreover, while this Awakening was linked to social reform in New England and the Midwest, it focused almost exclusively on personal salvation in the South, at least partly to avoid the issue of slavery that divided denominations into Northern and Southern branches after 1830.

"The Battle Hymn of the Republic" shows clear Northern influences with its call to remake the country according to God's will and a sense of what His will entailed, a sense that many white Southerners did not share. Howe began her song with a highly personal testimony that suggests a conversion experience and a terrifying vision of judgment brought down on the country:

> Mine eyes have seen the glory of the coming of the Lord,
> He is trampling out the vintage where the grapes of wrath are stored,
> He has loosed the dreadful lightning of His terrible swift sword,
> His truth is marching on.

Nothing could stand before God's glorious truth and his "terrible swift sword" while the dark red liquid of the grapes of wrath spread across the land. The next verse combines religious and martial images as light struggles against darkness. A just sentence has been handed down, and sacrifice on the altar may be necessary. Howe wrote:

> I have seen Him in the watch fires of a hundred circling camps,
> They have builded Him an altar in the evening dews and damps,

I can read His righteous sentence by the dim and flaring lamps,
His truth is marching on.

The third verse is rarely included in published versions today, perhaps because of its hostile stance toward the Confederacy. After the gentler images of the second stanza, Howe let her anger show, suggesting that failure to "crush the serpent" would be dealt with harshly. Instead of a dimly lit judicial setting, she now saw fiercely illuminated weapons as God marched inexorably onward.

I have read a fiery gospel, writ in burnished rows of steel;
As ye deal with my contemners, so with you my grace shall deal;
Let the Hero born of woman, crush the serpent with his heel;
Since God is marching on.

Although the nation faced a difficult crisis, Howe moved to a strong affirmation that with awakening virtue and religious fortitude, God and country would prevail.

He has sounded forth the trumpet that shall never call retreat,
He is sorting out the souls of men before His judgment seat,
Oh, be swift my heart to answer Him, be jubilant my feet,
Our God is marching on.

The final verse builds on the image of souls and hearts responding to God's trumpet, by calling for a sacrifice "to make men free," a sacrifice Howe thought could only be compared to the one Jesus had made when "He died to make men holy." From the darkness of sin at the start of the song, Howe has taken the singers to glory and beauty, and suffering people to freedom from slavery and sin:

In the beauty of the lilies Christ was born across the sea,
With a glory in His bosom that transfigures you and me,
As He died to make men holy, let us die to make men free,
His truth is marching on.

Camp meetings answered this militant hymn with a different song of war and faith, this time one of peace. In "I Ain't Gonna Study War No More," African Americans took the imagery of gathering "Down by the Riverside" from an old revival song and added to it a rejection of war.[6] Although abolition of slavery via the Thirteenth Amendment (1865) occurred soon after the war, many ex-slaves endured the burden of the conflict while it was going on, and they faced hostility, often overt, from angry, white neighbors after the war. The song begins with the affirmation, "I'm gonna lay down my sword and shield, down by the riverside and study war no more." Later verses describe the singer's intent to "put on my long, white robe" and to walk or talk with "the Prince of Peace." Many African-American religious songs describe life after death, and this can certainly be interpreted as depicting an end to either war or the struggle of life. But given its origins in the spirituals that emerged shortly after the Civil War, singers must have had that all-too-real conflict in mind.

♯ ♯ ♯

The powerful influences of religious folk songs can be demonstrated by the continued, and indeed growing, use of both "Amazing Grace" and "We Shall Overcome."[7] These two songs, both staples in Protestant hymnals, have become standards in American civic ceremonies and have even spread abroad. Both can be considered folk songs in that at least a few verses of each have gone into the oral tradition and their melodies are widely recognized. Virtually all religious folk songs come from the Protestant tradition, white and black. It is fair to say that no Catholic or Jewish songs—let alone Muslim, Buddhist, or Hindu—have become widely recognized in the American oral tradition, with the possible exception of "Ave Maria."

A brief history of religion in America, with a focus on the role music has played, will help set a sampling of songs in context.[8] It is a commonplace but true assertion that religion played a central role in the founding of England's colonies in North America in the seventeenth century. Three groups of English Protestants had set their stamp on certain colonies by the end of that century. In New England, Calvinist dissenters from the Church of England's emphasis on church hierarchy settled first in Plymouth colony (the Pilgrims in 1620) and then Massachusetts Bay (the Puritans in 1629). By the end of the century, a Quaker presence was evident in the middle colonies, first in New Jersey and then in Pennsylvania. Elsewhere, the Church of England, the established church of the mother country, dominated with varying degrees of public support.

Of these, music historians generally give the Puritans the most attention. Among the Puritans, the singing of the Psalms was the prevalent form of singing until the very end of the seventeenth century. Verses from the book of Psalms might be edited to fit the rhythms of the tunes that were common, but they still were considered the word of God. A few common tunes, sharing two or three basic meters, were used with these songs, with no one melody permanently associated with any one psalm. A song leader might specify which tune a congregation should use on a given morning, but then the singers set their own starting note and tempo. Some even sang different tunes. Since many people were illiterate and songbooks were expensive, the common pattern was for a leader to "line out" the next line or verse to be sung and the congregation to repeat it. To sing a psalm took a long time, and the sound was not altogether harmonious, however satisfying it may have been to the singers.

In the eighteenth century, the number of different religious groups in the colonies multiplied from immigration, from the effects of the First Great Awakening (c. 1725–45), and from the rising appeal of new Protestant sects like the Methodists and Baptists. During the religious revivals of the First Great Awakening, quarrels over proper theology, the form of worship, the training of clergy, and the place of music in the service left congregations divided. Although a few Africans and African Americans converted to Christianity as early as the seventeenth century, most became fellow believers with their white neighbors and masters at the end of the eighteenth century, responding with special enthusiasm to the energetic services and egalitarian messages of the Methodists and Baptists. While the First Great Awakening generally emphasized the need for a conversion experience by an individual (similar to being "born again," in today's terms), the trend in theology after 1725 was to give the individual believer greater authority and control over his or her salvation and to offer a gentler faith from which many more could be confident of attaining heaven than the Puritans thought possible.

Two major trends in religious music occurred during the eighteenth century. Hymns, often inspired by scripture but clearly the thoughts and words of mere mortals, came to play an important part in religious services. The first great hymnologist was Isaac Watts, whose songs arrived on this side of the Atlantic shortly after 1700 and, once they gained support, remained popular until well into the nineteenth century. Other hymn writers of note include John and Charles Wesley, who were active as missionaries during the early settlement of Georgia, and John Newton, whose "Amazing Grace" ultimately became America's favorite hymn. The other significant change came with the advent of regular singing and the rise of singing schools. The advocates of regular singing urged their congregations to adopt more system and discipline in their religious music. Psalms and hymns were to be sung with a more vigorous tempo, all singers should start in the same key, and the flourishes, slides, and grace notes that singers used to personalize their own singing were to be eliminated. Trained singers formed choirs to set standards for their congregations, both in the selection and the performance of songs.

Of religious songs that crossed into the folk tradition, we will start with lyrics linked to white Protestants. "Wicked Polly" is a song with clear roots in Puritan theology. It may have originated in Rhode Island in the first half of the eighteenth century, but the song spread widely from there.[9] One of the central tenets of Puritan beliefs was that the chance for salvation came only through God's grace. Good works or living a virtuous life were important for securing the offer of salvation, but mere mortals could not force God to save them by their actions. Moreover, at a time when life expectancy was low and death might come to anyone at any time, colonists of all Protestant persuasions believed that one should be prepared to die at any moment. "Wicked Polly" tells the tale of a young woman who foolishly challenged both these doctrines; the song warns others not to repeat her folly, lest they too would die "in sin and deep despair."

The opening verse calls for "young people who delight in sin" to hark to this sad story. The second stanza is the most critical, for it is there Polly not only rejects the warnings of her friends to prepare her soul for death but also commits the heresy of asserting she can turn to God when she is ready and He will no doubt save her. The lyrics declare:

> She went to frolic, dance, and play,
> In spite of all her friends could say,
> I'll turn to God when I get old,
> And He will then receive my soul.

The third verse is the climax of the song, for it is there we learn she has made a serious mistake, realizing the error of her ways after being taken suddenly ill. The verse also reminds listeners that death brings separation from family, permanently when some are saved and others damned. Puritan families often suffered from anxiety over the possible separation of parents and children in the afterlife.[10] Theirs was not a faith to encourage hope that the circle would be unbroken.

> On Friday morning she took sick,
> Her stubborn heart began to break,
> She called her mother to her bed,
> Her eyes were rolling in her head.

The ensuing stanzas echo Jonathan Edwards's famous sermon, "Sinners in the Hands of an Angry God," as Polly understands her fate and is confronted by the King of Terrors. She tells her mother, "Your wicked Polly's doomed to Hell" because her "soul is lost." To her father, she reports sensing "the flaming wrath begins to roll" before succumbing to physical and spiritual agony. Leaving little to imagination, the lyrics inform us:

> She gnawed her tongue before she died,
> She rolled, she groaned, she screamed and cried,
> O must I burn forever more,
> Till thousand, thousand years are o'er?

In case the message escaped anyone's comprehension, the final verses drive it home. Two typical stanzas remind the young not only that salvation comes from God but also that preparation for death is prudent.

> Young people lest this be your case,
> O' turn to God and trust His grace,
> Down on your knees for mercies cry,
> Lest you in sin like Polly die.

> Oh sinners! take this warning far,
> And for your dying bed prepare,
> Remember well your dying day,
> And seek salvation while you may.

It would take a truly hardened or foolish young sinner to ignore these stern warnings.

At the end of the eighteenth century, "Amazing Grace" embraced the old beliefs about God's saving grace, but it did so with a gentler, more optimistic, more universal message.[11] This great hymn, written by John Newton, a sailor and slave trader turned obscure English country parson, was probably first sung at a New Year's service in 1773. What tune was used is uncertain, for the familiar melody, known as "New Britain," was first linked in print to the hymn in the shape-note classic, *Southern Harmony*, in 1835. The power and appeal of this song, from 1773 to the present, may come from some intuitive sense by listeners and singers of the personal testimony behind it. Newton's life took frequent turns, many encompassed by his famous hymn. Newton was the son of a sea captain and followed his father to sea at an early age. He soon lost whatever religion his mother had instilled in him, living a wild and dissipated life, and eventually participating in the slave trade. After several brutal and even degrading years in Africa, Newton sailed for home aboard a slave ship. In March 1748 the ship was struck by a powerful storm, and in the midst of the tempest Newton suddenly realized the sorry state of his soul. It might make a better story if he had immediately renounced his former life and worked against the slave trade from that day forward, but that is not the case. Newton remained at sea and in the slave trade until he took a job as a customs collector in 1755. Nine years later, after much study and introspection, he managed to persuade the Anglican hierarchy to ordain him and appoint him to the small parish of Olney. There he began to write hymns with some success. Only later did he commit fully to the abolition of slavery and the trade in which he had once engaged.

Knowing about Newton's life enhances the understanding of "Amazing Grace," but the hymn's appeal does not depend on that. Whereas "Wicked Polly" reminded singers that God punished sinners with everlasting torment, Newton chose to celebrate God's love and forgiveness, and the redemptive power of "Amazing Grace." He may have been looking back on the transforming moment of his life as he wondered with awe:

> Amazing grace! (how sweet the sound)
> That saved a wretch like me!
> I once was lost but now I'm found,
> Was blind, but now I see.

Other sinners can share his sense of amazement that wretches like them can also have hope.

Many Americans know the first verse but not the following five stanzas, arranged in a type of life course of the soul. The storm at sea and Newton's spiritual awakening certainly resonates in the second stanza:

> 'Twas grace that taught my soul to fear,
> And grace my fears relieved;
> How precious did that grace appear,
> The hour I first believed!

Throughout the years, the third verse has spoken as directly to singers as the second, as they have struggled with their own personal dangers, labors, and temptations. Newton rejoiced:

> Through many dangers, toils, and snares,
> I have already come;

'Tis grace that brought me safe thus far,
And grace will lead me home.

After celebrating his rescue from near spiritual death, Newton testified to the place God would play in his life until he died:

The Lord has promised good to me,
His word my hope secures;
He shall my shield and portion be,
As long as life endures.

Whereas death brought Polly to hell and its torments, Newton hoped for better things, as he anticipated:

Yes, when this flesh and heart shall fail,
And mortal life shall cease;
I shall possess, within the vail,
A life of joy and peace.

Even the end of time and the world as he knew it held no fears for Newton, who believed:

The earth shall soon dissolve like snow,
The sun forbear to shine;
But God, who called me here below,
Will be forever mine.

Many Americans share the sentiment expressed in a verse that was added in the nineteenth century and is well enough known that Uncle Tom sings it in Harriet Beecher Stowe's attack on slavery, *Uncle Tom's Cabin*. After receiving a near-fatal beating, Tom comforts himself with the previous two verses and then adds:

When we've been there 10,000 years,
Bright shining as the sun,
We've no less days to sing God's praise,
Than when we'd first begun.

Although both can legitimately be considered folk songs, the gentler, more optimistic message of "Amazing Grace" has clearly appealed to more Americans than "Wicked Polly." Both address the proper relationship between God and individuals, but few Americans would endorse the sense of powerlessness inherent in the former song. Many may have felt like wretches at some point in their lives, but Newton gives them encouragement, not fears of "flaming wrath." In the descriptive terms used by students of religious music, "Amazing Grace" is clearly a "hymn of praise," while "Wicked Polly" warns sinners of the folly of their ways, providing for their "edification."

An important musical innovation occurred at the start of the nineteenth century. In 1801 William Little and William Smith published the first shape-note tune book, followed by a similar work in 1803 by Andrew Law. Both assigned shapes to the basic notes on the scale, with Little and Smith using a triangle for fa, an oval for sol, a square for la, and a diamond for mi. This was to aid in learning to read music and to sing in parts. Purists and advocates of the old regular singing scoffed at this innovation as unnecessary for any real musicians, but it caught on. The *Kentucky Harmony*, published in 1816, includes 144 tunes, many from old folk songs and ballads, and is an early example of folk hymns based on old, familiar music. William Walker's *The Southern Harmony* of 1835 includes 209 songs and sold around six hundred thousand copies in five editions by the time of the Civil War. In 1844 Benjamin Franklin White and E. J. King published *The Sacred Harp*, giving a new name to the style of singing and a collection of songs that remained in use until well into the twentieth century. Sacred-harp or shape-note singing, also known as *fasola*, started in New England before spreading to the Midwest and the South. It endured into the twentieth century in the South, among both white and black congregations. The music has distinctive harmonies that take time to get used to but which are powerfully engaging.[12] The various parts produce harmonies that hover between major and minor scales, helping to produce the unique and readily identifiable sounds.

The nineteenth century saw the continued diversification of American Christianity. The Second Great Awakening led to many new congregations and to the use of camp meetings as places for revivals. Many African Americans joined Christian churches, eventually forming their own separate congregations when white churches proved less than welcoming. Religious reformers and innovators brought new messages to the country; among the best known are Joseph Smith and the Mormons, William Noyes and the Oneida Community, Anne Lee and the Shakers (though she arrived in this country in the eighteenth century), and William Miller and the Seventh-Day Adventists. Many originated in the "burned-over district" of upstate New York, so named for the frequent religious enthusiasms that swept like fire through the people there. Catholics began to arrive in significant numbers after 1830. Revivals after the Civil War made effective use of new gospel hymns that followed the example set by Dwight Moody and Ira Sankey.[13] African-American spirituals had long been a part of black religious experience, but they were introduced to—and enthusiastically accepted by—white audiences in the North and in Europe (and the rest of the world) by the Fisk Jubilee Singers after 1871, when this student choral group set out to raise money for its struggling university.

One great American religious folk song probably dates from the start of the nineteenth century and the Second Great Awakening: "When the Saints Go Marching In." This song has a definite collective, if exclusive bent as the singer longs to "be in that number, when the saints go marching in." It is easy to imagine this being sung at a camp meeting by hundreds of voices. A belief common in the Second Great Awakening, and of religious reformers like William Miller, was that the end of days was imminent. Thus verses anticipating "when the trumpet sounds the call," "when the sun refuse to shine," and "when the moon runs red with blood" before the saints would gather, leaving sinners behind, are critical parts to this song. For a people fond of imagining themselves as chosen, with a special mission reshaped from religious to political in the nineteenth century, it is not a long step from marching into heaven with the saints, to marching into other lands as part of manifest destiny, with its duty to civilize other nations. Secular saints believed they were among the numbers charged to "overspread the continent allotted by Providence for the free development of our yearly multiplying millions."[14]

One striking folk hymn from the nineteenth-century shape-note tradition is "Wondrous Love."[15] This song was popular in the South, where revivals emphasized personal salvation. Apparently taking heed of the old question, Why should the devil have all the good tunes? some anonymous author took the music to an old English ballad, "Captain Kidd," and wrote new lyrics that resonate well with "Amazing Grace." While "Captain Kidd" does provide a moral message in that the infamous pirate was hanged for his crimes, it contains many vivid images of the "much wickedness" he did. For those who knew the old song, the new lyrics must have been both shocking and reassuring. The first of three simple verses begins by remarking on the blessing, similar to "amazing grace," of "what wondrous love is this . . . that caused the Lord of Bliss to bear the dreadful curse for my soul." Echoing the subsequent stanzas of Newton's hymn of sin and redemption, the next verse rejoices, "When I was sinking down, beneath God's righteous frown, Christ laid aside His crown for my soul." Newton's concluding lines are paralleled here by, "And when from death I'm free, I'll sing and joyful be, and through eternity I'll sing on." Later, Americans encountered the tune as it returned to more secular folk songs, such as "She'll Be Coming 'Round the Mountain" or "Peg and Awl."

Just before the Revolution, Ann Lee brought a small group of followers from England to upstate New York and established the reform communities known as the Shakers. Mother Ann was known for her singing, and the musical tradition lasted after her death in 1784 with a great outpouring of "gift songs" in the 1830s and 1840s.[16] One of these, "Simple Gifts," has become familiar to most Americans in the twentieth century, though more for its melody than its lyrics. The Shakers emphasized simplicity in their lives and surroundings in the midst of the material changes engulfing America as the Industrial Revolution transformed most aspects of life. They believed strongly in celibacy, one reaction to the questions about family life that were emerging at the time. They were also known for their intricate social dances involving separate lines of men and women who never mingled. Dancing has often been frowned on by other religious groups for its sexual nature, so perhaps the Shakers' energetic dancing released some sexual tensions.

"Simple Gifts" celebrates the grace that comes from attaining simplicity in life, a state of being that can be considered a true gift; by dancing one will "come 'round right," achieving the goal of simplicity.[17] The lyrics are themselves wonderfully plain and direct:

'Tis the gift to be simple,
'Tis the gift to be free,
'Tis the gift to come down where we ought to be,
And when we are in the place just right,
'Twill be in the valley of love and delight.

When true simplicity is gained,
To bow and to bend we will not be ashamed,
To turn, to turn will be our delight,
Till by turning, turning,
We come 'round right.

To seek the gifts of being simple and free, and to end "where we ought to be" in the "valley of love and delight," whether by bowing and bending or some other action, may have struck many striving Americans as naive, but others must have admired the Shaker goal of achieving "true simplicity."

A lovely little hymn that asks "How Can I Keep from Singing?" serves in many ways as an inspiration for this whole book. The song was first published in 1869 by Robert Lowry, a writer of gospel music; Ira Sankey wrote a different tune for it.[18] In recent years the song has come to be associated with the Quakers, possibly because Pete Seeger said he learned it from a woman who told him she learned it from her Quaker grandmother. It does appear in Quaker hymnals, and recently composed verses make specific reference to Friends, but its origins are clearly in the revivalist tradition. The sentiment in it testifies to the power of song to comfort and sustain us in times of trial, with the declaration in the first verse, "My life flows on in endless song, above earth's lamentations," and the conclusion, "Through all the tumult and the strife, I hear that music ringing, it finds an echo in my soul, how can I keep from singing?"

The second verse picks up the theme of comfort in time of turmoil, giving rise to music by way of rejoicing. In 1869 many Americans could easily have had both the recently concluded Civil War and more general social change in mind when they sang:

> What though the tempest loudly roars,
> I hear the truth, it liveth,
> What though the darkness 'round me close,
> Songs in the night it giveth.
> No storm can shake my inmost calm,
> While to that rock I'm clinging,
> Since love is Lord of heaven and earth,
> How can I keep from singing?[19]

Given the Quaker history of being persecuted for their pacifist beliefs, including during the Civil War, one can see why these lyrics would have appealed to many Friends. In the midst of the Cold War and its accompanying political persecutions by advocates of right-wing political correctness, Doris Plenn added the following lines to sustain once again any friends or Friends who might be the victims of oppression.

> When tyrants tremble sick with fear,
> And hear their death knell ringing,
> When Friends rejoice both far and near,
> How can I keep from singing?
> To prison cell and dungeon vile,
> Our thoughts to them are winging,
> When Friends by shame are undefiled,
> How can I keep from singing?[20]

As black Americans turned to Christianity in significant numbers after Independence, they adopted white religious music but also put a distinctive stamp on religious singing with their own musical preferences based on African practices. One common feature in African singing, evident in the religious music of African Americans, is the use of call and response. Although similar to the lining out of hymns, it is in essence quite different. Whereas lining out involves a song leader providing the next segment of lyrics to be repeated by the congregation, call and response places different musical tasks on the leader and the responders.[21] The leader is responsible for moving the song along and introducing new, often short statements appropriate to the emerging sentiment of the song. Many such statements come from a free-floating collection of verses that move easily from one song to another, enabling the leader to keep a song going for as long as the group desires, shaping the meaning by extemporaneous editing. The group responds with repeated supporting lines, certainly at the end of each verse, but often at the end of each line, validating the leader's message and urging the leader on. In call and response, the melody differs in each part. The tasks are not the same, but the whole is clearly greater than the sum of its parts.

African-American religious songs of the early nineteenth century tended to emphasize only those parts of the Christian message that had special meaning to their singers' lives. Until the Civil War, about 90 percent of the black population lived in the South as slaves. Free blacks gravitated toward the cities, both North and South, but their lives were exceedingly hard, and they faced racial prejudices, even among whites who opposed slavery. Black Americans drew different messages and hopes from the ferment of the Second Great Awakening.[22] Identifying with stories of the Hebrews' escape from bondage, slaves and free blacks found Moses an appealing subject for songs. Likewise, Jesus, a Lord more loving and just than any slave master, and one more powerful in righting wrongs, is commonplace in their songs. Some rejected the preaching of Paul, which masters often used to teach obedience.[23] Faced with a life in bondage, a status inheritable by their children as well, many slaves found the book of Revelation to be an inspiration for songs, with its vision of the end of days, the last judgment, and a new world unlike the present reality.

Release or escape via death before the final sorting out of souls meant death offered little terror to slaves. Endurance looms large in their songs; many trials had to be endured before they could lay their burdens down and cross over into the Promised Land. Crossing over water to a better life and reunion with loved ones echoed the desire to return home to Africa felt by many captives. Finally, slaves found song a way to convey hidden messages within the hearing of their masters, reflecting African customs that often used song to express criticism and hostile comments that would not have been acceptable in everyday speech. Certainly some of the hidden messages were not terribly difficult to decode, unless masters were not paying attention to their subordinates or chose to ignore what they heard as difficult to challenge, especially when a slave might respond that the song was from the scriptures. No doubt some songs were rarely sung if any whites were within hearing distance.

African-American religious songs rapidly diverged from white sacred music in the nineteenth century. One of the first collections of African-American religious music was a hymnal based on white collections and assembled and published in 1801 by Richard Allen, the founder of the African Methodist Episcopal Church in Philadelphia.[24] Isaac Watts and the Wesleys supplied many of Allen's choices, but he may have written a few of the hymns himself. By 1820 white visitors to black churches were commenting on differences in how they sang and what they sang about. In the South, where slaves were deliberately kept illiterate, African-American religious singing soon developed its own body of material, performed in its own distinctive style. The compilers of the first great collection of slave songs, *Slave Songs of the United States*, published in 1867, remark at length in its introduction of how difficult it was to use standard musical notation to capture the singing of the slaves on paper.[25] The compilers, particularly Lucy Garrison, had written down the music as they heard it. They note the ability of the singers to "keep exquisite time in singing" and how they "do not suffer themselves to be daunted by any obstacle in the words." Paper and pen "convey[ed] but a faint shadow of the original" singing, whether individual or collective. In their own way, the compilers emphasize the distinctive quality of black singing, with lead singers often "improvising" and the others "basing" the leader according to "their own whims," with rhythms and tonal variations that "produce the effect of a marvelous complication and variety, . . . rarely with any discord."[26] Twentieth-century collectors of African-American folk songs found it desirable to include separate chapters on religious songs.[27] While Newman White recognizes the distinctive qualities of African-American songs, he also believes their religious music was quite similar to that of the white camp meetings and backwoods churches, however different it might have been from the mainline hymnals.

African-American religious folk songs are many and varied, some still widely known and sung; others are less popular but continue to convey important messages. One place to begin is with two of the "sorrow songs" W. E. B. DuBois identifies as expressing life under slavery.[28] Release is the theme of "Swing Low, Sweet Chariot," which the singer believes is "coming for to carry me home." DuBois calls this the "cradle song of death," though it might also be interpreted via a more worldly metaphor as a call for the conductors of the Underground Railroad to lead the person home to freedom. In any case, the singer looks "over Jordan," the way to heaven, and spies "a band of angels coming after me." Despite the burdens of life, the weary traveler still feels "my soul is heavenly bound." This is no isolated person facing God all alone, but one who expects to be reunited with fellow sufferers in a better world, one who can exclaim, "If you get there before I do, . . . just tell my friends that I'm a coming too."

"The End and the Beginning" is how DuBois describes "My Lord! What a Mourning" and its contemplation of the end of days as described in the book of Revelation. The title of this song has a subtle double meaning. To the ear, *mourning* is indistinguishable from *morning*, and both are appropriate for the context of the song. The former tends to emphasize the laments of sinners left behind at the last judgment, while the latter celebrates the glorious dawn when the saints will go marching in. Which word a singer or hearer understands may say something about that individual's personality, faith, and current situation. In either case, the song asks, "Sinners, what will you do, when the stars begin to fall?" If the answer to the question, "Will there be time to find salvation?" is negative, then sinners will be left to "weep for the rocks and mountains," desperately but futilely listening for "the shout of victory." The shout may be that of the individual, but "shouts" were common in African-American music, both religious and secular, and generally accompanied by rhythmic movement in a circle that bordered on dancing. In the twentieth century, the preaching of "John, the Revelator" was still a powerful image for religious songs.[29]

"Sinner Man" combines many themes in African-American religious songs.[30] Sinners loom large in the body of folk songs, both as reminders of whose company to avoid and as the ones the songs address directly with the message to mend their ways. Rejected by God with the admonition, "You should have been a praying," the sinner is asked, "Where you going to run to?" Seeking a hiding place in nature at the end of days offers no help because rocks are melting, the sea is boiling, and the moon is bleeding—all familiar metaphors from other songs. Finally Satan, another very real and common presence in religious folk songs, appears to say, "Step right in," welcoming one of his own home.

Secret and not-so-secret messages abound in African-American religious folk songs. *Slave Songs of the United States* includes "There's a Meeting Here Tonight," which may have alerted slaves to a religious gathering after sundown, meetings that frequently were not approved by the masters. "Steal Away to Jesus" may have sent the same message, though it could also refer to escaping North or finding comfort in faith, or even in death. The story of Paul and Silas brought hope via song, and perhaps a sense of outwitting the master.[31] Acts 16 tells the story of how Paul and Silas meet a slave woman who is being exploited by her master as a fortuneteller because she is possessed by a spirit. Paul casts out the spirit, thereby rendering this slave property worthless to her master, and for this he and Silas are imprisoned. As they sing and pray for deliverance in jail that night, an earthquake strikes, destroying the jail and opening the way for them to escape. But Paul insists on remaining, to be set free by the court because as a Roman citizen he should not have been treated this way. For slaves to sing of slave property destroyed and prisoners miraculously set free would have sent a challenge to their masters; yet had the slaves been questioned, they could easily have replied they were only setting a Bible story to song. Since slaves understood their masters' predilection to have them taught Paul's messages of obedience rather than the more radical acts of Moses or Jesus, there is special irony in using Paul as a model of resistance to slavery.

Several verses use the common metaphor of the train to heaven, a celebration of one of the great technological wonders of the nineteenth century and a possible allusion to the Underground Railroad. Slaves may have intended a strictly religious meaning when they cautioned, "Straight up to heaven and straight right back, ain't but one train on this track," and continued, "People keep coming, but the train done gone," recalling the admonition to be prepared at all times. But they could readily have used such verses to communicate about more imminent escape.

Many songs speak directly of salvation and the way to heaven. Titles alone, a number of them from the 1867 collection, illustrate the point. Many a "Poor Wayfaring Stranger" had to "Walk the Lonesome Valley" where "Nobody Knows the Trouble I've Had." Often faced with a "Rocky Road," one still struggled onward because "I Can't Stay Behind" and "No Man Can Hinder Me," while friends might offer such encouragement as "O Brother, Don't Get Weary," or a reminder that we "ain't got long to stay here." It might be necessary to climb "Jacob's Ladder" or "go down in the valley to pray," studying about "The Good Old Way" before one could "Lay This Body [or Burden] Down" in preparation to saying, "I'm Going Home" to "Build a House in Paradise" where "The Sabbath Has No End." Some took comfort in the belief that the social inequities of this world would be gone in the next, or even reversed. In "Get a Home in That Rock," the "rich man Dives he lived so well, when he died he had a home in hell"; whereas, "poor man Lazarus, poor as I, when he died he had a home on high." A less stark but nonetheless pointed comment on social class came through the observation, "If 'ligion was a thing that money could buy, de rich would live and de po' would die." But "de Lord he wouldn't have it so, so de rich must die, just de same as de po'." No doubt, when slaves and later freed blacks sang of sinners and Satan, they had some very real examples in mind.

Ultimately, all one could hope for regarding the "light from the light house" was to request, "Let It Shine on Me." Leadbelly refers to this spiritual, with its tune echoing "Amazing Grace," as coming from slavery days, and he demonstrates how Baptists sang it slowly, the Methodists picked up the pace, and the Holy Ghost believers gave it real swing.[32] The enduring power and appeal of African-American religious songs is illustrated by the way "I'll Overcome Some Day," first published by Charles Tindley in 1900, was transformed into the more secular "We Shall Overcome," first by the Southern Tenant Farmers' Union in the 1930s, then by striking African-American tobacco workers in 1945, and ultimately by the civil rights movement in the 1960s.[33]

♯ ♯ ♯

Songs of war also express Americans' search for personal and national salvation and redemption. War songs fall into several different categories: marching songs (which frequently carry additional messages), patriotic songs intended to boost morale and inspire loyalty, ballads that spread the news and celebrate victories, soldiers' songs that comment on their life (often with bitter humor or satire), and songs of lament and sorrow expressed by those left behind. Les Cleveland draws the distinction between war songs that belong to popular culture (these are generally produced and marketed commercially and have patriotic messages) and songs that are more appropriately considered folk songs because they arise from the people, frequently as a form of protest with subversive intent.[34] Soldiers often take current or at least familiar tunes and use them in parodies. Death, never frequent in popular songs, is common in folk songs from war.

Folk songs from times of war are often topical and intimately related to immediate events, barely outlasting the war that gave rise to them. Some, however, strike a chord that rings over several generations, as is evident in a

selection of songs from American wars starting with the colonial era. Before
the Revolution, American wars involved the native peoples who were being
dispossessed, rival European empires, or both. The earliest conflicts between
Great Britain and other European powers involved the Spanish, followed by
wars with the Dutch. But the most significant and long-lasting struggle began
in 1689 with the French and lasted until 1815. Until 1763 the colonies joined
the mother country in opposing the French; but during the Revolution, the
emerging United States turned to this long-time enemy for assistance.

One of the earliest ballads from a colonial war is "The Ballad of
Schenectady."[35] Little remembered and probably seldom sung, this ballad
illustrates how songs spread both news and propaganda. In 1688 William of
Orange and his wife, Mary, accepted the throne of England from Parliament
to bring England into William's war with Louis XIV of France, a conflict
that would last long after both monarchs had died. During the summer
of 1689, a joint English–Iroquois force attacked Montreal from Albany. On
February 8, 1690, a French–Algonquian force retaliated, walking down from
Canada and assaulting not Albany but its smaller, more exposed neighbor,
Schenectady. Although troops were stationed in Schenectady, they had left
the gates unguarded, perhaps doubting anyone would walk from Canada in
the middle of winter. When the 114 French and 96 Indians fell on the city
at night, they burned 70 houses, killed 62 residents, and took 29 captives. A
few escaped, traveling to Albany to warn that city and get help. Soldiers soon
pursued the raiding party and managed to rescue some of the prisoners.

According to its title, the ballad was written the next summer by one
of the soldiers after he had returned to Albany. It has also been attributed
to Dr. Richard Shuckburgh, who has sometimes been credited with writing
"Yankee Doodle," though his authorship of either is doubtful.[36] The opening
lines echo "Chevy Chase," a British ballad about a 1388 battle on the border
between England and Scotland; that ballad was considered old in 1595 and
was among the most popular in the colonies.[37] The structure of the stanzas
is clearly based on "Chevy Chase," and the tune fits. Unlike nineteenth-
century visual representations of the massacre, which portray only Indians
as assaulting the town, the ballad makes it clear that the French were the
principal perpetrators and prime enemy, referring to their Indian allies only
in the next-to-last verse. The brutality of the attack and the horrors of life
on the frontier are evident from this account: we hear of "the cruel blow,"
murder committed "without shame or remorse," and "miseries of that night,"
which produced "great agony." The ballad reports the pursuing soldiers were
so enraged that "they took scarce one alive" when they caught the raiders.

The French are portrayed as "thievish rogues" who stoop to using "bloody Indian dogs." What the British Mohawk allies may have thought of the latter jibe is unclear, for the ballad recognizes their contribution to the chase.

BALLAD OF SCHENECTADY BY WALTER WILIE,
ALBANY, JUNE 12, 1690

God prosper long our King and Queen,
Our lives & safeties all,
A sad misfortune once there did
Schenectady befall.

From forth the woods of Canada
The Frenchmen tooke their way
The people of Schenectady
To captivate and slay.

They march'd for two and twenty dais
All thro' the deepest snow;
And on a dismal Winter Night
They strucke the Cruel Blow.

The lightsome sun that rules the day
Had gone down in the West;
And eke the drowsy Villagers
Had sought and found their rest.

They thought They were in Safetie all,
And dreampt not of the Foe;
But att Midnight They all awoke,
In Wonderment & Woe.

For They were in their pleasant Beddes,
And soundelle sleeping, when
Each door was sudden open broke
By six or seven Men.

The Men and Women, Younge & Olde,
And eke the Girls and Boys,
All started up in great Affright,
Att the alarming Noise.

They then were murther'd in their Beddes,
Without shame or remorse;
And soon the Floores and Streets were strew'd
With many a bleeding corse.

The Village soon began to Blaze,
Which shew'd the horrid sight:—
But, O, I can scarse Beare to Tell,
The mis'ries of that Night.

They threw the Infants in the Fire,
The Men they did not spare;
But killed All which they could find,
Tho' Aged or tho' Fair.

O Christe! In the still Midnight air,
It sounded dismally,
The Women's Prayers, and the loud screams
Of their great Agony.

Methinks as if I hear them now
All ringing in my ear;
The Shrieks and Groanes and Woefull Sighs
They utter'd in their fear.

But some ran off to Albany,
And told the dolefull Tale:
Yett, tho' We gave our cheerful aid,
It did not much avail.

And we were horribly afraid,
And shook with Terror, when
They told us that the Frenchmen were
More than a Thousand Men.

The news came on the Sabbath morn
Just att the Break of Day,
And with a companie of Horse
I galloped away.

But soone We found the French were gone
With all their great Bootye;
And then their Trail We did pursue
As was our true Dutye.

The Mohaques joynd our brave Partye,
And followed in the chase
Till we came upp with the Frenchmen
Att a most likely Place.

Our soldiers fell upon their Reare,
And killed twenty-five;

Our Young men were so much enrag'd
They took scarce One alive.

D'Aillebout Then did commande,
Which were but Theevish Rogues,
Else why did they consent and goe
With Bloodye Indian dogges?

And Here I end the long Ballad
The Which you just have redde;
I wish that it may stay on earth
Long after I am dead.

Between 1689 and 1763, when the French finally surrendered Canada to
the British, these two rivals went to war several times and spent many years
of peace preparing for the next conflict. Folk songs from these wars acted as
propaganda, celebrated victories, and created heroes. In 1759 British General James Wolfe died while taking the city of Quebec from his opponent,
Montcalm, who was also fatally wounded. Wolfe's death was the subject of
a series of ballads and paintings. One collection of ballads relating to the
colonial period concludes with five celebrating Wolfe's triumph and lamenting his death.[38] The best-known ballad, "Brave Wolfe," reprinted regularly
until the 1850s and collected from singers into the twentieth century, sets
the narrative of the victory in the context of lost love, recognizing that
Wolfe had become engaged shortly before embarking for America. Versions
vary, but Wolfe is represented as asking his love to remember him, lest he
be "undone forever." When his fiancée receives word of him, it is not of a
glorious victory, but "bad news" that "they stole my love while I was sleeping."[39] Thus the fiancées and wives of officers suffered the loss of their men
just as the women of the common soldiers did, though presumably few of
the former ever had to dye a dress red to support herself and her children
on the street.

The American Revolution produced numerous ballads and satires from
both sides of the conflict.[40] Songs arose from specific events leading up to
the Revolution, like the regulator movement in North Carolina (1765–71), or
served as patriot propaganda before and during the war.[41] Many were highly
topical and so quickly fell out of use once events ceased to be of interest.
Others have retained their appeal.

"Yankee Doodle" is the most prominent folk song from the Revolution,
though its origins trace to the colonial wars, probably at least to 1745.[42] J. A.
Lemay argues that "Yankee Doodle" has three sources, reflected in different

motifs. The oldest may be in the form of songs sung during harvest time, particularly when husks were being taken off ears of corn. The second, which he dates to 1745 on the basis of logic and internal evidence, comes from the unexpected conquest by ill-trained colonial volunteers of the great French fort at Louisbourg, Cape Breton Island. Lemay reads the verses as self-mockery from the surprise over this victory, not as British insults from an effort to retake the same fort in 1758. (The British had returned it to the French via a treaty in 1748.) The final source is, of course, the Revolution, when soldiers from small towns and farms laughed at themselves and their wide-eyed innocence when they first came to military camp and encountered more men than they had ever seen before. This is the source for such well-known verses as "Father and I went down to camp, along with Captain Gooding, and there we saw the men and boys as thick as hasty pudding," or "There was General Washington . . . giving orders to his men, I guess there was a million." The country rube marvels at the waste, the size of the guns—"as big as mother's basin"—and even the drums.

Certainly the British relished the song, initially playing it as they marched out of Boston on their way to Concord and Lexington on April 19, 1775; but being made to "dance to it till we were tired" on the way back to town may have made them feel less enamored of it.[43] Other lyrics composed during the war were sung to the tune.[44] But it is clear that when Americans sang the song, they not only were making fun of themselves but also of the British soldiers' contempt for their untrained opponents, who nonetheless prevailed.

Satire is also evident in "The Junto Song," a ballad that explained the war to those who could not read the extensive pamphlet literature written by such men as John Adams or Thomas Jefferson.[45] "The Junto Song" was not the first song to present the American side of the dispute with Great Britain to the general public. As early as 1765, when the Stamp Act was the object of protest, Americans could sing of the "Taxation of America."[46] Over the next decade, the conflict became more complicated, and deep philosophical questions about the nature of government were raised. Americans came to believe in the value of republics, a form of government that required virtuous citizens willing to act in the public interest.

"The Junto Song" uses these beliefs to good effect. Following the British retreat from Concord and Lexington, and before Bunker Hill, three British generals arrived in Boston to take command of the troops. Americans labeled them the *Junto*. This song, published in a New York newspaper in September 1775, was ostensibly sung by them and indicates British colonial policy. One question that concerned the colonists was what new taxes would be used for. An answer, bribes, appears in the first verse when the Junto states, "'Tis money makes the member vote and sanctifies our ways, it makes the patriot turn his coat, and money we must raise." The chorus then adds, "And a taxing we will go will go, and a taxing we will go," deliberately recalling the old, familiar folk song "A Begging We Will Go." Thus corruption of the political system is the aim of the taxes, a point reinforced in the second verse, where Americans learned the money was to pay "our ayes and noes," certainly in Parliament and perhaps in the colonial assemblies. With nothing left to tax in England, Parliament sent taxing laws abroad to make the colonists "bend to Britain's supreme power" via the sword and "leaden balls a shower." After threatening to burn Boston, the Junto has "second thoughts," deciding to test "what fraud can do . . . and see what bribes avail." The final verse links violence and the corrupt use of tax revenues as it summarizes the generals' policy:

> We'll force and fraud in one unite,
> To bring them to our hands;
> Then lay a tax on the sun's light,
> And a king's tax on their lands.

Anyone foolish enough to believe British reassurances that small taxes were not worth quarreling over would have been reminded of the colonial tendency to see tyranny behind any governmental action and that taxes on stamps and tea would soon be followed by levies on more basic essentials, though perhaps not the sun's light.

When the British soldiers surrendered at Yorktown in 1781, effectively ending the war and securing American independence, tradition records that the British band may have played an old English ditty, "The World Turned Upside Down."[47] "Yankee Doodle" had poked fun at the poorly trained continental soldiers, and for the most part, the British army had been able to go where it pleased and conquer whatever territory it wanted to. But now the unthinkable had happened. The most powerful country in the world had been defeated by its colonial offshoot. No wonder this old nursery rhyme may have seemed appropriate.

> If buttercups buzzed after the bees,
> If boats were on land, churches on sea,
> If ponics rodc mcn, and grass ate the corn,
> And if cats should be chased into holes by the mouse,
> If mommas sold their babies to gypsies for half a crown,

If summer were spring, and the other way 'round,
Then all the world would be upside down.

The Continental army would not have been so surprised, but it would have enjoyed the joke and its enemy's dismay.

The War of 1812 is a curious conflict, arguably fought at the wrong time and against the wrong enemy. As the French Revolution followed the American in 1789, and war between Great Britain and France resumed in 1793, the newly formed United States was asked to choose sides in a conflict in which it wanted no part. For almost twenty years, both European nations bullied the United States, attempting to force its support. Although James Madison and Congress finally decided to declare war on the British in 1812, the country had been insulted more seriously in 1807, and the French were equally plausible opponents. A few songs celebrated American naval victories but did not last long in American memory. Our national anthem emerged from an old English drinking song that provided the melody for a set of lyrics that celebrates American endurance in the face of a British bombardment of Fort McHenry, near Baltimore. But the most notable American victory, and one that produced the best songs, came at New Orleans, early in 1815 and after peace had been signed in Europe but before the news had crossed the Atlantic.

In 1822 Samuel Woodworth published "The Hunters of Kentucky," though he may have written it shortly after the battle.[48] Sung to the tune of "Unfortunate Miss Bailey," or occasionally "Yankee Doodle," this ballad combines several themes in celebrating Andrew Jackson's victory over the British. Larger-than-life individuals have long been a part of American folklore, from Mike Fink to Paul Bunyan to Pecos Bill. The hunters from Kentucky who joined Jackson in driving the British from New Orleans fit this mold, for they were not only a "hardy, free-born race," ready to face any "daring foe" who should invade the country, but they did so because each man "was half a horse, and half an alligator." As at Bunker Hill, the British forces, "arrayed in martial pomp," advanced against the American lines where the soldiers "snugly kept [their] places," not firing until the enemy "were so near we saw them wink." Sexual overtones are evident when the song relates how British Colonel Packenham bragged he would seize not only the city's cotton but also its women "of ev'ry hue it seems, from snowy white to sooty." In the end, the British found "*lead* was all the *booty*," leaving the Kentucky hunters "all our *beauty*," as they successfully "protect[ed] ye ladies." This song may have provided Jackson's presidential campaigns in 1824 and 1828 with one of the more singable election songs in American history.

Around 1945 a high school principal and history teacher known as Jimmy Driftwood wrote "Battle of New Orleans" as a means of helping his students learn about the past. His lesson plan was successful beyond his wildest dreams. Johnny Horton won a Grammy in 1959 for the song in the country and western category. Even more remarkable, the song became a hit in Great Britain, recorded by Lonnie Donegan. Although we know who wrote the song and of its commercial success, it has some claim to folk song status because it became widely popular, and its verses may have gone into the oral tradition. The music was taken from an old fiddle tune, "The 8th of January," which was the date of the battle. The principal addition of Driftwood's song was to introduce the role played in defeating the British by a local Cajun named Jean Lafitte, who the song refers to as a pirate, recognizing his uncertain relationship with the law.

In 1846 the United States went to war with Mexico. In the peace treaty of 1848, the United States acquired much of what is now its Southwest, and Mexico found its territory cut in half. Texas, which won its independence from Mexico in 1836, had already been added to the union in 1845, and California, also a former Mexican territory, would be admitted as a state in 1850. This was part of the extraordinary expansion of the country, from the Louisiana Purchase in 1803 to the Gadsen Purchase in 1853. With the decision in the Missouri Compromise in 1820 to prohibit slavery in most of the Louisiana Purchase, many Southerners pursued territorial ambitions against Mexico as a place to extend slavery.

One song from that conflict deserves attention, if only because of its later influence: "Green Grow the Laurels."[49] This song was familiar to the Irish immigrants who had enlisted in the army and fought in Mexico. The story goes that the Mexicans who heard the song did not understand the lyrics but adopted a paraphrase of "green grow" as their name for the Yankee invaders, henceforth known as *gringos.* In the twentieth century, Oklahoma author Lynn Riggs wrote a not-very-successful folk opera titled *Green Grow the Lilacs.* Riggs's opera was eventually transformed into one of the great Broadway musicals, *Oklahoma.*

The song itself could easily have been included in the previous chapter, for it raises serious questions about relations between men and women. The soldiers in Mexico may have sung it to express their fears of some Matty Grove appealing to the girls they had left behind, or perhaps, since the lyrics make specific reference to letters, to their worries about receiving "Dear John" letters. The original may have been sung from the female point of view, but it was easily given a gendered twist. Thus one typical verse begins,

"I oft-times have wondered why women love men, and oft-times I wonder why men would like them." If a woman is singing the song, she may finish it: "From my own sad experience I very well know, that men are deceitful wherever they go." To which a man might respond, "They're [women] men's ruination and sudden downfall, and they cause men to labor behind the stone wall [prison?]." Other stanzas lament, "I once had a sweetheart but now I've got none," and speak of the receipt of a letter "saying you write to your love and I'll write to mine."

The chorus, as modified from its British origins, reads:

> Green grow the laurels, all sparkling with dew,
> I'm lonely my darling since parting with you,
> But at our next meeting I hope to prove true,
> And change the green laurel for the red, white, and blue.

In the original, the first line sometimes reads, "Green grow the laurel and so does the rue," referring to traditional associations of virginity with laurel and the loss of virginity with rue. Thus the song hints at a young woman who has lost her virginity to a soldier, "deceitful wherever they go." Some versions suggest she intends to follow him, since the chorus concludes with "and change the green laurel for the orange and blue," possibly referring to regimental colors. Another interpretation translates "orange and blue" into "oregano blue," the herb of fidelity. In any case, the song addresses anxieties and fears stemming from separation during war.

The "Battle Hymn of the Republic" is one of the best-known songs from America's bloodiest war.[50] By the time Howe wrote her lyrics, the tune was already widely in use in the war as "John Brown's Body," a Northern song with an abolitionist viewpoint. Although Lincoln initially claimed to be fighting the war to preserve the Union and oppose secession, Northern abolitionists, both black and white, believed he should make it about ending slavery. Preserving slavery was certainly what many white Southerners had in mind when they supported secession. Following the Union victory at Antietam in September 1862, Lincoln responded to the antislavery voices by promising to issue an Emancipation Proclamation on January 1, 1863, if the war had not ended. The popularity of "John Brown's Body" makes it clear that many soldiers were already sympathetic with that goal, for Brown was a well-known martyr to the cause of abolition and a hated figure in the South for attempting to foment a slave revolt with his raid on Harper's Ferry in 1859. Brown seized the federal armory at Harper's Ferry but was soon captured by Robert E. Lee and executed for his actions.

The soldiers who marched to this song recognized and identified with the spirit of Brown when they sang, "John Brown's body lies a-mould'ring in the grave, but his soul goes marching on." They also included him among their number and invoked God's blessings on their own efforts, proclaiming, "He's gone to be a soldier in the army of the Lord." One of the bluntest verses makes it abundantly clear where they thought virtue lay in the conflict when they compared Brown to his and their opponents:

> He captured Harper's Ferry with his nineteen men so true,
> He frightened old Virginny 'til she trembled thru and thru,
> They hung him for a traitor, they themselves the traitor crew,
> But his soul goes marching on.

Adaptations of Steffe's hymn tune did not stop with either "John Brown" or the "Battle Hymn." White Southerners bravely responded with "we'll hang Abe Lincoln from a sour apple tree," but they may have been shocked when black soldiers in the Union armies offered their own interpretation of events:

> We are done with hoeing cotton, we are done with hoeing corn,
> We are colored Yankee soldiers as sure as you are born,
> When Massa hears us shouting, he will think it's Gabriel's horn,
> As we go marching on.

Few melodies are as instantly recognized by Americans, or evoke as much emotion as "Taps," another song with roots in the Civil War.[51] In 1862 General Daniel Butterfield was commanding a unit of the Union army in the Peninsular Campaign in Virginia. Butterfield had been dissatisfied with the bugle call for the end of day and had been working on a substitute in his own mind. He called one of his buglers in, and together they worked out a suitable, playable version. Butterfield instructed his own command to use the new call, but it proved so appealing that it spread quickly to nearby units. Soon Confederate troops within earshot began to use "Taps," continuing the folk adoption of a song through aural transmission. It was eventually given words, but few know them, or even of them. The four-note melody is enough.

One could easily write a whole volume on the songs of the Civil War, though many never crossed over from the commercial sector into the folk tradition. "Dixie" certainly did for the Southern side. The Northern song "When Johnny Comes Marching Home Again" clearly served the need for propaganda; it celebrates Johnny's glorious return from war, when "the men will cheer and the boys will shout, and the ladies they will all turn out, and we'll all feel gay when Johnny comes marching home."[52] In fact, many soldiers did not come home, and many who did were unable to march. So common were injuries during this war that a whole industry making prosthetic limbs developed after the conflict.[53] The old Irish song that provided the tune for "When Johnny Comes Marching Home Again" is perhaps a more realistic assessment and was known in the United States at the time. The tune, a variation of "Captain Kidd," was used again in the twentieth century for a popular song in the folk style, "Ghost Riders in the Sky."

The Irish version, sometimes known as "Guns and Drums," is sung from the perspective of a woman welcoming home the wreck of her husband. It begins, "With your guns and drums . . . the enemy nearly slew you." Later verses ask, "Where are your legs that used to run?" and bitterly observe, "You haven't an arm, you haven't a leg" and will "have to be put with a bowl to beg." The recurring motif in the last line of the chorus grieves, "Johnny, I hardly knew you," a cry that is equally powerful whether it refers to her trouble recognizing him or her regret that they had too little time together before he went to war. Faced with the fact that "they're rolling out the guns again," this wife and mother promises, "They'll never take our sons again, Johnny I'm swearing to you." Few songs are so direct about the likely outcomes of war for the soldiers and their families, while blame is shared between Johnny, who was attracted to his "guns and drums," and the powerful "they," who are rolling out the guns again to feed the children of the poor to the dogs of war.

Between the Civil War and World War I, the United States fought many battles with the Indians within the country and a brief skirmish with the Spanish in 1898. Neither produced any memorable folk songs. World War I, however, gave rise to several enduring songs. Both the Lomaxes and Carl Sandburg include songs from that war, many from the perspective of the soldiers, in their volumes printed within a decade and a half of the war's end.[54] Often these songs have a biting, satirical edge.

Perhaps the best-known song from World War I is "Mademoiselle from Armentieres," or "Hinky Dinky, Parlee-Voo," whose tune is similar to "When Johnny Comes Marching Home Again."[55] Sandburg claims that this song has been sung more often and with more different verses than any other. It is easy to see why, as it is as much about attitude as it is about content. In a structure similar to the newly popular blues, each verse repeats one line twice, followed by commentary, and then concludes with "hinky dinky, parlee-voo," a linguistic reminder that this war and France were unlike anything most American soldiers had ever encountered. The song can be repeated easily and endlessly, as long as anyone has another verse to offer. Many stanzas offer satire, some with special attention to the officers. One such observes, "The captain he's carrying the pack," apparently an unusual activity for an officer, since the soldiers "hope to the Lord it breaks his back." Another comments that while "the officers get all the steak . . . all we get is the belly-ache." But the preponderance of verses, whether acceptable in polite company or obscene, concern the mademoiselle. Many play off American stereotypes of the French as sexually liberated and imaginative. In 1927 Sandburg included verses remarking that the mademoiselle never wore underwear and that "many and many a married man, wants to go back to France again," drawn by selective memories that meant a soldier "might forget the gas and shell, [but he'll] never forget the mademoiselle."[56]

Soldiers used songs to register complaints about all sorts of conditions. "A Rookie's Lament" adopts the attitude of "Yankee Doodle," an American innocent confronting the army.[57] Pleased that there are "no cows to milk and drive" in the army, the soldier is nonetheless amazed by shower baths and signal flags. Broken legs are treated by the army doctor, though the physician might prescribe "C.C." pills (cocaine?) for a leg "just badly bent." The topics of songs like "The Company Cook" or "The Sergeant, He's the Worst of All" are self-evident.[58] Another song asserts that soldiers, however crude and brutal their service, must be going to heaven because "We've Done Our Hitch in Hell."[59]

Both Sandburg and the Lomaxes included in their collections a song of social commentary about the privileges of class and rank: "If You Want to Know Where the Privates Are."[60] Ascending through the ranks, we discover the privates spend their time "up to their necks in mud." Sergeants are still on the frontlines but are more secure "clipping the old barbed-wire." The captains are near enough to be "drinking the private's rum," but higher-ranked officers are "down in their deep dugout." The generals, however, are safely "back in gay Paree." The singer attests to the truth of this realistic portrait of the glories of war by asserting in every case, "I saw them."

In keeping with Les Cleveland's observation that folk songs about war recognize the possibility of death, both the Lomaxes and Sandburg included "The Hearse Song," one of the bluntest reminders of the purpose of war—killing people—in folk song tradition.[61] The song consists of three basic parts. The first reminds living soldiers to remember when they see the hearse rolling by that "the hearse's next load may consist of you." Once dead, soldiers should not expect to be treated with respect, as the grave diggers will "lower you down," and then "they'll thrown in dirt and they'll thrown in rocks,

and they won't give a damn if they break the box." But the final indignity
is reserved for after one is dead and buried, for it is then that:

> Oh, the bugs crawl in and the bugs crawl out,
> They do right dress and they turn about,
> Then each one takes a bite or two,
> Of what the war office used to call you.

This is true gallows humor, a form of whistling past the graveyard, or laughing
at death. A similar need of school children confronting their own mortality for
the first time meant variations of this verse were heard in elementary school
yards in the 1950s, albeit stripped of any obvious references to war.[62]

Neither World War II, the cold war, the Vietnam War, nor more recent
conflicts have produced any distinguished folk songs. Protest songs have
abounded, but most have not lasted. Some folk songs, however, have provided
the tune for military songs from these conflicts. Woody Guthrie's "Reuben
James," commemorating the lives lost by the sinking of an American destroyer in the North Atlantic almost two months before Pearl Harbor, was set
to "Wildwood Flower." Bob Dylan's "Blowin' in the Wind" addresses both
war and racism with a tune modified from a slave song from the Civil War,
"No More Auction Block for Me." During the Vietnam War, pilots composed
verses to the tune of "Red River Valley," reflecting not on lost love but on
comrades lost and dangers faced in air raids in the Red River Valley of North
Vietnam. The folk process continues to be evident by the now-common appearance of yellow ribbons on trees and automobiles when American soldiers
are off at war, a custom with deep roots but clearly given a boost by the
popular song "Tie a Yellow Ribbon 'Round the Old Oak Tree." Not only did
that song provide the impetus for the wide adoption of the custom, but the
folk process modified the original meaning of the song—in which the ribbon
was to indicate whether a man just out of prison should bother to get off the
bus as he came home—to an unequivocal welcome home for soldiers.

CHAPTER 4

"Take This Hammer"

Work and the Labor Movement

"The Ballad of John Henry" is one of America's best-known folk songs. John and Alan Lomax began their first collection, *American Ballads and Folk Songs*, with this famous song, while Howard Odum and Guy Johnson devoted a separate chapter to the ballad in *Negro Workaday Songs*.[1] Versions abound, testifying to its wide circulation among singers. For years scholars searched diligently, but to no avail, to find the "real" John Henry, believing from the lyrics that he hammered in the Big Bend Tunnel on the C&O Railroad around 1870. In a remarkable piece of historical detection, Scott Nelson recently connected a John William Henry to the Lewis Tunnel, east of the Big Bend but still on the C&O. Henry, born in New Jersey, had received a ten-year sentence in Virginia for housebreaking in 1866. He was contracted out to work on the railroad in 1868; but like so many convicts, he never returned alive, perhaps killed not by a race with a steam drill but by hazardous conditions or the brutal demands of tunneling that overtaxed his five-feet-one-inch frame. In some ways, it might have been better if John Henry had not been identified, for the ballad clearly speaks to and about all American workers caught up in the Industrial Revolution, which profoundly altered economic relationships in the nineteenth century. Workers, individually and collectively, faced not only the technological changes of the machine age but also the legal and economic innovations of industrial capitalism.[2]

"John Henry" expresses a number of important themes, but none so central as the confrontation of man and machine. We associate the machine age with factory production, and rightly so, but working men and women confronted mechanical counterparts to their place in the workplace as they labored in mines, sweated in fields, and hammered on the railroads. In some ways, the story of the Industrial Revolution replacing men and women with machines is summed up in the following verse:

> Well the Captain cried to John Henry,
> I'm going to bring that steam drill 'round,
> I'm going to bring that steam drill out on the job,
> Going to whup that steel on down.

Faced with this challenge from the boss and his mechanical companion, John Henry refuses to accept obsolescence and asserts, "A man ain't nothing but a man, but before I let that steam drill beat me down, I'll die with a hammer in my hand." To keep up in his race with the steam drill, John Henry had to swing two hammers weighing nine to fifteen pounds each, instead of the usual one hammer. Confronted with a smug inventor "who thought he was mighty fine," John Henry "drove fifteen feet while the steam drill only made nine"; but "he hammered so hard that he broke his poor heart, and he laid down his hammer and he died."

Later singers, faced with the same option but more familiar with the power of the machines and the economic system, and more interested in survival, used "Take This Hammer" to proclaim, "This hammer it killed John Henry, but it won't kill me"; and as far as the captain was concerned, "Tell him I'm gone."[3] John Henry was heroic and capable of great feats, and his story was widely known and greatly respected among African Americans. His near-mythic qualities are suggested by the prophecy that is included in many versions: when he was a child, "sitting on his momma's knee, he picked up a hammer and a little piece of steel, said hammer's going to be the death of me." But he was no Hercules, or even Paul Bunyan, and, as the prophecy foretold, the hammer did him in.

In the nineteenth century, nature was an opponent from which riches might be won via agriculture or other extractive industries. But nature did not give up those riches easily. Some versions of this ballad suggest it was not the race with the machine that killed John Henry but that the task of subduing nature was beyond human powers. A typical verse reflects this sentiment:

> John Henry went up to the mountain,
> His hammer was by his side,

But the mountain so tall, and John Henry so small,
That he laid down his hammer and he died [or cried].

The ballad recognizes many of the dangers inherent in work in the nineteenth century, both for the workers and for their families. As John Henry, or any other hammering man, drove his drill into the mountain to make a hole for blasting powder, a shaker had to hold the drill and turn it so the loose pieces of rock fell out. After asking his shaker to sing to support his effort of swinging two hammers, John Henry reminds him, "If my hammer misses that steel, tomorrow going to be your burying day." In most of the versions John Henry also has a wife, who is profoundly affected by his death, a common occurrence in the nineteenth century, when occupational hazards were great and insurance virtually nonexistent. Although the means of expressing it vary, Polly Ann demonstrates her loyalty to her man. A common story line has her picking up his hammer to finish the job, driving steel "like a man." Other versions have her stepping up to his grave to say, "I'm always true to you," or pledging to take a pilgrimage to the place where her man "fell dead." A number of versions use lines adopted from a Child ballad, "The Lass of Roch Royal," to remind listeners that Polly Ann has lost her economic support and companion.[4] These lines are quite familiar, asking, among other things, "Who's going to shoe your pretty little feet?" and "Who's going to kiss your ruby-red lips?" That the original ballad was about a young mother and child denied financial support may not have been known to the singers of "John Henry," but the situation was similar and all too familiar at the time. Perhaps if Polly Ann had been asked, she would have advised John Henry to walk away from the contest, or at least to use only one hammer, even if it meant losing.

♯ ♯ ♯

Songs relating to work fall into two broad categories. The first consists of songs that arise from a particular occupation or type of work. Many songs were intended to make work easier by helping pass the time while doing a boring job, by setting an appropriate pace to keep the boss content without exhausting the workers, or by establishing a rhythm for joint action, such as rowing or hauling on ropes. Other songs comment on occupations, offering descriptions of the demands of the job and observations about coworkers and bosses, frequently via satirical remarks.

The second category includes songs connected to the labor movement and efforts to unionize. Many of these songs were composed to address specific events and issues, and so they are not as clearly folk songs as those in the first category, nor have they all survived for as long. Songs from the labor movement were first and foremost intended to create and express solidarity among workers. Many offered social commentary directed at class conflict or the dangers of particular lines of work. Although all these songs were stimulated by the transformations associated with the Industrial Revolution and capitalism, some union movements, such as the Knights of Labor and the International Workers of the World (also known as the IWW or the Wobblies), were more inclined to singing than others; the successes and failures of unionization influenced the creation and spread of songs as well.

Time looms large in work and labor songs. Work songs could be used to establish rhythms to pace and coordinate joint efforts. Certain pre- or proto-industrial occupations, such as farming, logging, or whaling, were closely linked to seasonal cycles, so many songs would have been more appropriate to one time of year than another. The increasing dominance of clock time is one of the profound but often overlooked results of the Industrial Revolution. Miners and especially factory workers were subject to work disciplined by the clock and the demand that all workers start and stop at the same time. Songs comment not only on this aspect of clock time but also on the dangers of speed and trying to make up for lost time. The latter is addressed more extensively in the next chapter on transportation with regard to wrecks.

♯ ♯ ♯

Understanding the transformation of the American economy in the nineteenth century helps to make sense of work songs. Until the twentieth century, the American economy was solidly agricultural. In 1800 only about 5 percent of the population lived in cities, and the cities were not very large. Until 1920 over half the people lived in rural areas. Because the United States is so large and includes such a wide range of environments, agriculture varies notably from one part of the country to another, if only because of the increasing length of the growing season as one moves south and the decline in rainfall as one moves west. Both affect choices of agriculture. Cattle herding, for example, is easier to do on wide-open grasslands and may be better suited to that environment than plowing the land for crops.

In addition to farming, extractive industries exploited natural resources for economic gain from the earliest years of European presence in North America. Fishing and logging attracted colonists from the beginning, as did mining, though the long-hoped-for gold proved elusive in what became the eastern United States, so miners had to settle for less exotic ores like iron or copper. Most of the songs that have endured from these industries date from the nineteenth century, many stimulated by European immigrants, such as Welsh miners, who had traditions of singing about their work.

During the nineteenth century, the Industrial Revolution added new forms of work to the American economy in factories and on large-scale construction jobs. Clock discipline brought many workers together in factories, but work in textile mills or iron foundries was often too noisy and hectic to encourage singing on the job.[5] Thus many of the songs of the Industrial Revolution were intended to be sung at home or in union meetings. The most notable exception comes from songs that emerged from the great construction projects of building the railroads, canals, and highways, for there laborers could sing while they worked. Revolutions in transportation were significant components of the Industrial Revolution, whether transforming old modes like shipping, or providing new ways to get around like the railroads. Songs from the transportation revolution follow in the next chapter.

♯ ♯ ♯

Agriculture was the heart of the American economy until well into the twentieth century. The nature of particular crops and animals affected work rhythms, which in turn influenced the songs that arose from that particular type of work. At the same time, the way work was organized also affected the songs, as individual farmers working alone produced one type of music, while gangs of workers sang other types of songs. In addition, agricultural songs can be divided into field songs and barn songs. Both helped to pass the time during repetitive, boring tasks; both helped to set the pace and rhythm of work; and both helped to coordinate efforts when joint action was needed.

Work in the fields went more easily with songs. Leadbelly sang a number of songs from his own work experience, songs designed to set an efficient pace for a gang of workers picking cotton. A good song leader could establish a pace that would not prove too taxing to the hands but would keep the boss content; a song leader who was angry with his coworkers could set an unpleasantly fast tempo with his singing. The content of a song might send a variety of messages. One of Leadbelly's well-known songs, "Pick a Bale of Cotton," contains a brag or challenge about the amount of work the singer can do. When the lead singer boasts he can "pick a bale a day," this is an exaggeration because a cotton bale weighs over five hundred pounds. In his songbook, Leadbelly might claim he could pick one thousand pounds a day by hustling, "jump down, turn around," but his coworkers might well have asked, "How in the world can I pick a bale a day?" If they complained too much, the leader could respond that he has a "little baby sister" who can pick a bale a day.[6] In "Cotton Fields," Leadbelly reflected on the hard life of a cotton picker when he observed, "When them cotton balls got rotten, you couldn't pick very much cotton."[7] Friends might wonder why a worker left one part of the South to come to another when regardless of the place, "you didn't make very much money in them old cotton fields at home." Such a song might be sung while picking, but it also set the pace for hoeing the fields to keep the weeds down.

Not all picking or hoeing songs comment exclusively on the work at hand. In 1959 Alan Lomax recorded a group of prisoners on Parchman Farm in Mississippi hoeing at a brisk pace and singing "Berta, Berta," in which instructions to "raise 'em up higher, let 'em drop down" are intermingled with an imagined conversation with Alberta "livin' at ease" back home.[8] The prisoner tells his woman to marry someone else if she pleases, covering his despair over his long time left to serve and his anxiety over her willingness to wait with the excuse, "[I] might not want you when I go free."

African-American farmers working alone in their fields often developed their own unique and highly individualistic songs or "hollers" by which they could communicate over long distances to family or neighbors. The blues may well have had roots in these songs. Leadbelly sang an example of one such holler his Uncle Bob used to ask his wife to "Bring Me Little Water, Sylvie" when he got "hot and dry" from plowing.[9]

Once certain crops had been harvested, they needed to be processed in the barns. Tobacco had to be stripped and dried, corn husked, grains thrashed. The roots of "Yankee Doodle" have been traced to corn-husking songs, and the following verse identifies the various stages of processing corn.[10] The first line is about husking, the second about using a corn machine to take the kernels off the cob, the third about parching the corn, and the last about making meal.[11]

> Corn-stalks twist your hair off,
> Cart wheel frolic round you,
> Old fiery dragon carry you off,
> And mortar pestle pound you.

Other verses describe the social scene of a husking bee, including the celebrations when the job was done and the neighbors all had a "duced frolic," during which many would become "drunk as sots." From verses in the corn stalks tradition regarding sexual improprieties at frolics, it is easy to imagine some of the songs warning about courtship and marriage passing among the workers at a husking bee.[12]

Songs of the loggers naturally follow those of agriculture because many farm boys earned extra cash during the winter by working for timber companies. Moreover, access to timber was always one consideration in selecting a farm site, for trees provided housing, heat, fences, and tools. Farmers and shanty-boys were often rivals for the affections of young women, with the cash available to the latter frequently proving attractive.[13] Although forests were common in the South, most of the best-known logger songs come from the North in an arc stretching from Maine to Wisconsin, with occasional extensions into Canada. Most date from the middle to the end of the nineteenth century, when logging and the songs moved west.[14]

Although most of the loggers' songs comment on the rigors of their life, at least one echoes the familiar complaint that the girls left behind are not always true. The story of Jack Haggerty and his "Flat River Girl" was popular among loggers at the end of the nineteenth century.[15] Apparently Jack had proved as attractive as many shanty-boys to his beloved Annie, and he worked hard and risked danger in the woods to make the money to give her "jewels and the finest lace." One day Jack received a letter in which Annie informed him "from her promise herself she'd relieved" and that when he next saw her she would "ne'er be a maid." The song does not tell if a farm boy won her hand, or some roving gambler, but the news left Jack in despair and sent him wandering, perhaps to sea or perhaps out West.

Logging was hard, dangerous work, generally done in remote areas during the winter months. Winter not only was a time when extra hands could be recruited off the farms but also when the woods were freer from insects and undergrowth, and snow made it easier to skid the logs out to the rivers, down which the logs would float to the sawmills when the ice melted in the spring. Although axe men on Southern prison farms sang as they chopped together, few songs seem to have developed in the Northern forests to assist in the actual work. But during the long, cold nights back in the shanties, the men would sing to amuse themselves with songs about their work.

The process of recruitment produced one familiar song that wryly remarks on deceitful bosses and hard conditions. Telling a common story, the song proved popular in reference to "Canada-I-O" and later "Michigan-I-O," perhaps by way of Pennsylvania. It sounded such a resonant chord among young men lured off to work by false promises that later versions no longer referred to loggers but to buffalo hunters and railroad builders.[16]

The tale begins with an offer from a labor recruiter to "spend one winter pleasantly" in the woods of Canada or Michigan, or some other remote place. The promise of good wages and transportation enticed not only the singer but also another twenty-five to thirty men. As the trip to the woods began, however, the singer reports, "Our joys were ended, and our sorrows did begin." Tough bosses, hard work, bad food, and unpleasant living conditions meant the workers "suffered worse than murderers," so that when the winter was finally over and the men returned home, all they wanted to do was "tell others not to go to that forsaken God Damned place called Canada-I-O," or "Michigan-I-O," or "the range of the buffalo."

A song from Michigan in the 1840s called "The Shanty Boys" or "Cutting Down the Pines" offers numerous details about the logger's life.[17] It begins with the observation that a lumbering crew was composed of farmers, sailors, mechanics, and tradesmen who left their homes and sweethearts for the lure of the woods and high pay. Once there, the men were divided into "choppers and sawyers . . . [who] lay their timber low," along with skidders, yardsmen, and teamsters, who dragged the logs out of the forest to the river, where they would be floated down to the mills in the spring. The workday began about four o'clock in the morning, when the crew was rousted out. After great confusion finding "caps, mitts, socks, rags and shoe-packs" left near the stove to dry overnight, and eating a solid breakfast, the crew headed out into the woods to cut and haul timber until noon. A lunch of pork and beans, and pie was hastily consumed, at least partly so as not to lose one's share, followed by a few minutes smoking "till everything looks blue." After an afternoon spent like the morning, the crew returned to the shanty with "cold and wet feet," ready for supper. At the end of their long day, the loggers were generally ready for bed by about nine o'clock, but not before a round of songs and stories. The next morning, the whole routine started all over again. The song ends, as did the lumbering season, with spring and the melting snow and ice, when it was time to "lay down your saws and axes" so the loggers could "risk their dear lives" taking part in the dangerous trip with the logs down the swollen, cold river.

Miles from home or the nearest town and cooped up with other young men in crowded conditions, the logging crew put a premium on getting along. But tempers did flare occasionally. "Blue Mountain Lake,"* collected from Yankee John Galusha in 1939 and based on real men known by Galusha

*Words and music collected, adapted, and arranged by Frank Warner. TRO-© Copyright 1971 (Renewed) Melody Trails, Inc., New York, NY. Used by permission.

and his wife in the 1870s, tells the story "'bout the rackets we had 'round the Blue Mountain Lake" in the Adirondacks.[18] The heart of the matter was the friction between the crew and Bill Mitchell, "as mean a damn man as you ever did see," who kept the shanty. Apparently Mitchell did not carry his share of the load but "lay 'round the shanty from morning to night, and if a man said a word he was ready to fight." Early one morning, one of the loggers had enough and "knocked hell out of Mitchell," with the shanty keeper's wife looking on with approval. George Griffin, the head of the whole operation, found he had "nothing to say" about his foreman's woes when the "boys came and took him away." The final two verses have nothing to do with this incident. One celebrates Nellie, the cook, who despite being "short, thick, and stout" was nevertheless "the belle of Long Lake." The second anticipates a brief respite from the labors with a Christmas season spree midst the lures of Glens Falls.

Two of the best-known songs of the shanty boys address the dangers associated with floating the logs down to the mills in the spring: "James Phalen" and "The Jam on Gerry's Rock."[19] Certainly falling trees and dangling limbs posed hazards in the woods, as did the sharp tools of the trade, but nothing threatened the men's safety like a jam of thousands of logs on a swollen river. Men who were willing to risk their lives to break up jams could make up to three times the wages as those who preferred to stay safely on shore. "James Phalen" or "Jim Whalen" is a simple story of a young man who, seduced by his foreman's flattering talk of his bravery to "do as we are told," tried to break up a dangerous jam. The song has been identified with a real event on the upper Mississippi in 1878. The moral of the story is clearly stated, advising the "jolly raftsmen" to "be cautious before it is too late, for death's still lurking 'round you."

"The Jam on Gerry's Rock," widely known but without precise historical roots despite years of searching, is more complex. The victim in this song is not one of the men taking orders but "the foreman, young Monroe." There is a suggestion that Monroe courted death (the wages of sin) in the eyes of some of his men, for he set out to break up the jam on a Sunday. Regardless of this hint of moral indignation, the song is essentially sympathetic in its descriptions of the courageous Monroe's battered body, which they "found all bruised and mangled on the beach" downriver. In some versions, only his battered head is found. Monroe's loss is mourned not only by his comrades but also by his "promised bride." Some sense of the solidarity among loggers is portrayed by the "liberal subscription she received from the shanty-boys that day," along with Monroe's wages from the firm. In true ballad tradition, however, the brokenhearted girl dies shortly after her man and is buried beside him. Surely many families worried that this might be the fate of their young men who worked in the woods.

Work on the water also produced many folk songs, whether derived from rowing, sailing, whaling, or simply loading and unloading ships. The songs coordinated collective actions: pulling oars, hauling ropes, or lifting heavy objects. The stressed beats for common action are easy to hear in recordings of these songs, especially when the singers grunt or exhale; it takes some imagination to hear the beats when reading them. The lyrics of the songs may relate to the task at hand, may comment on some person or event, or may be irrelevant, but the words are incidental to the beat.

The importance of the beat is evident in Leadbelly's recordings of such songs and is especially clear in the collection of work songs on Alan Lomax's CD *Southern Journey, Volume 13: Earliest Times*. Timber cut in the Southern forests was often shipped elsewhere. Loading forty- to fifty-foot logs on board a swaying ship was no easy task, requiring numerous hands working in unison. "Old Tar River" rambles on about a letter from Major Bailey, saying, "Old Tar River gonna run tomorrow," but the point is in the rhythms that let the work get done.[20] Although the purpose of singing "Pay Me" was to make the timber "light" during loading, this song offers some social commentary as well.[21] The chorus makes it clear that the men are working for wages, but they are unsure of whether they will, in fact, be paid, for they repeatedly request, "Oh pay me, pay me my money down, pay me or go to jail, pay me my money down." They have heard the captain remark, "Tomorrow is my sailing day," and they hope he will not leave without settling his debts. Few African Americans would have been willing or able to put a captain in jail for cheating them of their wages. The workers also understand class and social privilege when they wish they were "Mrs. Alfred Jones's son" because then they could "stay in the house and drink good rum." If Mrs. Alfred Jones's son had happened to be watching the work, he might well have found himself subject to the same kind of satire a Southern academic faced when he paused to see if he could determine what a nearby road crew was singing. As he finally caught the gist of the song, he found the men were singing, "White man settin' on a wall . . . wastin' his time."[22]

Rowing was another activity in which songs served to coordinate effort, with the tempo easily varied to fit the weight of the boat or the length of the journey. In much of the coastal South, rivers and bays provided the easiest means of travel, whether for a social visit or for moving goods. "Michael, Row the Boat Ashore" is full of religious imagery, but it is essentially a rowing song from the Georgia Sea Islands, where ships had to anchor in the surf off shore, and goods and passengers had to be rowed to land.[23] Admonitions like "brother, lend a helping hand" or "sister, help to trim the sail" can be understood metaphorically as assisting on the road to salvation, but they can also be taken literally as requests to aid in the immediate work. "Row the Boat, Child" was recalled by Peter Davis for Alan Lomax in 1960 as a song he had learned from his grandfather, who would sit in his chair and make rowing motions as he sang.[24] Much of the song is a simple repetition of "come row the boat, child," with a few touching reminders of the effort involved when the singer says, "Child, I'm tired . . . lemme go home."

On board ship, sailors had any number of songs to aid in hauling on lines or turning capstans to raise anchors.[25] Leadbelly learned "Haul Away, Joe" from men who worked on the Mississippi River, but this was clearly adopted from deep-water sailors.[26] As he sings this song, the points at which the crew is expected to "haul away" are unmistakable. Similarly, instructions to "Heave Away" are present in one of the few secular slave songs noted by William Allen and his associates in 1867.[27] A modest social comment is included when the sailors remark they would rather spend their time courting than working.

The life of a sailor was often hard, and long weeks or even months on board ship were punctuated with brief sprees on shore. Songs abound about shore leave and its perils. To the question "What Shall We Do with the Drunken Sailor?" one answer is to "put him in the jail till he wakes up sober." Verses to "Blow the Man Down" tell tales of the chance encounters a sailor might have on shore, varying from being accused of crimes by a "saucy policeman" to taking up with a "handsome young damsel" who might well prove to be married, or at least older than she looks.[28]

Whaling as a distinct occupation produced its share of songs. In the seventeenth century, whaling was often done via day excursions from shore in relatively small boats. By the eighteenth century, longer voyages of up to a year were common, with crews recruited from the same social strata as shanty boys. Unlike the loggers' repetitious but strenuous days, whalers faced long periods of boredom punctuated by a few hours of terrifying effort to kill the immense whales, and then more hours of stressful work to harvest the blubber in a rolling sea, often with sharks swimming around, before the carcass rotted.[29] Longer voyages to remote parts of the world became common in the nineteenth century. To pass the time, whalers sang of their life at sea and of those they left behind.

One of the classic whaling songs, "The Greenland Whale Fishery," was popular on both sides of the Atlantic; it has possible British origins of around

1790, though most American versions place it in the middle of the nineteenth century.[30] The song relates a voyage that in one version began in 1853, "on June the 13th day." Almost immediately the crew is struck by the forbidding environment of the seas around Greenland, so they soon "wished ourselves back safe at home again, with our friends all on the shore." With the spotting of a whale, the heart of the story begins:

> We struck that whale and the line paid out,
> But she gave a flourish with her tail,
> The boat capsized, and we lost four of our crew,
> And we never caught that whale, brave boys—

All ships were very hierarchical in their arrangements, with extensive power held by the captain and mates, and almost none by the crew. Relations between the captain and crew depended on the personality of the master and his familiarity with his men. A British version of the song from the 1820s reports that the captain lowered his flag in response to the loss of his men. But class differences are recognized in some versions, which criticize the captain's heartless attitude about their deaths:

> Bad news, bad news our Captain cried,
> For it grieved his heart full sore,
> But the losing of the hundred barrel whale,
> It grieved him ten times more, brave boys—

Whatever money the crew might make on the voyage, and they generally worked for a predetermined proportion of the take, their attitude about Greenland is hostile, as the following verse makes evident:

> O Greenland is a dreadful place,
> It's a land that's never green,
> Where there's ice and snow, and the whale fishes blow,
> And the daylight's seldom seen, brave boys—

The last line is intriguing because during the summer months the waters off Greenland have prolonged daylight, though a voyage that began in mid-June may have had to remain off Greenland long enough to encounter the dark months of the year before the hold was full. In the 1850s, however, mid-winter voyages to the Greenland bays where the whales were wintering became common.[31] Or perhaps "daylight" was simply a corruption from a verse lamenting that "ale" was seldom seen.

Miners produced a number of engaging songs. Because mining was noisy and the working quarters were often cramped, singing generally did not accompany the work. Occasionally miners entertained each other with songs while they waited for cars to come to carry away loose coal and ore, but that was unusual.[32] Many mining songs fall into the category of commentary on the occupation.

"Drill, Ye Tarriers, Drill" is associated with hard-rock miners who extracted ore or dug tunnels for railroads. It has been traced back at least to 1888 but may have originated during work on the transcontinental railroad in the 1860s.[33] Like other occupational songs, it makes observations on the life of miners and their relations with the bosses. Perhaps the best-known set of verses revolves around the hard-nosed approach bosses took toward pay. In a highly personalized account, foreman Dan McCann, "a blame mean man," docks Big Jim Goff a dollar. The previous week a "premature blast" had sent Big Jim flying, an unfortunately common accident. Big Jim survived, and when he asks why he is a dollar short in his pay, he is told, "You were docked for the time you were up in the sky," though his temporary absence from work was hardly his fault. At best, the pay was not exceptional, for the chorus suggests it was necessary to "work all day for the sugar in your tay [tea]." Months might "roll by" with no pay forthcoming.

In addition to accidental explosions, other aspects of the work came in for comment. Singers might worry that tunnels will "cave in and we all [get] badly hurt." If the men were digging in wet rock, then "mud about six feet deep" made life miserable. The bunkhouse was often cold and dark, and full of snoring men, which made sleep difficult, even for exhausted miners. Just as the loggers on Blue Mountain Lake celebrated their cook Nellie, the tarriers sang the praises of their boss's wife, a large woman who baked pies and bread, though she baked them hard or hot as the "hobs of Hell." Canalers shared in this tendency for working men to sing dubious praises of their cooks.

In his remarkable study of recorded miners' songs, Archie Green identifies "Only a Miner" as "the American miner's national anthem, known wherever coal or metal ore was found in our land."[34] Much of the chapter on "Only a Miner" is devoted to tracing the origins and descent of the song and how various performers transformed it, but Green does recognize how the song resonated with miners' lives. Followers of particularly dangerous trades like mining often used songs as a means to name and confront the hazards they faced and to provide some psychic relief. Green argues that "Only a Miner" is more a lament than a ballad, "intended to evoke an emotional tone of resignation rather than narrate a specific tragedy."[35] Perhaps its offer of consolation was what made it appeal so widely, for there was no need for another specific ballad in an industry that "produced more disaster songs" than any other line of work, starting with the ballad on the Avondale, Pennsylvania, fire in 1869, "Avondale Mine Disaster."[36]

But the song has a clear social message as well, commenting on the lives of workers too often considered expendable in the American economy. Green traces the origins of the song to a poem written in 1877 by "Captain Jack" Crawford, a rival of "Buffalo Bill" Cody. Crawford claimed to have been moved to write his poem, which begins, "Only a miner killed," by hearing someone in Virginia City, Nevada, dismiss the sight of the body of a local miner with those words on the very day in 1877 that the newspapers were full of the death of Cornelius Vanderbilt.[37] Echoing a sentiment expressed by slaves before the Civil War, Crawford remarked that however impressive Vanderbilt's grave might be compared to the miner's, "beyond, all are equal, the master and slave." Green believes that "Only a Miner" was created from Crawford's lines sometime in the 1880s. Although one can hear resignation in the chorus, there is more than a hint of bitter irony over the casual dismissal of a miner's death and the equally casual assumption that his replacement will be quickly found.

> He's only a miner been killed in the ground,
> Only a miner and one more is found,
> Killed by an accident, no one can tell,
> His mining's all over, poor miner farewell.[38]

The three stanzas reminded miners and their families, and any concerned sympathizers, that "their dangers are great" and many miners have met their "sad fate . . . shut out from the daylight and their darling ones, too." As with a soldier's wife, who faced severe poverty and possible starvation if her husband was killed, a miner's "dear wife and little ones, too" faced hard times if he was crushed by a boulder "while working for those whom he loved." The final lines evoke the fallen comrade's memory and seek God's pity and protection for his fellow workers, who recognize "how soon we may follow, there's no one can tell." During labor troubles in the coalfields in the 1930s, Aunt Molly Jackson added several verses to the song from a woman's perspective, making the financial problems faced by the survivors the central theme.[39] Whatever the attitude of most Americans, any husband, father, brother, or son killed in a mining accident was never "only a miner."

Building and maintaining the railroads produced many memorable songs in addition to "John Henry." While "John Henry" is clearly a ballad, "Take

This Hammer," notable for its instinct for survival, is unmistakably a work song, with powerful accents on beats where hammers would strike together to crack rock or drive spikes into ties to hold the rails in place. Song catchers of the 1920s often indicated the point at which blows would be struck.[40]

Another task that required coordinated effort involved placing long, heavy rails on the ties and then lining them up precisely. Lining track continued after construction because rails had to be kept in good condition despite the wear and tear of the trains and changes in the weather. Songs designed to aid in lining track not only provided a distinct beat on which rails might be lifted or pry-bars shoved, but they sometimes contained specific instructions for the workers. Leadbelly's "Linin' Track" makes use of familiar verses from other songs to set the rhythm and pace for the workers, and it presumably can be kept going for as long as necessary.[41] "Boys, Put Yo' Hands on It" includes commands to "put yo' hands on it," "set it on time," "pick up high," "jump at it," and "raise your hand higher."[42]

Many different ethnic groups contributed to the building of the railroads, from African Americans in the South, to Chinese in the West, to Irish all over the land. The experiences of the latter were chronicled in a familiar song in which an Irish laborer works his way through the 1840s, with comments on the problems each year brought as "Pat worked on the railway."[43] The song was first mentioned in 1864 but may date from the previous decade. Versions vary, and the form is perhaps more memorable than the actual content, making new verses easy to compose. Representative verses suggest that opportunity in the New World proved elusive, but of course the potato famine in the 1840s left many Irish with few choices but to leave. One such version reports:

In 18 hundred and 41,	I put my corduroy britches on,
In 18 hundred and 42,	I left the old world for the new, Bad cess to the luck that brought me through,
In 18 hundred and 43,	'Twas then I met sweet Biddy McGee, An elegant wife she's been to me,
In 18 hundred and 45,	I found myself more dead than alive,
In 18 hundred and 46,	I found myself in a hell of a fix,
In 18 hundred and 47,	Sweet Biddy McGee she went to heaven, If she left one kid she left eleven,
In 18 hundred and 48,	I found myself at the Pearly Gates,
In 18 hundred and 49,	I found myself at the end of the line.

Instead of streets paved with gold, all the immigrants found was a roadbed to be paved with gravel, ties, and steel rails, at much effort and for little reward.

‡ ‡ ‡

Efforts to organize workers in the United States began in the 1790s as urban artisans tried to gain some control over their wages. The Philadelphia cordwainers (leather workers) led the first strike by a "permanent" union in 1799 and produced the first union song. In 1805 eight members were convicted of conspiracy because of their efforts to raise wages. By the end of the nineteenth century, hundreds of songs had been published in union newspapers, and the twentieth century saw the continuation of the trend of labor groups to use songs for solidarity and information.[44] Labor groups may rank third after religious and military organizations in producing songs for collective use. A brief history of the labor movement as it emerged as part of the Industrial Revolution makes clear why and how the issues that concerned workers were expressed in song. Many of these songs never went into oral circulation, and certainly many did not remain in use for long, but they do reflect a good deal of the social and economic history of the time. They also illustrate the conflict and anger that accompanied the economic transformation of the United States.

The confrontation between man and machine, vividly portrayed in "John Henry," is also the subject of "Peg and Awl." In its early years, the Industrial Revolution altered only a few industries, among them textiles, metals, transportation, and shoe manufacturing. Shoe making was often done in the homes of the workers in the early years, and one key step was the fastening of the upper parts of the shoe to the sole. This was done by using an awl to punch holes in the upper and the sole, and then connecting the two with pegs, hence the name of the song. "Peg and Awl," sung to the same melody as "She'll Be Coming 'Round the Mountain" and many other folk songs, addresses the problem faced by workers who were being displaced by machines. It follows the same structure as "Paddy Works on the Railway," referring to a sequence of years and what each brought. Most versions place the action in the first decade of the nineteenth century, even though the first pegging machine was invented in the 1830s and the replacement of pegged with sewn uppers occurred about 1860. Regardless of whether the date is off in the song, technological unemployment is what matters.[45]

The song opens in 1801, with the singer hard at work as he declares, "In the year of eighteen and one, . . . Peggin' shoes was all I done." The next couple of verses reinforce the first. The problem emerges when the singer worries that a new machine, "prettiest thing I ever seen," will force him to "throw away my peg . . . my awl." John Henry may have been able to keep up with the steam drill for a brief time at the cost of his life, but the pegger cannot and will not compete with the technological marvel. Since it "pegs a hundred pair to my one," he will have to find work where humans can still compete.

The early Industrial Revolution in the United States is generally associated with textiles, beginning with Samuel Slater memorizing the plans for mechanized looms to get them out of England in 1789 and continuing with the creation of the mills in Waltham, Massachusetts, in 1813. The New England textile factories depended in the early years on the labor of young women who left their family farms, if only for a few years, to earn some money in the mills. They were closely supervised at work and in the company-run boarding houses where they had to live. The hours were long and the work was tedious, if not always physically taxing.[46] When mill owners tried to extract more profit from the labor of the girls by speeding up the pace or requiring them to tend more machines, they discovered that the farm girls could easily go back home to the family farm. As a result, in the 1830s the owners began to replace the local girls with immigrant workers, who were more vulnerable to coercion but were also more prone to organize.[47]

Between 1828 and 1834 the Working Man's Party founded branches in sixty-one cities and established over fifty labor newspapers to spread its message, sometimes by the publication of songs. Early issues of the papers focused on mechanization and reducing hours. A general strike in Philadelphia in 1835 won a ten-hour day for workers, though Saturday remained a workday. In the 1830s attention began to shift to factory conditions, including child labor. Reduced wages led to strikes in the Lowell, Massachusetts, mills in 1834 and 1836.

Two songs from the labor press in 1834 illustrate what was on the minds of workers and their families at the time.[48] The first is in the form of a monologue from "The Little Factory Girl to a More Fortunate Playmate." It begins as the factory girl recalls how "we used in summer fields to play" and then asks if the other girl still does so, for she, the factory girl, now tends a "dull and tedious wheel." She tells her "fortunate playmate" that the latter "Cannot think how sad, and tired, and faint I often feel." Her parents try to make her life better, but she only has time to "snatch the meal" her mother has prepared, and when she is asleep her dreams are disturbed by fears of oversleeping and facing exorbitant fines for being late. She recalls hearing her father mourn, "Oh better were a grave, than such a life as this for thee, thou little sinless slave."

The issues of child labor and class privilege are also prominent in "The Factory Girl." The song begins when a father wakes his "hapless darling" to a meager breakfast in a dark room so she can "haste" to the factory. The family is in dire straits, with no mother and the father out of work. The child recognizes the dilemma the family faces and understands that though "they killed my little brother, like him I'll work—and die." The day at the factory indeed proves to be her last, as she has no strength to walk home that evening. After watching his child struggle all night on her bed, unaware of her surroundings, the father sees her spring up at the sound of the morning bell. She shrieks, "'Tis time!" and falls down dead. An even more bitter verse concludes with a vignette of the mill owner's daughters going to a meeting that night, where "their tender hearts were sighing, as the negroes' wrongs were told, while the white slave was dying, who gained their father's gold." Decades later, Carl Sandburg found the same sentiments still evident in these few short lines of "The Poor Working Girl," sung, so he thought, both to pass the time and as social comment:[49]

> The poor working girl,
> May heaven protect her,
> She has such an awf'ly hard time;
> The rich man's daughter goes haughtily by,
> My God! Do you wonder at crime!

A panic in 1837 dealt a severe blow to the early labor movement. Although there was some activity during the 1840s and 1850s, major union organizing did not reappear until after the Civil War, when the conflict between labor and capital emerged as a dominant issue for much of the next century. Farmers also found themselves vulnerable to the manipulations of large railroad corporations, and tenant farmers were dependent on their landlords. Songs celebrating bandits like Jesse James or Cole Younger may reflect rural hostilities toward the banks and railroads the outlaws attacked. One of the earliest songs expressing rural discontent with the new economy rose out of the Patrons of Husbandry, or Grange movement, organized about 1867 to combat railroad rates, credit restrictions, and unpredictable prices on a world grain market.

"The Farmer Is the Man" is an unmistakable reminder of the central place of agriculture in the American economy and a catalog of the problems facing those who tried to earn a living from the land in a new economy in which the ephemeral seemed to carry more weight than the real.[50] The recurring image in the song is clear: "The farmer is the man who feeds them all." Despite his critical role as foundation of the economy, the farmer "comes to town with his wagon broken down," where he confronts banks and merchants who give him "credit to the fall," only to "lead him from the land" when his crops fail to cover his loans. The lawyer, the butcher, the preacher, and the cook all "go a-strolling by the brook," ignoring their dependence on the farmer. Although the economy may struggle somewhat when "the banker says he's broke, and the merchant's up in smoke," it will survive these paper failures. But "it would put 'em to the test if the farmer took a rest, [for] then they'd know that it's the farmer feeds them all." In the new world of banks and credit, however, the farmer's influence on the economy did not seem to match his productive prominence, as too often, "with the interest rates so high . . . the mortgage man's the one who gets it all."

Not all rural problems stemmed from remote, faceless corporate entities. Land was the key to economic independence, but too often land was controlled by a few wealthy men who then rented it to their neighbors. As early as the 1840s, labor papers published songs with such suggestive titles as "Song of the Land Pirate" or "The Landless."[51] In the twentieth century, the issue remained pertinent, with the Bentley Boys recording "Hard Times in the Country, Down on Penny's Farm."[52] This song describes the difficulties faced by George Penny's tenant farmers, who work long hours for meager crops, only to be cheated by the landlord when it comes time to settle accounts. When the landlord shows up with a wagonload of rotten peaches, the renters pay "him for a bushel but don't get a peck," which makes for "hard times in the country, down on Penny's farm." Local merchants might extend credit to the sharecroppers; but if they could not pay their bill in the fall, the merchants would make a call to the sheriff, and the renter would be off to the chain gang.

Unionization was a slow process in the United States because for many it ran counter to basic American values, such as property rights, free markets, and individualism. Moreover, businessmen were skilled at linking union activity to foreigners, who were sometimes more radical in their politics than native-born American workers. But businessmen themselves were rarely opposed to combining to deny the rights of workers to be properly compensated for their labor. Nor were they particularly concerned about workers' safety. Miners were among the first to organize successfully, though not without violence. Miners also used songs in their struggles, learning from the experience of German and Welsh miners who brought their musical traditions with them when they migrated to this country.

"Buddy, Won't You Roll Down the Line" comes from a strike known as the Coal Creek Rebellion. It was organized by the Knights of Labor in Tennessee in 1891–92 to protest wages and working conditions; but as the strike wore on, it came to focus on the use of African-American convicts as strike breakers. The Knights of Labor were first organized in 1869 and became a national union in 1878, advocating one union for all workers. They promoted equal wages for equal work, cooperatives, worker-owned factories, no convict labor, easy credit, and an eight-hour workday. A surge of membership took them from about twenty thousand in 1879 to about seven hundred thousand in 1886. They organized the first Labor Day parade in 1882, which was recognized by Congress in 1894. The violence associated with the Haymarket rally and bombing on May 3, 1886, hurt the Knights of Labor, especially after seven German anarchists were accused, with virtually no evidence, of throwing the bomb, and four of them were hanged. Although the Coal Creek Rebellion was instigated by the Knights of Labor, the final settlement in 1892 was with the United Mine Workers of America (UMW), which had been formed in 1890.[53]

The issue of using convict labor, which came to dominate the Coal Creek Rebellion (also referred to as the Insurrection, or Troubles), stemmed from the aftermath of the Civil War. After slavery was outlawed in 1865, white Southerners found other methods to ensure African-American workers would remain on the job at low wages. Various terrorist organizations emerged to intimidate recently freed slaves. Sharecropping arrangements soon trapped many ex-slaves into debt peonage from which they could escape only when the landlord decided their accounts had been settled. The legal system assisted in controlling labor by arresting many black males on minor or trumped-up charges and sentencing them to extraordinarily long terms on prison farms or chain gangs.[54] Wealthy individuals and corporations quickly discovered they could make large sums of money by leasing the convicts from state and local officials for work on private projects. Governments enjoyed the extra income and did not worry overmuch if the convicts never returned home alive. In 1891 J. C. Powell wrote a book about his experiences overseeing convict labor, which he titled *American Siberia*, linking the abuses of the system to Czarist Russia.

In 1891 white miners in Tennessee went out on strike. The strike affected a number of communities but was eventually associated with Coal Creek, now Lake City, near Oak Ridge. The owners responded by leasing African-

American convicts from the Tennessee Coal, Iron, and Railroad Company, generally known as the TCI. This latter corporation, presided over by Thomas Platt, the head of New York's Republican Party, had extensive holdings in coal and iron mines in the South. Faced with involuntary black strikebreakers and a remote and unresponsive corporate opponent, the white miners attacked the camps where the convicts were being held overnight and set them free. Governor John Buchanan called up the local militia and, after several violent confrontations, subdued the miners and kept the new convicts in place working the mines. But this action cost him reelection, and by 1896 the state had outlawed future use of convicts as scabs.

Several songs resulted from the Coal Creek Rebellion. Uncle Dave Macon, one of the early stars of the Grand Ole Opry, made the best-known song, "Buddy, Won't You Roll Down the Line," popular.[55] Harry Smith included Macon's 1928 recording in his *Anthology of American Folk Music,* suggestively placing it between several blues by Blind Lemon Jefferson and just before Mississippi John Hurt's version of "Spike Driver Blues," in which the singer refuses to die with a hammer in his hand. Macon grew up in the vicinity of Coal Creek and may have learned some of the songs directly from the convicts, or from people living in the area, where he drove a wagon as a boy. He took the basic story and reshaped it into a song from the perspective of the convicts. Archie Green, the leading historian of the links between the rebellion and its songs, sees Macon's version as humorous—which it is, compared to some of the others—but it still tells the tale of a hard life. Macon's version, which he sang with great gusto, begins by setting the context, a necessity for audiences who may have been unfamiliar with the actual events:

> Way back yonder in Tennessee,
> They leased the convicts out,
> Put them working in the mines,
> Against free labor stout,
> Free labor rebelled against it,
> To win it took some time,
> But while the lease was in effect,
> They made 'em rise and shine.

The chorus, echoing similar lines from other songs, produces the title. Coal miners were paid according to the weight of coal they dug every day. The coal was hauled out of the mine in little cars, often pulled by mules or donkeys, and weighed outside. Thus miners depended on the men and boys who ran the cars to get sufficient coal out to meet their daily quota.

The chorus is basically a call from the miner to his buddy with the car, to roll down the line. A hard-working car man would be a *darling*. Hence the chorus, with several of these lines, repeats, "Buddy won't you roll down the line, yonder comes my darlin' coming down the line."

Three verses address working conditions faced by the convicts. The first notes the demand for labor:

> Every Monday morning,
> They've got 'em out on time,
> Marched them down to Lone Rock,
> Just to look into that mine,
> March you down to Lone Rock,
> Just to look into that hole,
> Very next thing the captain says,
> "You better get your pole."

Macon follows this general demand with comments on the food, noting that it was not very good; but after a hard day in the mines, the workers were so hungry they would eat almost anything. Macon may have used humor here, but he is also wryly satirical and sensitive to the convicts' situation:

> The beans they are half done,
> The bread is not so well,
> The meat it is all burnt up,
> And the coffee's black as heck!
> But when you get your task done,
> And it's on the floor you fall,
> Anything you get to eat,
> It 'ud taste good done or raw.

Macon also understood the social conditions surrounding the strike, for in the final verse he includes a direct barb aimed at the owners and operators, one that many working-class Americans would have related to, whatever their occupation:

> The bank boss he's a hard man,
> He's a man you all know well,
> And if you don't get your task done,
> He's gone you give you *halleluiah*,
> Carry you to the stockade,

And it's on the floor you fall,
The very next word that you hear,
"You better get your pole."

Other songs from the immediate years of the Rebellion, such as "Coal Creek Troubles" and the "Lone Rock Song," are longer and more specific, but they only reinforce Macon's overall criticism of the use of convict labor.[56] "Coal Creek Troubles" opens with a vow to tell the truth about "how hard the millionaire will crush . . . the miner toiling underground . . . to clothe his wife and children." The politics of the day are noted when the song remarks how "the corruption of Buchanan brought the convicts here, just to please the rich man." The miners receive praise for giving the convicts "no abuse" but instead turning "the convicts loose." This remarkable combination of class solidarity and self-interest across the color line occurred five years before *Plessy v. Ferguson* declared segregation constitutional, and in the midst of frequent lynching in the country. The "Lone Rock Song," a curious blend of verses put together by the convicts, is less overtly political, but it nonetheless makes its point. Several stanzas directly address the ill treatment of the convicts and the lack of respect shown to them. The head man shows up at the mine, "poke[s] his head in the hole," and demands, "Nigger gimme that coal." The guards bully the convicts with their shotguns, and if the convicts "don't get [their] task" completed during the day, then, from being counted at night to the next morning, "the nigger catches hell." The song is personalized with a reference to Charlie Medlick, who died while driving a cross entry to the tunnel, thus highlighting the dangers faced by all the men and the death that could come to any one of them. Two additional verses, taken from older folk songs, long for better times with one's girl in New Orleans or sitting in one's chair reading the morning paper.

In 1897 a strike called "the spontaneous uprising of an enslaved people" sent over two hundred thousand workers out of the soft-coal mines of Pennsylvania, Ohio, Virginia, and West Virginia.[57] After twelve weeks, the UMW signed the first agreement organizing a major industry in the United States. With this success, more miners joined the union, about 20 percent of them African American. Several weeks after negotiations ended, the union newspaper published a song called "Miner's Lifeguard," rallying the workers to stand together.[58] In the chorus, the miners are reminded, "Union miners stand together, heed no operators' tale," before they are given the highly practical advice to "keep your hand upon the dollar and your eyes upon the scale." The latter lines, repeated at the end of each stanza as well, clearly refer to the problem of honest recording of the weight of the coal being dug. The advice to keep one's hand upon the dollar may reflect the habit of many companies of paying in scrip (local company money) that could be used only in company stores, whereas miners preferred dollars that could be used anywhere.

The song begins with a comparison of mining to sailing and the need to be brave in facing the dangers of both livelihoods:

> Miner's life is like a sailor's
> 'Board a ship to cross the wave;
> Every day his life's in danger,
> Still he ventures being brave.
> Watch the rocks, they're falling daily,
> Careless miners always fail.

The struggle may have been long, but the song encourages the miners to persevere, for "soon this trouble will be ended, [and] union men will have their rights." Miners may have faced dangers similar to those of sailors, but the song also compares them to the recently freed slaves when it refers to "many years of bondage, digging days and digging nights." Slaves had been cheated of the value of their labor, just as miners were via dishonest practices at the scales; so the goal was simple—to achieve a time "when by honest weight we'll labor," receiving full pay for work done. After warning the workers not to be swayed by "newspapers' false reports," the song returns to the analogy, with sailors urging the miners to "trust in their safe lifeboats," referring, in this case, to "Jehovah." The religious reference is understandable since the lyrics were set to the tune of a recent religious song, "Life's Railway to Heaven," published in 1890.[59] In a blunt reminder of the need for the union to better their lives, the penultimate stanza links the problem of being cheated by the company to the poverty of their lives:

> You've been docked and docked again boys,
> You've been loading two for one;
> What have you to show for working
> Since this mining has begun?
> Overalls, and cans for rockers,
> In your shanties sleep on rails.
> Keep your hand upon the dollar
> And your eyes upon the scale.

The song concludes with a reminder and an optimistic promise, asking the miners to "bear in memory" that "God provides for every nation, when in union they combine."

With the success of this strike, miners presumably had more honest weights recorded and could hope to improve their standard of living. Despite the victory, the dangers of the mine still remained, the companies were still firmly in control, and change came slowly. Florence Reese used song in 1931 to ask the striking miners in Harlan County, Kentucky, "Which Side Are You On?" Reese was moved to write this song, which eventually became widely known, when the local sheriff ransacked her home while looking for her husband, a strong union organizer. In 1931 the struggle was still so violent and dangerous that, at least in Harlan County, there could be "no neutrals there," and, as she reminded her neighbors, "Us poor folks haven't got a chance unless we organize."

In 1947 Merle Travis, a Kentucky-born miner's son, wrote two remarkable songs pointing to the problems miners still faced a half century after the first successful strikes.[60] The most famous of Travis's songs, "Sixteen Tons," not only celebrates the toughness of the miners but recalls that the use of scrip in company towns still meant that many a miner could complain, as did Travis's father, "I owe my soul to the company store," because life in the mines only made a person "another day older and deeper in debt." "Dark as a Dungeon" warns young men to avoid the mines, where "the danger is double and the pleasures are few." According to Travis, only a "lust for the lure of the mines," comparable to an alcohol or drug addiction, could explain why anyone would choose to work where "the demons of death often come by surprise."

As miners were beginning to have some successes in organizing, the general labor movement underwent dramatic changes. The Knights of Labor were hurt by reaction to the Haymarket affair in Chicago in 1886. Violence between union men and Pinkerton "detectives" during a strike at the Homestead steel mill in 1892 turned many Americans against unions. In 1894 President Cleveland called out federal troops in the name of protecting mail delivery to end the railroad strike against the Pullman railroad car company. No doubt many Americans clearly remembered the great railroad strike of 1877, when the first national strike in American history led to troops being called out, over one hundred fatalities, and the building of armories in many American cities in response to fears of class warfare.

As the nineteenth century came to an end, parts of the labor movement went in separate directions. In 1886 Samuel Gompers organized the American

Federation of Labor (AF of L) to link skilled workers on the basis of specific crafts. Gompers was interested in practical issues like hours and pay, caring little for theory and less for social revolution. The AF of L was not prone to songs as a means of fostering solidarity. Gompers's main competition came from the Congress of Industrial Organizations (CIO), a movement based on uniting workers in whole industries, whatever their craft. The CIO suffered from being linked to the failures at Homestead and Pullman. The IWW (or the Wobblies) emerged in the mines and lumber camps of the Northwest around 1893. The IWW, led by Big Bill Haywood, was among the most musically oriented of all union movements and was clearly the most radical. It emphasized class conflict and espoused a program of syndicalism in which the state would be replaced by one universal union.

Two of the best-known labor songs are products of the Wobblies: "Solidarity Forever" and "Joe Hill." "Solidarity Forever" is a truly angry song. The lyrics were written by Ralph Chaplin in 1915, just after an IWW-led strike in the Kanawha Valley in West Virginia. Labor had reason to be angry in 1915. Many workers struggled to earn five hundred dollars a year, and their families had to send several members into the workplace simply to make ends meet. Work was dangerous, and businessmen took advantage of the influx of immigrants to keep wages low and to replace lost workers with another pair of hands. In 1914 over 921,000 miners faced long-term health problems like black lung disease, caused by breathing coal dust, and short-term problems like accidents. From 1884 to 1912 about 43,000 miners died in accidents, and thousands more were injured.[61] Between 1878 and 1910, 242 major mine accidents killed 5,835 workers. In 1913 alone, 25,000 died in factory accidents, and another 700,000 were injured.

Two incidents in 1913 and 1914, in which miners' families lost their lives, reminded workers of their place in the American economy. Both were later remembered and labeled as massacres in songs by Woody Guthrie. In 1913, during a labor conflict in the copper-mining town of Calumet, Michigan, seventy-three children were crushed to death after panic spread among those in attendance at a union-sponsored Christmas party in the local Italian hall when thugs barricaded the doors and then cried, "Fire!" A year later miners, and the labor movement in general, mourned the deaths of twenty men, women, and children in Ludlow, Colorado. The miners, who were on strike against the Rockefeller-owned Colorado Fuel and Iron Company, had set up a tent city after being expelled from their company houses. A combination of Colorado militiamen and hired "detectives" fired machine guns into the tents and then set fire to them, suffocating the women and children who had taken shelter from the expected bullets in foxholes dug within the tents.[62]

Finally, Chaplin and other Wobblies would have been upset in early 1915 over the case of fellow union member Joe Hill, who was executed late that year after a trial widely protested as unfair for a murder he may never have committed. Hill, himself memorialized in song, was one of the most prolific of the IWW songsters, responsible for converting the union into a singing organization, according to Chaplin.

In this context, it is no wonder "Solidarity Forever" is angry. In addition to ire, IWW radicalism is also evident in the lyrics. The first and last verses, along with the chorus, stress the importance of and power to be gained by uniting to achieve the workers' goals. The four intervening stanzas express the IWW anger and class antagonism toward the "greedy parasite" with whom the workers had nothing in common. The lyrics share the sentiment expressed in "The Farmer Is the Man"—that too many Americans had forgotten who had, in fact, built America and made the economy run. Using the tune of "The Battle Hymn of the Republic" linked that earlier crusade against one form of oppression to another. "Solidarity Forever" needs no extensive explication of its meaning. Here it is in its entirety:

> When the union's inspiration through the workers' blood shall run,
> There can be no power greater anywhere beneath the sun,
> Yet what force on earth is weaker than the feeble strength of one,
> For the Union makes us strong.

> *Chorus:* Solidarity forever, solidarity forever, solidarity forever,
> For the Union makes us strong.

> Is there ought we hold in common with the greedy parasite,
> Who would lash us into serfdom and would crush us with his might?
> Is there anything left to us, but to organize and fight?
> For the Union makes us strong.

> It is we who ploughed the prairies, built the cities where they trade,
> Dug the mines and built the workshops, endless miles of railroad laid;
> Now we stand outcast and starving, 'mid the wonders we have made,
> But the Union makes us strong.

> All the world that's owned by idle drones is ours and ours alone,
> We have laid the wide foundations, built it skyward, stone by stone,
> It is ours! Not to slave in but to master and to own,
> While the Union makes us strong.

They have taken untold millions that they never toiled to earn,
But without our brain and muscle not a single wheel can turn;
We can break their haughty power, gain our freedom when we learn,
That the Union makes us strong.

In our hands is placed a power greater than their hoarded gold,
Greater than the might of atoms magnified a thousandfold;
We can bring to birth a new world from the ashes of the old,
For the Union makes us strong.

"Joe Hill," written in 1935 by Earl Robinson and Alfred Hayes, is a much
more optimistic song, celebrating the union movement and the enduring
spirit of Joe Hill. Joel Hagglund was born in Sweden and moved to the United
States in 1901 at the age of nineteen. He joined the IWW in 1910 and by 1913
had contributed thirteen songs to the union songbook. He was arrested in
January 1913 in Salt Lake City on a murder charge. Although some believed
him guilty—and historians have differed on this—Woodrow Wilson tried to
intervene on his behalf, and protests about the trial were held throughout
the United States and abroad. Hill, as he had become, was shot to death by
a firing squad in November 1915. He is remembered for sending a telegram
to Big Bill Haywood the day before he died, instructing his fellow union
members, "Don't waste time mourning. Organize." Thirty thousand supporters attended his funeral in Chicago. After he was cremated, his ashes
were distributed to many foreign countries and every state except Utah,
since Hill had specifically said he did "not want to be found dead there."

"Joe Hill," written twenty years after his death, is a fitting memorial to
the musical union organizer, clearly following his instructions not to waste
time mourning but to get on with the union business. It is a wonderfully
singable song, as many have found. The essence of the song is that Joe Hill
comes to the singer in a dream and declares that, while his body may have
been shot in Utah, his spirit lives on wherever and whenever union men
and women are fighting for their rights. Not believing his eyes, the dreamer
insists, "The copper bosses killed you, Joe," to which Hill responds, in one
of the more memorable lines of the song, "'Takes more than guns to kill a
man,' says Joe, 'I didn't die.'"

In the final verses, Joe's life and death become symbolic of the ongoing
efforts to achieve social justice, reminding union members that whatever
the fate of an individual, as long as the union remains strong, the work will
go on. Building on the belief that there is more to a man than his body, the
next verse has Joe tell his comrade, "What they forgot to kill went on to

organize." Moreover, his spirit is still alive, so that "where working men are out on strike, Joe Hill is at their side."

"Solidarity Forever" and "Joe Hill" became widely known among union members and their supporters. But they, like many other union songs, never spread beyond the labor movement. "We Shall Not Be Moved" is an exception. In the 1930s union members adapted the old hymn "I Shall Not Be Moved" to their purposes, singing, perhaps while on a picket line or when faced with a difficult decision:

> **We shall not**, we shall not be moved,
> **We shall not**, we shall not be moved,
> *Just like a tree standing by the water,*
> *We shall not be moved.*

The song is what Lee Hays of the Weavers once called a "zipper" song, eminently adaptable to multiple situations and able to be kept going for as long as anyone in the group can think of another line to "zipper" in where the boldface type is. The chorus, in italics, with its powerful image of a mighty tree firmly rooted near the nourishing waters, just keeps on going. Thus union members could easily celebrate, "The union is behind us, we shall not be moved," or in a more confrontational situation they could rally each other with, "We will stand and fight together." In the 1960s civil rights demonstrators made the song a vital part of their musical repertoire. Civil rights marches required the same courage and unity as walking the picket lines, and songs both bolstered spirits and helped pass the time. Many of the verses from "We Shall Not Be Moved" could be used directly, or with only minimal editing. Others, such as "We are black and white together," were more directly applicable to the current situation, though this particular verse connected to unionizing efforts in the South, to link black and white workers in common cause, despite a long tradition of racial hostilities that had been dented when the Coal Creek miners had freed the convicts in 1891.

CHAPTER 5

The Man Who Never Returned

Ships, Trains, and Other Transportation

In 1948 Walter F. O'Brien ran for mayor of Boston as the Progressive Party candidate. When the Metropolitan Transit Authority's (MTA) recent fare increase from five to ten cents became an issue during the campaign, Jacqueline Steiner and Bess Lomax Hawes (Alan Lomax's sister) wrote a song about a man named Charlie trapped on the Boston subway because he did not have another nickel to "get off of that train."[1] Their song is a parody of several old folk songs that tell similar stories of men who left their wives and families never to return. "Charlie and the MTA" urged the citizens of Boston to vote for O'Brien or else Charlie might have to "ride forever 'neath the streets of Boston," another man "who never returned." Charlie is quite possibly the dumbest character in American popular culture after Lois Lane, who never figured out Clark Kent looked like Superman with glasses. The song relates how he rode the subway bemoaning his fate, with his wife coming "down to Scollay Square Station every day at quarter passed two," whereupon she would use an open window in the car to "hand Charlie a sandwich as the train [came] rumbling through." But it never dawned on him to ask for the other nickel. We cannot be sure about his wife, but she may have been glad to be rid of such a dim bulb at the cost of one sandwich a day. A decade later, the Kingston Trio went to the top of the charts with this obscure campaign parody.[2]

"Charlie and the MTA" is an important song not only because of its place in the folk revival of the later 1950s but also because of its roots in a critical part of American history. One of the central subplots of the Industrial Revolution is the transportation revolution, which transformed Americans' ability to travel about their country and communicate with each other.[3] The story begins in the seventeenth century with ships; picks up its pace in the nineteenth century with turnpikes, canals, and railroads; and finishes in the twentieth century with automobiles, airplanes, and subways. As new technology was invented and adopted, dangers from accidents were plentiful, and separation from death or migration happened frequently. In 1865 Henry Clay Work, one of America's popular composers at the time, explored this theme with "The Ship That Never Returned" when he wrote romantically of a young man who set sail as "commander on a ship that never returned."[4] In 1903 several songs about the "Wreck of Old '97" recounted the crash of a mail train trying to make up time on the Southern Railroad.[5] One common stanza warned wives not to "speak harsh words to your true loving husband," for he might "leave you and never return." The theme of separation via transportation must have struck a chord with Americans, because even before the "Wreck of Old '97," writers had used the melody and theme to compose "The Hand-Car That Never Returned," "The Train That Never Returned," and "The Parted Lover."[6] Apparently Charlie eventually got off the MTA and retired to Florida; folk singer Rod MacDonald discovered him in Palm Beach County in 2000, where Charlie cast a ballot that was "never returned." Walter O'Brien's daughter heard the song and approved.[7]

♯ ♯ ♯

It is hard to overstate the significance of the transportation, or perhaps more accurately, communication revolution in creating the United States as a continental nation and world power. In 1787, when a new constitution was proposed for the emerging country, the United States stretched about fifteen hundred miles along the Atlantic coast from Maine to Georgia. Although the western border had been set at the Mississippi River in 1783, few Americans lived more than one hundred fifty miles from the Atlantic Ocean. When the first census was taken in 1790, it reported just under four million people in the country. Despite this thin population, scattered mostly on farms along the eastern seaboard, many Americans worried that such an extensive territory and large population could not be successfully governed as a republic. They feared tyranny from too many contending and conflicting interests competing at a center of government that lay days, if not weeks, away by horseback. Some believed the people would be better off with two or three smaller republics instead of one big one. In what may well be the single most important essay on American politics, James Madison reassured his fellow citizens in the *10th Federalist* that a large country was actually desirable, as all those contending interests would offset each other, reinforcing the constitutional provisions of separation of powers to check and balance against abuse of power. But it is doubtful even Madison would have believed the country could work successfully "from sea to shining sea" with a population of one hundred million by 1920. Following the Louisiana Purchase in 1803, the United States quickly expanded across the continent, with California admitted to statehood in 1850 and the Gadsen Purchase putting the last piece of the contiguous forty-eight states in place by 1853.

What made it possible for the United States to become a continental nation—and avoid a monarchy or some other highly centralized form of government—was the transportation revolution, a revolution celebrated in song. The true measure of distance is the time it takes to get from one place to another, and by the end of the nineteenth century Americans could send a message across the continent more quickly than they could to the next town when Madison wrote his essay. A survey of the new innovations is instructive. Turnpikes began to improve overland travel before the end of the eighteenth century. Although the first experiments with steamboats occurred in the 1780s, Robert Fulton's *Clermont* stimulated the rapid expansion of this form of travel after 1807. Steam soon moved from riverboats to ocean-going vessels, and by mid-century, iron hulls provided larger, more secure ships. Canals, including the Erie, which opened in 1825, allowed bulk commodities to be moved easily over short and then long distances. The first railroad was built in 1829. Although bicycles and automobiles did not make their contribution to the revolution until the very end of the nineteenth century, they were followed in 1903 with the first airplane flight at Kitty Hawk.

Other forms of communication aided and abetted the desire to get in touch rapidly. Samuel Morse invented the telegraph in 1833, and it was in wide use a decade later. The 1840s saw the advent of mass-circulation newspapers along with books and magazines. The telephone was added to the mix in 1876. The ability to record sound was demonstrated before the end of the century, and improvements in quality and price meant that by 1924 Vernon Dalhart could sell over a million copies of the "Wreck of Old '97." There were ten thousand movie theaters by 1910 and five hundred radio stations broadcasting to over three million receivers by 1922. Although none of the changes in communication were celebrated in folk song, they did have an effect on music, both because Americans no longer had to depend on their own talents for amusement and also because people could now hear and learn new songs more readily. It is no accident that the 1920s saw great expansions in the recording and sale of "race" and "hillbilly" records, and the collection and publication of folk songs. What were once local songs, known to only a few, could now reach a national audience. When John Lomax set out to collect folk songs from African Americans in 1932, he deliberately went to prisons, places where he assumed, perhaps mistakenly, singers would not have been exposed to new types of music via radio or records.

Railroad songs dominate the music stimulated by the transportation revolution. Indeed, one could write a whole book on that topic alone, if Norm Cohen had not already produced a very large and excellent one already.[8] It is tempting to start with train songs, if only because so many are so good; but the chronological order of significant innovations leads first to deep-water ships. Ships have been the preferred way to move bulk cargo long distances for several thousand years. During the last millennium, inventions made longer voyages out of sight of land possible. The compass indicates direction, even during cloudy days or at night. Well before the American colonies were established, navigators could approximate how far north or south of the equator they were. In the eighteenth century, precise clocks finally let sailors determine how far east or west they were of any given point. Improvements in ship construction and sails made vessels more secure, maneuverable, and able to hold the provisions needed to cover long distances. Over the course of the fifteenth and sixteenth centuries, Portuguese sailors learned the regular patterns of wind and currents in the Atlantic as they pressed south around Africa. Thus Columbus built on many years of innovation and discovery when he sailed west in 1492, intending to get to China and Japan.

Despite the growing security of long-distance voyaging, sailors faced many dangers recognized in their songs. Then, as today, powerful storms and rogue waves could sink ships. Once a ship cleared port, it was vulnerable to attack by national enemies or pirates, with the distinction not always obvious. All ships had to be prepared to protect themselves by gunpowder or speed. On board, sailors faced the reality of officers who exercised command with little heed to the interests or ideas of their men. Ship's captains were absolute monarchs in their domain, and a sailor's fate depended on the officer's personality.

The English, some of whose colonies formed the original United States, came late to the colonizing venture and had to be content with Spanish and Portuguese leftovers. One region the Spanish had explored and left largely unsettled was the coast of North America north of St. Augustine, Florida. In 1587 a group of English investors, Sir Walter Raleigh among them, planted a colony at Roanoke, in modern North Carolina. The threat of the Spanish armada the next year prevented reinforcements from being sent until 1590, by which time the colony had disappeared.

Sir Walter, however, was active in other colonizing ventures, and one familiar song has been traced to one of his voyages. The song, known here as "The Golden Vanity," was first published in 1682 in a broadside in which the ship's name was the *Sweet Trinity* and Raleigh was the captain.[9] The song is widely known, and its extensive circulation in the oral tradition is made evident by the many variations in the name of the ship and the identity of the enemy it encountered. The enemy is of some consequence, for the heart of the story is a blunt reminder that ships at sea often had to protect themselves when they met other vessels, and that courage in the face of danger did not depend on social status. The tale is also one of heroism and betrayal, embedded in a web of class antagonisms. It is perhaps the latter part of this story that took it as far inland as the Ozarks, for surely mountain folk had few fears of seafaring.[10]

The ballad begins by naming the "lofty ship" that "sailed upon that low and lonesome, low, . . . sailed upon that lonesome sea." The story quickly moves to the action, with the second stanza reporting: "She had not been from port, but two weeks or three, when she was overtaken by a Turkish revelee," a ship from the then-powerful Ottoman Empire. A cabin boy steps up in the midst of the anxious crew and asks the captain, "What will you give me if them I do destroy, if I sink them in the low and lonesome sea?" The captain, clearly desperate to save his life, ship, and possibly cargo, promises the boy "Five thousand pounds and my daughter for his bride," if he can sink the Turkish raider. The boy accepts the offer, despite the danger to his own life, and jumps into the sea to swim to the enemy ship. Once at the Turkish revelee he "had a little tool that was made for the use, and he bore nine holes in her all at the once, and sank her in the . . . lonesome sea." But this heroic act was not to be rewarded, at least not in most versions of the song. When the boy returns to the *Golden Vanity*, the captain refuses to take him back on board, realizing that his promise will lead not only to an inappropriate marriage for his daughter but also to the loss of an extraordinary sum of money. Faced with this betrayal, the boy realizes that to take revenge on the captain by sinking his ship would also doom his mates, and so he accepts his own death without drilling holes in the *Golden Vanity*. Some singers do not like this courageous and selfless outcome, and they edit the song either so that the boy is rescued or he takes his revenge regardless of the crew. But for most singers, the tale remains one of danger on the high seas, heroism, and betrayal.

Not all dangers worthy of commemoration by song came in human form. Virginia, England's first permanent colony in the Americas, was settled in 1607. A voyage in 1609, bringing supplies and reinforcements, encountered a violent storm and ended up shipwrecked on Bermuda. Fortunately, the survivors found thousands of hogs on the islands for food and ample cedar trees to build new ships. It took almost a year before the aptly named *Deliverance* and the *Patience* were ready to complete the voyage to Virginia; but upon their arrival, the survivors were greeted with surprise and joy. When Sir Thomas Gates, briefly Virginia's governor, and Captain Newport, captain of the ship, returned to England late in 1610, their tale became a sensation. The best-known response to the shipwreck is William Shakespeare's *The Tempest*, though it focuses more on the "brave new world that hath such people in't."[11] Perhaps the length of the title of "Newes from Virginia of the happy arrival of That famous and Worthy Knight, Sir Thomas Gates, and well reputed and Valiante Captain Newport, into England," explains why this ballad on the tale never achieved the renown of Shakespeare's play, or maybe the song's quick segue into a promotional piece for the colony undercut its appeal, for in truth, Virginia was little more than a death trap in its early years.[12] Nonetheless, the ballad probably beats the bard in celebrating how "these gallant worthy wights" survived, despite the fact "the seas did rage, the windes did blowe, distressed were they then, their shippe did leake, her tacklings breake, in danger were her men."

The dangers confronted by sailors and the uncertainties faced by their families remained a subject for songs into the nineteenth and twentieth centuries. Henry Clay Work's "The Ship That Never Returned" relied on the intrinsic appeal of this theme in 1865, though his emphasis on loved ones left behind is in keeping with the nineteenth-century tendency to view death from the perspective of the survivors.[13] Although Work's song was composed for commercial reasons, its standing as a folk song is evident in its use as a parody, as noted earlier. The heart of the song as it relates to ocean voyages is in the chorus, with its lament about the uncertain fate of sailors and their ships: "Did she ever return? She never returned." When voyages could easily last for several years and letters from far-off ports depended on accidental encounters with ships on the way home, it was common for "her fate, [to be] yet unlearned; tho' for years and years there were fond ones watching, but the ship—she never returned." The actual body of the song is overtly sentimental, with a "feeble lad" leaving his "aged mother" and his "loving wife" to pursue "health and strength" in a "far off country" in the hopes of earning "one more bag of the golden treasure [that] will last us all through life." Little did his family know as they sent "loving signals" to the ship "while a form was yet discerned," that "a last poor man set sail commander, on a ship that never returned." No doubt this story was familiar enough to many Americans to appeal in its literal form, but it also may have resonated with those who were critical of the eager and heedless pursuit of the dollar in the mid-nineteenth century.

As ships became larger and more secure, and Americans believed they could conquer nature, confidence in technology became common. Perhaps nothing so well exhibits this attitude, shared on both sides of the Atlantic, than the construction and promotion of the "unsinkable" *Titanic*. When this powerful ship went down on her maiden voyage in April 1912, many took it as a moral lesson. At least 125 songs were copyrighted in one year about the disaster, repeating a centuries-old tradition of memorializing disasters in moralizing songs. But different people drew different lessons.

Leadbelly's version of "Titanic" draws on news reports, other folk songs, and an African-American perspective of the event.[14] The song begins with a reference to the ship's band playing "Nearer My God to Thee" as the *Titanic* sank, bidding the great liner "fare thee well." In his spoken introduction to the song, Leadbelly comments that this song, which he learned from the great blues-man Blind Lemon Jefferson, was the first he ever played on the twelve-string guitar that became his signature instrument. His driving accompaniment sounds as if it could easily be fitted to a railroad song, which is not inappropriate since Leadbelly's second and third verses clearly draw on railroad songs. In verse two, once the ship was loaded, the "Captain hollered, 'All aboard,'" while the wreck is described in the third verse as happening as the "Titanic was comin' 'round the curve," a direct reference to "Casey Jones" and other ballads about train crashes. Newman White suggested in 1927 that many of the *Titanic* songs were based on old songs about a long-forgotten steamboat wreck on the Mississippi. This too would make sense, though the railroad influence is unmistakable.[15] The fourth and fifth verses report the scene as the ship sank, highlighting the custom of the women and children going into the lifeboats first, with the men remaining behind.

So far, Leadbelly's "Titanic" has been unremarkable, but the last two stanzas set it apart. The recordings issued under the title of *Last Sessions* were made on tape and published on long-playing records. As a result, Leadbelly was not constrained by the roughly three-minute capacity of most records at the time and was able to comment on his songs. In introducing "Titanic," he remarked that he normally only sang the last two verses to "colored" audiences; but because he trusted the white people he was with, he would sing them the whole song. According to the two verses, Jack Johnson, the great African-American heavyweight champion, had tried to board the ship but was told by the captain, "I ain't hauling no coal." In response to this insult, the song reports that when Johnson learned about the wreck he did the Eagle Rock, a popular dance of the era. Although the Johnson story is false, Leadbelly and Jefferson used a basic summary of the *Titanic* story as a means to make a sharp comment about race relations under the doctrine of legal segregation. African Americans may not have been entirely dismayed by the demise of many rich, white people whose passages may have been paid for by the work of blacks who could not even get on the ship.

A 1927 recording by William and Versey Smith offers different moral lessons, not only commenting on class distinctions but also recalling age-old warnings of the need to prepare for death.[16] The Smiths sing "When That Good Ship Went Down" with a powerful beat reminiscent of complex African rhythms, and they add call and response, all with the repeated refrain, "It was sad when the great ship went down." They begin their version with references to family, noting that "husbands and wives, children lost their lives . . . when that great ship went down." The social hierarchy on board ship and in death was connected by a stanza that commented:

> When that ship left England it was making for the shore,
> The rich had declared they would not ride with the poor,
> So they put the poor below, they were the first to go.[17]

After repeating the lines on family and social class several times, the Smiths finish with a warning that echoes from the eighteenth century. Although the passengers were a "long ways from home," many had "friends all around." Feeling safe and secure on the unsinkable *Titanic*, they were surprised "that the time had come, Death came riding by, sixteen hundred had to die." Truly, "it was sad when that great ship went down."

The moral message in Almeda Riddle's "The Titanic" is, as Alan Lomax has observed, "unusually stern and pious, certainly in content but also in delivery."[18] Lomax recorded Riddle in 1959, at which time she claimed she could still remember the disaster. The moral meaning was significant to this inhabitant of the Ozark Mountains, far removed from the Atlantic and its icebergs. At the heart of Riddle's version is a contrast between a sense of carelessness and confidence among the rich, and the ultimate fate and judgment that waits us all. The *Titanic* set sail for New York "with a cargo of wealth untold." Although brief mention is made to the presence of lower-class passengers, Riddle is more concerned with those who spent the night leading up to the disaster "revel[ing] in room and hall, . . . never [giving] a thought of their danger, till the ice ripped open the floor." In addition to the general scene of sin and debauchery, made worse by human pride, Riddle blames the captain. Whether she is referring to the rumor that he was going too fast for the conditions, or to some other flaw in his character, justice was served, as "the slayer now died with the slain." God's justice is made even more evident in a verse that concludes that, whether drowned or rescued, "We'll all be made right in God's judgment, the crooked will all be made straight."

Given the recent success of films on the *Titanic* and continued interest in salvage operations, it is easy to understand why the disaster was used by singers to convey not only the story itself but also moral messages. When earlier songs warned about the perils of ocean travel, they focused on the power of nature and the dangers of evil men. Certainly the *Titanic* story contains both, though the iceberg plays a very small role in many songs. Although early-twentieth-century songs are more explicit in criticizing the privileges of class and race, and in warning that pride and arrogance are recipes for a fall, recent interest still reflects these attitudes.

The American Great Lakes are sufficiently large to present most of the dangers of deep-water sailing. Gordon Lightfoot's "The Wreck of the Edmund Fitzgerald" is too recent to be considered a folk song, but its style and content certainly resonate with the songs we have been discussing here. "The Bigler" offers an amusing contrast, however, for instead of dangers and powerful ships, this song tells the story of a timber ship notorious for its lack of speed.[19] At no point during the journey from Milwaukee to Buffalo is the *Bigler* ever in danger, nor does anything dramatic happen to her. With a strong wind and in full sail, the *Bigler* "might have passed the fleet ahead if they'd hove to and wait." But instead the *Bigler* crew has to make do with the fantasy that they are driving the fleet "on before." Indignity in the form of getting stuck on a mud flat while being towed through the passage between Lakes Huron and Erie, and smashing into another ship while out of control continue the saga. The *Bigler* eventually arrives at Buffalo, with its saloons and promises of better times ashore.

The humor of "The Bigler" is matched by songs from the antithesis of deep-water sailing: canalling. In 1816, the year before construction started on the Erie Canal, the United States had fewer than one hundred miles of canals. By 1840 the total stood at 3,326 miles, almost all through relatively flat and well-watered lands north of the Ohio and east of the Mississippi.[20] Many short canals provided links between nearby natural resources and shipping points, or offered a means around an obstacle in a river. The Erie Canal, built between 1817 and 1825, was a notable exception. When the 364 miles of canal from Buffalo to Albany opened, it connected much of the upper Midwest with the eastern seaboard and provided a means of shipping bulk commodities to market at a reasonable price. Although the canal was later enlarged, it was initially forty feet wide and four feet deep. Travel across New York on the canal was by barges pulled by mules averaging about four miles per hour. An occasional town broke the monotony of vistas of fields and forests slowly gliding by and the immediate view of the rear ends of the mules. Passage through locks added to the excitement. To deal with their boredom, canalers composed and sang tongue-in-cheek songs about the dangers they faced while at work, likening their lives to those of deep-water sailors.

The majority of easily accessible folk songs from canal days are related to the Erie Canal.[21] Few of the surviving songs exist as anything more than fragments, however, with verses often floating from one version to another. The first song that appears in the Lomaxes' *American Ballads and Folk Songs* was, in fact, a composite assembled out of fragments they had collected in six different states, from New York to Texas to Washington.[22] Several themes recur in the songs of the Erie Canal, all humorous exaggerations of a hard life on the waterway. One of the most common is the saga of the "terrible storms we had one night on the raging canal." Despite sailing on a body of water four feet deep, such verses recount the dangers when "the wind began to whistle and the waves began to roll." The canalers are forced to "reef their royals" in the face of danger, just as sailors on clipper ships rounding Cape Horn into the roaring forties must. Of course, since they had to pass under bridges in country and town, canal boats had no masts or sails, let alone top royals four levels of sails up. The bridges, on the other hand, were very real dangers to inattentive crew or passengers, and the advice to "duck your nut" was sound. William Allen's 1915 celebration of his mule Sal contains the same advice in more proper English when he announces, "Low bridge, everybody down," meaning everyone should get off the top of the barge, where people liked to sit while traveling. Other "dangers" on the dreaded Erie included getting lost midst all the windings, contracting scurvy from long weeks on the water without vitamin C, encountering possible pirates, and springing a leak from striking "a chunk a Lackawanna coal." In the latter case, the captain comes to the rescue, springing back on board from the towpath and stopping the leak "with his old red flannel shirt." But the worst fear of many canalers is expressed in this chorus:

Oh the E-ri-e was a rising,
and the gin was getting low,
and I scarcely think we'll get a drink,
'til we get to Buffalo-o-o,
'til we get to Buffalo.

When the boatmen sang about being chock full up with barley and loaded down with rye, they had in mind both the solid and the liquid varieties of both grains.

Canalers were similar to lumbermen in making fun of their cooks. According to various songs, a canal boat cook was likely to be a maid of sixty summers or more. Furthermore, she was large, standing six feet tall in her socks; had a hand the size of an elephant's ear; could open the locks with her breath; and snored so loudly as to keep the crew awake. Her two virtues were a bright shiny nose that could be used as a headlight at night and a vivid red dress that could serve as a "signal of distress" when she was hoisted onto the mast in a storm. The beefsteak she served was often as "tough as a fighting dog's neck," prepared while she "play[ed] tag with the flies." If the cook did not provide enough material for satire, the animals pulling the barge were fair game. Not all of the mules were good pals; instead, they might be remembered as a "spavined" pair who needed constant attention via "cuss, kick, and swish," partly from the basic orneriness of the critter but also because they might start from the "playful horse flies" that liked to "climb" on the slow-moving and probably sweating animals.

In 1807 Robert Fulton demonstrated the utility of the steamboat for river commerce on the Hudson with his *Clermont*.[23] Two years later John Stevens did the same on the Delaware with the *Phoenix*. Even more remarkable, the *New Orleans* steamed from Pittsburgh to New Orleans in 1811, while four years later the *Enterprise* completed a round trip down and then up the Ohio–Mississippi corridor. By 1855 over seven hundred steamboats were active on the western waters, and many of these had grown to three hundred feet long, carrying several hundred passengers and tons of cargo. Eastern steamboats tended to be narrow, with deep hulls drawing considerable amounts of water. A new type of boat evolved on the Mississippi and its tributaries, where a wide beam and shallow draft were highly desirable. Captains exaggerated when they claimed they could sail in a heavy dew, but some big boats needed less than three feet of water to carry their load. When a leadsman tested the water and found its depth to measure *mark twain*, the twelve feet that term signifies was ample for most purposes and half way to "no bottom."

Folk songs that emerged from steamboat life are almost nonexistent in most standard collections. Fortunately, Mary Wheeler published a number of songs in 1944 that she collected from old men and women who had once worked on the steamboats at the end of the previous century.[24] Many of the songs she recorded fall into such categories as spirituals or love songs of interest to the crew. She also recorded work songs and occasionally even songs about the boats. The men who moved cargo on and off the steamboats had to carry heavy loads across often unsteady gangplanks as the boats nosed in to the shore. They sang to make the work go faster and to create rhythms for lifting and carrying. Sometimes the songs reflect their work. In "I'm Wukin' My Way Back Home" they sang, "My back is gittin' tired, an' my shoulder is gittin' sore," and they hoped that the "timber don't git too heavy . . . and the sacks too heavy to stack." What was equally important was that after "many a long day away from home . . . I'll be seein' you soon." Of course, the woman in question may have sent him out to work with the admonition, "You go back up the rivuh and carry some sacks, you kin git my kisses when the boat gits back." While he was gone, however, the deck hand might sing, "Ashes to ashes an' dust to dust, can't hardly tell what woman to trust."[25] For a man thinking about what was going on with his woman back home, it could be frustrating when "the boat's up the river and she won't come down."[26]

Given frequent songs about ship and train wrecks, and the very real dangers from high-pressure steam engines and snag-filled rivers, it is surprising that there are few folk songs about steamboat catastrophes. Perhaps such wrecks were so common that they evoked little comment, for the average life of a steamboat was said to be about five years. Workmen recognized that a "steamboat's a dangerous thing, . . . it's mighty strong, ef you give it steam enough, it'll shove it right along."[27] When the *City of Bayou Sara* burned in 1885, the rousters memorialized the disaster, implying that "two bright angels by [their] side" may have saved them from death. Similarly, when the *Gold Dust*'s boiler exploded in 1882, killing seventeen and injuring forty-seven, the black crew commented, "Ain't that a pity 'bout the Gold Dust men. Some got scalded, some got drowned, some got burnt up in the Gold Dust fire."[28] The *Gold Dust* explosion seems to have been an accident, but some wrecks occurred as captains raced, occasionally tying down safety valves to increase steam pressure. Fortunately, not all races ended badly, though the captain of the *James Lee* may have experienced some degree of humiliation when he heard "Katie an' the Jim Lee Had a Race."[29] A retired officer on the *James Lee* admitted that the only time his boat could beat the *Kate Adams* was when she had a heavy load on. Otherwise, as the men sang, "Katie threw the watuh in the Jim Lee's face," forcing the *Jim Lee* to "leave her mail," that is, to skip scheduled stops in order to keep up. No doubt the *Kate Adams* crew sang this with great pleasure, especially when in the company of men from the *James Lee*.

♯ ♯ ♯

No form of transportation has produced as many wonderful songs as the railroad. The train is a technological marvel whose sight and sound evoke great emotion. The arrival of the train, "train time," is an exciting moment, whether leaving, coming home, or meeting a person or package. Skillful musicians easily imitate the rhythm of the wheels over the joints, the chuffing of the engine, and the lonesome wail of the whistle. Alan Lomax sees both blues and jazz as rooted in the railroad song. The iron horse has become an icon not only in song but in visual art as well. In 1830 the United States claimed only seventy-three miles of track. A decade later, the country had laid 3,328 miles, a total that climbed to 30,636 by 1860. The first transcontinental route was completed in 1869, with similar routes making up part of the over 93,000 miles of rails laid down by 1880.[30] Rails reached their peak in 1920 with almost 253,000 miles of track in service.[31]

Railroads played a major role in shaping American society in the nineteenth century, beyond providing transportation. Railroad owners and operators were powerful political figures with great influence in Washington and the state capitals. Their influence over economic policy produced reactions among farmers and laborers, as seen in some of the songs about labor. Public financial support in the form of land grants to railroad corporations helped settle the West, and the decisions of remote companies often determined which communities would prosper and which would remain as backwaters, or even disappear. Railroad companies received over one hundred eighty million acres of land from federal and state governments, about 14 percent of all public lands. Even standard time zones, adopted in 1883, were an outgrowth of the railroads' desire to simplify their schedules.

Railroad songs come in many sizes and shapes. In addition to songs like "John Henry," which emerged from the construction of the railroads, folk singers made use of train wrecks, the train as metaphor for death, hobo songs, railroad blues, and prisoners' songs. "Casey Jones" and his wreck may be the only song to rival "John Henry" for its fame.

The power and speed of a train was both its great allure and its great danger. Newspapers from the middle of the nineteenth century are full of disasters, with rails breaking, bridges collapsing, trains jumping the tracks from excessive speed, and collisions resulting from faulty switches and signals. Perhaps the most common cause of disaster was the demand of the clock, which tempted engineers to race to make up lost time. Because almost all urban and industrial workers had become bound to the clock, this particular problem would have resonated with many Americans. "Casey Jones" was composed in the aftermath of a wreck outside Vaughn, Mississippi, on April 30, 1900, when engineer John Luther Jones from Cayce, Kentucky, was trying to make up ninety-five minutes on the *Cannonball Express,* southbound to New Orleans on the Illinois Central.[32] Wallace Saunders, a black man working in the roundhouse near where the wreck occurred, is credited with the first of many ballads about Casey Jones, though no copy of his words has been identified. Recordings of the song are many and varied, both in text and tone. Mississippi John Hurt offers two: one tells the story in a straightforward way, and a second demonstrates his wonderful ability to coax extraordinary train sounds from his guitar.[33] Norm Cohen begins his discussion of "Casey Jones" with the remarkable rendition by Furry Lewis that Harry Smith selected for the *Anthology of American Folk Music.*[34] Vernon Dalhart, one of the most popular country artists of the 1920s, recorded a version similar to Hurt's basic story, and Jerry Garcia of the Grateful Dead modeled his version on Hurt's as well.[35]

The true story is relatively mundane. Jones had been driving engines for ten years on the Illinois Central and had a reputation for being a "fast roller" who sometimes ignored railroad rules for the sake of speed. By the time the wreck occurred, Jones had made up most of the hour and a half in the 175 miles since he pulled out of Memphis. As the train rounded a sharp curve, Jones's fireman could see the tail end of a freight train still on the main track, even though it was supposed to be on the siding. He warned Casey of the danger, and as the engineer worked to slow the train, he told his fireman to jump, which the fireman did. But Jones died when the engine plowed into the back of the stopped freight train. Whether Jones was going too fast or the crew of the freight train had failed to place proper signals has never been conclusively determined. Photographs of the wreck show mangled cars and track in the middle of a flat field.

Although the details of the ballad vary according to the singer, some themes appear consistently, suggesting they resonate universally with those who valued the song. Versions often begin by reassuring listeners that "Casey Jones was a brave engineer," testifying to his courage in the face of the need for excessive speed to make up time. After telling his fireman "not to fear," he would ask his coworker to provide the needed water and coal to get the steam up, and then one or the other would "put his head out the window, and see the drive wheels roll"; that is, they would enjoy the power of the machine under their command as it rolled down the line. As they thundered down the rails and the train came "around the curve," they spied danger, not, according to the songs, a lowly freight caboose on the tracks, but a locomotive pulling an approaching passenger train, so the two were "bound to thump." To run into a standing freight train is not particularly heroic, and even suggests carelessness, but to die trying to save the passengers on both trains is the stuff of ballads.

Many versions of the song recognize the transient nature of railroad men that led mothers to warn their daughters away from such unreliable mates. A few have Casey's wife bidding him a sad farewell, but almost all have her comforting their children after the wreck and Casey's death that they would not suffer. Some offer the reassurance that the railroad would offer a pension; other versions indicate that while Casey was away, his wife found her children "another poppy on the Southern Line," perhaps in reaction to Casey's behavior that, according to one version, left the women of Kansas City and Jackson who normally dressed in red, donning black when he died. Despite the moral ambiguity of Casey's family life and his tendency to flout the rules of the road, his appeal was his courageous effort to follow orders and meet the demands of the clock, and his even more heroic self-sacrifice in slowing the train before the inevitable "thump."

Casey was celebrated in song as a "good engineer, but he's dead and gone." All along the tracks that night as he sped south, railroad workers knew who was running the Cannonball because of the way Casey made the whistle "moan" in unwitting anticipation of his fate. According to the legend, Casey's regret before he died was that he had "two more roads that he wanted to ride"; singers differ as to his preferences. To the end, Jones expressed the desire of many Americans to wander, a desire the railroads did so much to satisfy.

The "Wreck of Old '97" was even more popular than "Casey Jones." On September 27, 1903, Joseph "Steve" Broady was trying to make up lost time on the fast mail from Washington, D.C., to Atlanta on the Southern Railroad.[36] Coming down the grade on White Oak Mountain into Danville, Virginia, Broady was going too fast to make a curve at the bottom leading onto a trestle. His engine, along with the cars behind, jumped the track, hurtling seventy-five feet into a ravine. Nine people were killed, including Broady, who briefly survived the crash but, as the song told, "was scalded to death by the steam" when the boiler burst. Photographs show significant damage, right in town where the whole event interrupted a pleasant Sunday morning.

The song itself generated as fascinating a story as the wreck. As Norm Cohen shows, several ballads were composed shortly after the wreck, based in part on "The Ship That Never Returned" and its later parodies. When Vernon Dalhart's 1924 recording of the song sold over a million copies, several authors emerged to claim royalties for their efforts.[37] Although the front side of the record, "The Prisoner's Song," with a very similar tune, may have been responsible for the disk's success, the royalties for "Old '97" still amounted to over sixty-five thousand dollars in 1938, near the end of over ten years of litigation.

Early versions of the song are long, running to fourteen stanzas. Faced with the roughly three-minute limit of a 78 rpm record, Dalhart and others had to edit the song to its essence. In doing so, they made some interesting errors from mishearing whatever original they had used. The basic song begins with the engineer receiving his "orders in Monroe, Virginia," to make up the lost time, as this was "not '38 but old '97" and the train needed to "be in Spencer on time." Broady then climbed into the engine and told his fireman to "shovel on a little more coal," so that once they had crossed the White Oak Mountain they could "let old '97 roll." A warning verse follows in which listeners learn not only that the roadbed is "mighty rough" but also that a "three mile grade" lies on the far side of the mountain. Although the following verse indicates Broady was "coming down that grade doing ninety miles an hour," far too fast to make the curve at the bottom, and he was "found in the wreck with his hand on the throttle" and not the brakes, the reason for the wreck in the song is that while on the grade "he lost his airbrakes," leading to the "jump he made." Dalhart's version not only has Broady crossing a "wide old mountain" but also losing his "average" on the way down. While the first makes sense, the latter must have puzzled listeners. The song accurately reports Broady being "scalded to death by the steam." A telegram to the railroad offices in Washington reports that the "brave engineer" lies dead in Virginia, before the last verse offers a moral message. The conclusion continues the tradition of "The Ship That Never Returned" by warning wives never to "say harsh words" to their departing husbands, for they may "leave you and never return."

Numerous other ballads told similar stories with familiar moral messages. Norm Cohen devotes 105 pages to "The Fatal Run," including the two songs we have just examined.[38] One of the best known is "The Wreck on the C&O" or "Engine 143."[39] George Alley was the engineer on the *FFV,* the *Fast Flying*

Virginian, when his train struck a rock that had fallen on the track on October 23, 1890. Alley reportedly stood with his engine to the end, slowing the train sufficiently to save the passengers. According to the ballad, George's mother had warned him, "Many a man has lost his life trying to make up lost time," before suggesting he could still "get there just on time" if he would "run [his] engine right." A blunt assessment of the ultimate cause of the wreck comes in a chorus found in several versions: "Many a man's been murdered by the railroad." Not all wrecks, however, were caused by excessive speed and the demands of the clock and the railroad company. "The New Market Wreck" in 1904 occurred because the conductor misread his orders. A broken rail caused the crash of C&O number 5 in 1920, a landslide sent number 1256 off the track and into a river in 1925, and the brakes on number 1262 failed in the same year. The story is endless. Wives and mothers sent their men off to die sometimes heroic, but often needless deaths because of equipment failures or rash actions borne of company demands. The railroad promised excitement and escape, but at a cost.

Technological marvel that it was, and profound transformer of American life, the railroad was quickly adopted by both black and white Americans as a metaphor for life and death. The railroad—with its straight and narrow path, guiding passengers to a presumably desirable destination and moving along via a powerful force while under the care of an experienced and caring engineer and conductor—was an obvious choice for symbolic journeys through life. Within a few short years of the building of the first railroad in the United States, Nathaniel Hawthorne wrote the short story "The Celestial Railroad," reworking a pilgrim's progress to heaven. The songs "The Spiritual Rail-way" and "The Railway to Heaven" were among the first to use this metaphor.[40] "Life's Railway to Heaven," copyrighted in 1890, though based on an earlier poem, quickly became a popular hymn and provided both the tune and the general model for "Miner's Lifeguard" less than a decade later.[41] The first verse is indicative of the way the metaphor works:

> Life is like a mountain railroad, with an engineer that's brave,
> We must make the run successful from the cradle to the grave;
> Watch the curves, the fills, the tunnels, never falter, never fail,
> Keep your hand upon the throttle and your eye upon the rail.

Interestingly, the metaphor assumes we are all the engineers of our own lives, needing to a keep a hand on the throttle and an eye on the track, advice anyone who has listened to the songs of wrecks would surely appreciate.

Jesus is the conductor, while God, the superintendent of the whole operation, waits to welcome the travelers at the final "union depot."

Although the mechanical reality behind the metaphors was new, the message was often old, frequently centering on the need for spiritual preparation in the face of uncertainty about the time of death. Occasionally a blues singer might refer to the train as a release, contemplating laying his or her head on the rails to let the train "ease my troubling mind." But more often the train served as a metaphor for death, perhaps none so obviously as "Little Black Train."[42] As Scarborough observes, "The little black train here represents Death, and the passengers for whom seats are reserved appear not to be crowding eagerly around the ticket-window. This train . . . is uncertain in its time of arrival and departure. But a delay here brings forth no complaint against the management."[43]

The essence of "Little Black Train" is expressed in a verse repeated at odd intervals and serving as a semi-chorus. The version noted down by Scarborough from the Holy Rollers in Texas makes clear the warning to prepare:

> The little black train is coming,
> Get all your business right;
> Better set your house in order,
> For the train may be here to-night.

Or, as Woody Guthrie sang the final two lines, "You got to ride that little black train, and it ain't going to bring you back."

The song, appropriately sung to a variation of the melody of "The Roving Gambler," contains several distinct segments, biblical and secular, which may be included or omitted according to a singer's preference. The first part is based on the story of Hezekiah from 2 Kings 20. According to the song, the Lord warns Hezekiah to "set thy house in order, for thou shalt surely die." Being ill, Hezekiah does indeed "get his business all fixed right," in reward for which "God spared him fifteen years." After establishing Hezekiah as a model of good behavior, the song generally turns to modern-day sinners, though some versions refer only to the sinners. Among those warned of the approach of the little black train are barroom gamblers, who will not be able to cheat death; ballroom ladies filled or dressed "with earthly pride"; and owners of million-dollar fortunes, whose wealth will be of no avail once the train has come. One of the central components of Western attitudes toward death is the idea of judgment, with a trial based on the record of one's past life in the "Book of Life." In this song, the "Book" becomes a baggage car filled with "idle thoughts and wicked deeds, [which] must stop at the judgment bar."

In an echo of "Wicked Polly" and her foolish expectation that she could "turn to God when I get old," singers of "Little Black Train" sometimes include several verses about a young man who "cared not for the gospel light, until suddenly the whistle blew from the little black train in sight!" His desperate plea, "Death, will you not spare me, I've just seen my wicked plight," is of no avail, as "death had fixed his shackles about his soul so tight [so that] before he got his business fixed, the train rolled in that night." The Texas Holy Rollers added another story from the Bible, this time from Luke 12:15–21, in which a "rich fool in his granary said, 'I have no future fears.'" But as he stood planning how to store and expand his earthly wealth, "the God of power and might said 'Rich fool to judgment come; Thy soul must be there to-night.'"

Other folk songs emphasize the same theme. "This Train," bound for glory as it is, carries only the "righteous and the holy," with no room for liars, gamblers, midnight ramblers, jokers, or even cigarette smokers.[44] In a similar vein, "Oh, Be Ready When the Train Comes In," a song with a telling title, warns that:

> No harlot nor idolater, neither loafer,
> Will be counted in this holy train;
> Nor pipe-smoker, neither joker are permitted
> On this great clean train.[45]

A song made popular by the Fisk Jubilee Singers, "The Gospel Train Is Coming," and a variation, "The Gospel Train Am Leabin'," make it clear that all would be wise to be ready to "get on board" before the train departs. While "there is room for many a more," one does not want to be "left behind," especially since there is:

> No signal for another train
> To follow on the line,
> O, sinner, you're forever lost,
> If once you're left behind.[46]

"The Midnight Train and the 'Fo' Day Train" may "run all night long," carrying "your mother [father, sister, brother] away," but they only "run until the break of day."[47] Scarborough interprets this song as referring to trains that quite literally separated families; but if "the break of day" refers to that time "when the stars begin to fall," then this is clearly one more warning to prepare while there is time. Given the fact that Scarborough was collecting in the 1920s, just after the first great migration of African Americans out of the South began, this could also be a veiled reference to the trains heading north that white employers wished to keep secret from their black workers.

There were worse fates than missing the train to heaven. "The Hell-Bound Train" is one of several to use the device of an alcohol-induced dream to urge not only temperance but also preparation.[48] Aboard a train pulled by an engine damp with "murderous blood," in which "lager beer" was heated for steam "while an imp, for fuel, was shovelin' bones," rode a "mixed up crew" of passengers who "begged for the devil to stop the train" as it approached hell. But the devil "mocked at their misery," reminding his passengers, "You paid for the seats on this road, the train goes through with the complete load." Lest there be any doubt of the price of a ticket on this ride, the devil noted:

Ah, you've bullied the weak, and you've cheated the poor,
The starving brother you've turned from your door;
You've laid up your gold till your purses burst,
And given free pay to your beastly lust.

Not wanting to disappoint his deserving customers, the devil reassured them that because they had "paid full fare," that he would "carry you through, for it's only right you should have your due." Most versions offer a bit of relief at the end, allowing the drunk to awaken and reform his life.

Songs about real journeys abound. Despite the optimism and hope that must have accompanied many train trips to see family, find work, or experience new situations, most folk songs about railway journeys are laments of loss, separation, and the realization that often you can't go home again. The train whistle is for many an embodiment of loneliness, with its suggestion of distance, separation, and isolation. It is not accidental that songs refer to hearing engines "moan," whether it be Casey Jones rumbling through the night on his way to his doom, or the K. C. carrying someone's baby to or away from home.[49]

For many singers, nothing could be worse than being five hundred or nine hundred or ten thousand miles from home.[50] Listen to the voices crying over leaving, saying goodbye, coming home, pining a long way from home:

I'm a poor boy long way from home. . . .
. . . .

I wish a 'scushion train would run,
Carry me back where I come frum.

. . . .

I wish that ole engeneer wus dead,
Brought me 'way from my home.[51]

No more good time, woman, like we used to have,
Police knockin', woman, at my back do!
Meet me at the depot, bring my dirty clothes,
Meet me at the depot, woman, when the train comes down.[52]

Well, I thought I heard that K. C. whistle blow,
Blow lak she never blow befo'.
I believe my woman's on the train,
Oh babe! I believe my woman's on that train.

. . . .

Fireman, put in a little mo' coal,
Run dat train in some lonesome hole.[53]

Faced with an inability to bridge the separation, perhaps because "I got the blues, but I have n't got the fare," all one could do at times was "look down the Southern road an' cry."[54]

The pain of separation was a common experience, and many sang about it, using free-floating verses and collections of tunes with strong family resemblances. Folk song fans of a certain age are no doubt familiar with "500 Miles," a variant of one cluster introduced to the folk world by Hedy West and made popular by Peter, Paul, and Mary.[55] This is merely the most recent addition to the line that extends from "Reuben's Train" and "Train 45" to "900 Miles."[56] Echoes distant and close also can be heard between these songs and the cluster surrounding "The Longest Train" and "In the Pines." In some ways it does not matter whether the singer is five hundred or five thousand miles from home; whether he is going home or has "tears in my eyes, trying to read a letter from my home" to see if his woman will say the word to stop him from rambling; whether he will need to pawn his watch and chain to buy the ticket home; or even whether he is, like Reuben, "in trouble all his life," and thus unable to return. As anyone who has ever sung one of these songs can testify, it is the haunting melody that expresses the blues and may, if all goes well, carry them away. To keep the feeling real and alive, it is no wonder verses get borrowed to prolong the moment.

Norm Cohen devotes a whole chapter of his remarkable book on railroad folk songs to railroad blues.[57] One of those songs is called the "Cannonball

Blues," with both music and lyrics derived from the ballad composed in 1901 on the assassination of President McKinley called the "White House Blues."[58] As sung by the Carter Family, the "Cannonball Blues" echoes the theme of separation already noted, with uncertainty over who is leaving and who is staying behind. In one verse, the singer cries, "My baby left me, she even took my shoes, enough to give me those doggone worried blues," stating unequivocally, "She's solid gone." But two verses later the singer announces, "I'm going up north" and if "[my] luck don't change, I won't be back at all," and then, as if there was any doubt, "My honey babe, I'm leaving you."

The name "Cannonball" was attached both officially and informally to the fastest train on any railroad line. Casey Jones was driving the Illinois Central's Cannonball when he had his famous collision. But few Cannonballs are better known than the one that never existed, "The Wabash Cannonball."[59] In the second half of the nineteenth century, the American economy experienced three major depressions during which thousands of workers and their families struggled to make ends meet in a world with no social safety nets. Even between economic slumps, there was little an unemployed worker could do to support his family other than hit the road in search of work if local employers were not hiring. Thus it is not surprising that a number of folk songs about hobos and their life were written at this time.[60] Some, perhaps popular in the "jungle camps" where hobos congregated on the edge of town, celebrated the life and joked about their dreams. Others, possibly from the perspective of homeowners who had ragged men appear at their back door asking for work or food, were more critical. A few tried to remind their fellow citizens of the state of the economy, suggesting that many hobos were decent men trying to find work.

"The Wabash Cannonball" tells the story of a mythical journey across the United States, "from the great Atlantic Ocean to the wide Pacific shore," via a route no real train ever traveled. Although the song was first copyrighted in 1904, Cohen clearly shows its roots in an 1882 poem titled "The Great Rock Island Route."[61] One version of the chorus highlights its origins among wandering men:

> Listen to the jingle, the rumble and the roar,
> Riding through the woodlands,
> Through the hills and by the shore,
> Hear the mighty rush of the engine,
> Hear the lonesome hobo squall,
> Riding through the jungles on the Wabash Cannonball.

Although the last line of the chorus clearly refers to the world the hobos lived in, it replaces a line in other versions that referred to riding "the rods and brake-beams" under the trains, where the hobos clung when they could not get into an empty boxcar. Likewise, the end of the first verse often praises the Wabash Cannonball as "a modern [or 'regular'] combination." This seems to have replaced "she's the 'boes' accommodation" as the song became popular, possibly to distance the song from its roots, or maybe because of the normal shifting of lyrics in oral transmission.

"I'm Alabama Bound" was a song common among African Americans.[62] Heading south, the singer anticipates his journey will be successful so long as the train "don't stop and turn around"; but if "the train don't run, I got a mule to ride," a far less satisfactory form of transportation. Aboard the steamboat *Stacker Lee*, the verse goes, "Ef the Stack don't drown, I'm Alabama bound." Unfortunately, heading to and living in the South brought many African Americans face to face with a criminal justice system stacked against them. Several songs address the trains with language that symbolizes both confinement and freedom to many black men.

The loss of freedom began with being brought back to face trial. After admitting to abusing a woman, one singer of an untitled song declares, "I made a good run but I run too slow, . . . they put me on the train and brought me back."[63] Once the trial was over, and the guilty party sentenced "To Huntsville" in the Texas penitentiary system, the man and his woman might stand "upon that station platform . . . awaiting that train for Huntsville . . . for ten long years to stay."[64] After the convict had obeyed the sheriff's instructions to "get on that train," he could wryly ask anyone who saw his Lula to tell her he had finally, if involuntarily, "quit drinking and gambling, . . . and getting on my sprees." Asking any sympathetic bystander to "Look Where De Train Done Gone," a distraught prisoner facing ten or more years of hard labor might reflect, "If I had a-died when I was young, I would n't a-had this hard race to run!"[65]

Once in the penitentiary, the focus of the songs changes. Leadbelly, a man who had his share of experience with Southern prisons, sang of "Shorty George," the short train that brought prisoners' families out from Houston to visit their men at the Sugarland Prison but all too soon took them away again.[66] In this classic twelve-bar blues, Leadbelly remarks that the little train "ain't no friend of mine" because "he's taken the women leavin' the men behind." The same train was apparently used to transport convicts to the prison, for Leadbelly also comments that Shorty George "left a many po' man a long way from home."

Perhaps the best-known song linking trains to prisons is "The Midnight Special," made famous by Leadbelly but widely known across the South.[67] According to legend, the Midnight Special was a train that left Houston and passed Sugarland about midnight, reminding the prisoners of freedom and life on the outside, and perhaps bringing them hope of release. Although multiple versions exist, the essential message remains the same and is embodied in three parts, or themes, common to all the versions. One theme remarks on the bleak conditions in prison, where the bell gets the prisoners up to start the day with a meager meal at best.

> When you wake up in the morning, when the ding-dong ring,
> Go marching to the table, meet the same old thing.
> Knife and fork are on the table, nothing in my pan;
> Ever say anything about it, have trouble with the man.*

The song has frequently been localized by singers to the particular place they were arrested, with mention made of the men who took them down. Thus a second part of the song comments on the arrest, trial, and conviction in places as far apart as Houston or Paris, Texas, and Belmont, North Carolina. The third theme involves the prisoner looking out his cell window to see his woman, often called Rosie, coming for him. Sometimes all she has are a few amenities (a little coffee or tea) to make his life better, but sometimes she has a "piece of paper," a pardon, to give to the warden, telling him, "I want my man." Of course, the train could also bring bad news from home, as when Leadbelly received word that his "wife was dead." Unable to attend the funeral, cut off from this critical tie to the outside world, and possibly facing an end to visits for the rest of his sentence, Leadbelly responded:

> That started me to grieving,
> Whooping, hollering, and crying.
> Then I began to worry
> About my great long time.

The only hope was to have "the Midnight Special shine her light on me."

♯ ♯ ♯

*New words and new music adaptation by Huddie Ledbetter. Collected and adapted by John A. Lomax and Alan Lomax. TRO-© Copyright 1936 (Renewed) 1959 (Renewed) Folkways Music Publishers, Inc., New York, NY. Used by permission.

Modes of transportation that emerged in the twentieth century have produced few if any folk songs. "Charlie and the MTA" is based on older songs, and the subway is a short railroad that runs mostly underground. There are ample popular songs about automobiles, but none have become folk songs. It may be that car wrecks are too personal and private to merit memorialization in a folk song. Speed may kill, but cars rarely crash trying to make up lost time at the behest of a boss. Anyone who has ever studied attitudes toward death knows that the spectacular epidemic that, like an accident involving mass transit, kills a lot of people in a short time receives far more attention than the slow, steady, disease that one-by-one takes far more lives than any plague.

Travel by air has the potential for folk songs but has not yet produced any that have spread widely in the oral tradition. "The Wreck of the Shenandoah" was recorded by Vernon Dalhart after that airship was destroyed over Akron, Ohio, in 1925 with the loss of fourteen lives, but the ballad never achieved lasting popularity.[68] A quick search of the Mudcat Forum, a wonderful Internet source for lyrics and information on folk songs, shows no entries for songs about the crashes of the airships *Akron* in 1933 or *Hindenberg* in 1937, though Leadbelly wrote a song about the latter.[69] The *Hindenberg* disaster, was spectacular and widely reported, but it may have been unappealing for songwriters because of the increasing concern over the Nazi regime in Germany. In the 1930s Holy Rollers in Missouri and Arkansas adapted the old messages of preparation for the final journey home to heaven to "The Heavenly Aeroplane."[70] According to this song, "the Lord will come in his aeroplane" at the end of days to take all those who have a ticket "up to glory in His aeroplane." The airplane is portrayed as far superior to automobiles, which suffer from such metaphors for sin as "punctures, . . . muddy roads, . . . and broken axels from overloads." Woody Guthrie's last great composition, "Deportee," was written in 1948 after a "Plane Wreck at Los Gatos Canyon" took the lives of many migrant workers who were being deported back to Mexico.[71] But this plaintive ballad is about the callous treatment of migrant laborers, with the plane wreck only briefly mentioned. John Denver's "Leaving on a Jet Plane" and Gordon Lightfoot's "Early Morning Rain" both have the sound of a folk song and echo the sorrow of separation that is common in folk songs about ships and trains. Both have also been adopted by prominent and not-so-prominent folk singers of the late twentieth century. No doubt the two songs have begun to slide over into the oral tradition, if learning a song off a record or the radio counts. But neither has made the transformation yet. Perhaps when some scholar writes the sequel to this volume in fifty years, there will be folk songs about planes and cars.

CHAPTER 6

Just Lookin' for a Home

Traveling On

Oh, have you heard tell of Sweet Betsy from Pike,
Who crossed the wide prairie with her lover Ike,
With two yoke of cattle, an old yellow dog,
A tall shanghai rooster and one spotted hog?

Like Betsy, many Americans were on the move in the nineteenth century.[1] Betsy and Ike were traveling west to California in search of gold, but Americans had been heading west in search of a better future since the early seventeenth century, when the West was the Connecticut River Valley or the Blue Ridge Mountains. By 1850, when Betsy and Ike began their trek across the country, other Americans were already flocking to the cities in a flood that would turn the 5 percent who lived in cities in 1800 into an urban majority by 1920. Still others were pouring into the country from overseas, from Ireland and Germany when Betsy and Ike went west, but from other parts of Europe as the century came to a close. Between 1820 and 1920, approximately forty million people moved to the United States from abroad, some of whom joined Betsy and Ike in California, including a few from China.

In all probability, this was not Betsy's first move. Americans rarely picked up and migrated vast distances, but that does not mean they stayed in one place their whole lives; they still made moves that took them to new communities, counties, or states. Betsy's parents may well have been married in Virginia and moved first to Kentucky or Ohio before settling in Missouri, where Pike County is located.[2] Betsy could have been born in Virginia, or anywhere on the way to Pike County. Her trip with Ike across the plains and mountains would be the longest of her life, even though she would in all probability dwell in several different locations in the West. Although the proportion of Americans who joined Betsy in the gold rush was relatively small, the tendency to move was common. Throughout the nineteenth century, and on into the twentieth, only 35 to 60 percent of the people living in any American community, rural or urban, would be there ten years later.[3] Many migrated in the expectation of improving their standing in society; some actually realized that dream.

In setting forth with her "lover Ike," Betsy broke with the tradition of family migration, though only partly, since the song informs us that they married upon reaching California, a marriage that did not last for long. Many migrants traveled with their families or in a chain migration where one family member pioneered, with others coming along once roots had been planted. Others moved alone or as part of a group like the Mormons or Exodusters (African Americans who left the South for Kansas and Oklahoma after Emancipation). Betsy and Ike made their way west in a wagon train, but that group would have dispersed upon making it over the Sierras. Perhaps they sought an environment similar to Pike County, as many settled in places that reminded them of home, but the lure of gold may have overridden that impulse.

The trip was not without its trials and tribulations.[4] When the "Injuns came down in a wild yelling horde," Betsy crawled behind a wagon wheel to protect "her adored" with "musket and ball." In fact, Indians were often helpful to wagon trains, and as many migrants drowned as died from attacks. Diseases like cholera could plague a journey. Overall, mortality averaged about 4 percent for a typical party traveling west, about five times higher than was common in the rest of the population. In the desert "Betsy gave out and down in the sand she lay rolling about." Later, "the wagon tipped over with a terrible crash," possibly because it was overloaded; Betsy and Ike would not have been the only migrants who tried to take too much. Some claimed it was possible to start west with an empty wagon and gather enough discarded belongings by journey's end in California to furnish a home. Betsy and Ike appear to have caused a bit of a scandal with their accident when baby clothes were observed midst "all sorts of trash" that spilled out of the wagon, but the song reassures us "it was all on the square." The environment presented other difficulties.

They swam the wide rivers and crossed the tall peaks,
And camped on the prairie for weeks upon weeks,
Starvation and cholera, hard work and slaughter,
They reached California 'spite hell and high water.

"Seeing the elephant" was a common phrase for those who made it part way across but could not summon the courage to complete the journey.[5] Betsy apparently saw the elephant, for after the crash she "got up with a great deal of pain, and declared she'd go back to Pike County again." Ike sighed and embraced her, and then traveled on "with his arm 'round her waist," coaxing her forward. Left unreported is what she thought when they finally crested the Sierras and "looked down into old Placerville," while Ike rejoiced they had "got to Hangtown." But Betsy seems to have prospered in the mining camps with few other women around. Miners soon sought her out at dances, though she warned them not to squeeze her hard as she was still "chock full of strong alkali" from water holes along the way. Although Ike married her shortly after their arrival, he soon became "jealous [and] obtained a divorce." Perhaps he was right to suspect Sweet Betsy, because she accepted the divorce "with a smile, [saying] I've six good men waiting within half a mile."

Since Ike and Betsy headed west at the time of the gold rush, that presumably was their motivation. But the reasons people move are often complex. War and famine are among the most powerful *push factors*, along with religious or racial discrimination. Tales of streets paved in gold—or at least higher wages, political freedoms, and a more favorable climate—*pull* people to various destinations. Few move for one reason only, with combinations of push and pull both detaching people from their homes and directing them one place or another. Moreover, *intervening variables* affect choices along the way. Many Irish ended up in Boston during the potato famine of the 1840s because the British ships carrying the mail to Canada docked there instead of sailing up the St. Lawrence River. A promising-looking community, fertile soil, or an attractive woman or man might alter a migrant's final destination. Perhaps Ike and Betsy had more timid brothers and sisters who waited another twenty years to head west, when they could take an easy trip on the Union Pacific to San Francisco. Presumably the young lovers started voluntarily, though after Betsy saw the elephant, she continued only with Ike's "arm 'round her waist." Others had little choice in the matter. Had Betsy already married Ike in Pike County, she would have had less to say about heading west. Slaves who were caught up in the internal slave trade certainly had no control over their migration south and west. Occasionally individuals might move from complex patterns of push and pull, voluntary and involuntary. One can only wonder at the various motives of the individual to whom this brief ditty was addressed:

Oh, what was your name in the States?
Was it Thompson or Johnson or Bates?
Did you murder your wife
And fly for your life?
Say, what was your name in the States?[6]

We know nothing of what combination of guidebooks, letters, or rumors Ike and Betsy consulted when deciding what route to take or supplies they might need, but they surely had access to ample advice, not all of it accurate. The fact that they loaded "all sorts of trash" into their wagon suggests they were not entirely well informed, but at least they chose a better route to California than the Donner party. John Stone, the author of "Sweet Betsy," commented more explicitly on the problem in another song, "Crossing the Plains."[7] Stone urged all prospective Californians to "open wide your ears, if you are going across the Plains with snotty mules or steers." After poking fun at greenhorns who armed themselves to the teeth and grew out their beards to look "savage," Stone offered some practical advice. Food was one necessity, and the journey often took longer than expected. Stone, himself an overland veteran, pointedly noted:

You calculate on sixty days to take you over the Plains,
But there you lack for bread and meat, for coffee and for brains;
Your sixty days are a hundred or more, your grub you've got to divide,
Your steers and mules are alkalied, so foot it—you cannot ride.

Canteens filled with "poison alkali" from dangerous water holes at best left one's "bowels loose and free," if they did not lead one to "cramp all up and die." Cooking with "buffalo wood," including "some that's newly born," added extra zest to the journey and unique flavors to the meals. Arguments were frequent and disruptive, while many suddenly came down with headaches and coughs when faced with "stand[ing] a watch at night."

One alternative was to take a ship either all the way around Cape Horn or to Central America and, after crossing the Isthmus of Panama on foot, board another vessel to head north to California. This choice, however, offered only a different set of miseries, such as seasickness and abusive captains. Bad food and bugs were the common lot of all those headed west, whether by land or by sea, at least according to "Coming Around the Horn."[8]

Stone was sensitive to the problems women like Betsy faced on the trail when he wrote:

> The ladies have the hardest, that emigrate by land,
> For when they cook with buffalo wood, they often burn a hand;
> And when they jaw their husbands round, get mad and spill the tea,
> Wish to the Lord they'd been taken down with a turn of the di-a-ree.

The wagon tipping over was, perhaps, only the last straw for Ike's Pike County rose. Despite advice like Stone's, migrants, whether to the West or to more settled regions, often heard a welter of voices "booming," or promoting, communities, both settled and imaginary, leading to "overblown hopes" among those already inclined to optimism about their prospects.[9]

‡ ‡ ‡

Betsy and Ike were not the only migrants in songs to be motivated by love. Maybe it was her father who "was born in East Virginia" and moved to North Carolina, where he met "a fair young maiden, whose name and age [he did] not know." If this was Betsy's mother, her attraction was evident, sufficient to divert a young man to a different destination. Her hair was "a dark black color, and her lips were ruby red, on her breast she wore white lilies, where [he] longed to lay [his] head." But perhaps the courtship did not go well, since the singer sighed, "I'd rather live in some dark hollow, where the sun refuse to shine, than to see you with another, and to know you won't be mine." If the girl in question was "Pretty Saro," then we know he moved on because she "wants some freeholder that has houses and land," whereas this young man on the move was still too poor to buy her "all the fine things a big house can hold."[10] Despite the rejection, he vowed "to think of pretty Saro wherever I go." Perchance he went back and married her after finding success somewhere down the road, or he might have found another pretty girl on the way to Missouri, where he remembered Pretty Saro and the eastern mountains.

West was not the only direction lovers traveled. The "Red River Valley" tells the tale of promising love coming to an end when one partner decides to head back East.[11] The origins of this song are in some dispute. Canadians claim it was written in the Red River Valley that flows north through their

western plains, while others trace it to the United States. "In the Bright Mohawk Valley" places the song in upstate New York, but it is unclear whether
it originated there, or whether like one of the characters in the song, it
moved back East. The song begins with the prospect of farewells leaving a
fond heart breaking:

> From this valley they say you are going,
> I will miss your bright eyes and sweet smile,
> For they say you are taking the sunshine,
> That brightens our pathway awhile.

The chorus tries to delay the inevitable, when the one left behind urges her
departing lover:

> Come and sit by my side if you love me,
> Do not hasten to bid me adieu,
> But remember the Red River Valley,
> And the girl who has loved you so true.

After a number of sentimental verses, the girl appeals to her cowboy, "Think
of the fond heart you're breaking, and the grief you are causing to me," as
well the fact "you leave [me] behind unprotected." Toward the end of some
versions of the song, reference is made to "the dark maiden's prayer for her
lover," suggesting a Western origin about an Indian maiden who fell in love
with a white man, possibly a soldier. As he goes to his "home by the ocean,"
she hopes he will never "forget those sweet hours, that we spent in the Red
River Valley, and the love we exchanged midst the flowers."

Betsy and Ike had a fellow Pike County resident immortalized in a song
of unrequited love: "Joe Bowers."[12] Joe tells the sorry tale of courting a girl
named Sally Black, who would not marry him until he "had a little home
to keep his little wife." When Joe declared he would head to California and
the gold fields to "raise a stake," Sally cheered him on and sent him forth,
smothered in kisses. Despite the hard life in California, Joe persevered and
succeeded. Then a letter from home, written by his brother Ike, arrived and
devastated him. Joe read that in his absence "Sal was fickle, that her love for
me had fled." In fact, she had married a redheaded butcher. What aggravated
Joe the most was the news that Sally already had a baby, though "whether
'twas a boy or gal child, the letter never said, it only said its cussed hair was
inclined to be red." Not only were all his efforts mining gold for naught,
but Joe may have decided Sally wanted him out of the way before he even

left. The song does not tell us how long it was between the time Joe left Pike County and the time the redheaded baby was born.

‡ ‡ ‡

In 1910 John Lomax published the words to a then-little-known song that became one of America's favorites. "Home on the Range," first printed in a newspaper as early as 1873 and taught to Lomax by an African-American saloonkeeper in San Antonio, expresses great pleasure with the wide-open spaces and pristine environment of the West, with implied and explicit contrasts to the cities of the East.[13] As with songs like "Amazing Grace" or "The Battle Hymn of the Republic," many Americans know the first verse to "Home on the Range" but would be hard-pressed to sing any additional stanzas. Who but the most nature-phobic urbanite can resist the request:

> Oh give me a home, where the buffalo roam,
> And the deer and the antelope play,
> Where seldom is heard a discouraging word,
> And the skies are not cloudy all day.

Frolicking animals, cloudless skies, and boundless optimism appeal widely, so much so that the chorus repeats the last three lines of the first verse. But there is more. The song continues with a celebration of the "air so pure" and "breezes so balmy and light," declaring, "I would not exchange my home on the range for all of the cities so bright." No doubt many Americans were familiar with cities "so bright" at night but polluted by noxious fumes and decaying wastes during the day. Many, however, would have paused at the notion that the winds that sweep across the plains could be considered "balmy and light." Other verses praise "the wild flowers in this dear land of ours" and the curlew that screams from on high. "Bright diamond sands" stretching down to "where the graceful white swan goes gliding along like a maid in a heavenly stream" add to the romantic and peaceful image of the range. Anyone who has traveled across the plains, with the big sky extending in all directions, and who has looked to the heavens on a night unencumbered by the light pollution of the "cities so bright" can understand the following lines:

> How often at night when the heavens are bright,
> With the light of the glittering stars,
> Have I stood there amazed and asked as I gaze,
> If their glory exceeds that of ours.

The only hint of trouble in Eden, and it may not have bothered many pioneers heading west in the nineteenth century, were lines that recognize the land had long been inhabited. How many Americans, then or now, ever heard or paused to consider that:

> The red man was pressed from this part of the West,
> He's likely no more to return
> To the banks of Red River where seldom if ever
> Their flickering campfires burn.

"Home on the Range" is one of the rare optimistic songs associated with migration. Most take a far more pessimistic and cynical view of the experience, often expressed in the form of satire. The promise of streets paved in gold, or at least of more freedom and opportunity, often proved illusory. As high expectations and overblown hopes confronted the harsh realities of unfamiliar environments and hostile inhabitants, disillusionment set in, ameliorated to some degree by song.

The tendency to sing of the false promises of migration was evident in the seventeenth century. Virginia, the first permanent colony settled by the English in North America in 1607, was a terrible place. Instead of gold and natives to do the work, as the Spanish had acquired farther south, early settlers to Virginia found themselves faced with native leaders skeptical about the new invaders and expectations to work for the company that was sponsoring the venture. Jamestown proved deadly to many of the first colonists, with fewer than thirteen hundred still alive when a census was taken in 1624, despite over six thousand immigrants coming to the colony over the previous six years. The young men and few women who went to Virginia found a world little to their liking.

One song from the middle of the seventeenth century expresses the sentiments of "The Trappan'd Maiden: or, The Distressed Damsel."[14] The title implies trickery, or even coercion, in "recruiting" this servant girl, as *trappaning* often referred to being knocked unconscious and kidnapped. The song opens by asking the listener to "give ear unto a Maid, that lately was betray'd," to understand her tale of what she "suffer'd there, when that I was weary, weary, weary, weary, O." Despite gendered expectations of work in the seventeenth century that assigned fieldwork to men and domestic chores to women, the trepanned maid found that "the axe and hoe have wrought my overthrow." Five years of service, indicating an indenture, led her "to know sorrow, grief and woe." While her mistress had meat, she had "none to eat";

likewise, her clothes were "worn very thin" and her bed was of straw. Instead of beer, she had only water to drink, which, she said, left her "pale and wan, do all that e'er I can." It is hard to believe she would have been too pale after days spent in the sun with "plow and cart" or from carrying "billets from the Wood upon my back" and "water from the spring upon my head." If that were not enough, grinding grain and caring for the baby of the house added to her burdens. No wonder the song ends by warning others not to come voluntarily and indicating she would welcome the "chance, homewards to advance," where she would no longer be "weary, O."

New England, settled by the religious reformers known as the Pilgrims and the Puritans, came in for its share of criticism, even though the "starving times" did not last as long there as they had in Virginia, and society achieved stability quickly. "The Summons to Newe England" was reprinted in 1661 but probably dates from the 1630s, just as John Winthrop was envisioning his city upon a hill.[15] Clearly this is a song written by someone hostile to the Puritans' errand into the wilderness. It begins by summoning "the counterfeit Elect, all zealous bankrupps, puncks devout, preachers suspended, [and] rabble rout" to prepare to sail to New England, there "to build new Babel strong and sure, now call'd a Church unspotted pure." In addition to the constant, sarcastic reference to the hope of founding a church most pure, New England is described as a place where the need for work is at a minimum, running counter to the Puritans' admonition that idle hands do the devil's work and counter to reality as well. In the second verse, prospective migrants would have learned:

> There milk from springs, like rivers, flows,
> And honey upon hawthorn grows;
> Hemp, wool, and flax, there grows on trees,
> The mould is fat, and cuts like cheese;
> All fruits and herbs growes in the fields,
> Tobacco it good plenty yields.

Promises of venison and other game "so tame, that you with ease may eate your fill, take what you please," and flocks of birds that "cloud the light," are not entirely out of line with more objective descriptions of the resources of New England, but other verses exaggerate when they claim:

> There twice a year all sorts of grain
> Doth down from heaven like hailstones rain;
> You never need to sow nor plough,

There's plenty of all things enough;
Wine sweet and wholesome drops from trees,
As clear as crystal, without lees.

Should the promise of abundant nature not provide a sufficient lure, the song goes on to satirize the New England hopes for utopia based on a "Church unspotted pure." Although clearly meant critically, many Puritans would have rejoiced at the prospect of "no feasts or festival set daies" and welcomed a place where "no mass was ever sung . . . [and] surplice and cope durst not appear." They would, however, have objected strenuously to being accused of establishing a colony where "no discipline shall there be used . . . where lustes and pleasures dwell secure." The New England emphasis on "Christian liberty" and mutual effort and support is distorted into a promise that "t'avoide strife, each man may take another's wife, and keep a handmaid too, if need, to multiply, increase and breed." The song concludes with the suggestion that if enough of England's undesirables from its asylums and prisons, its Bedlams and Newgates, could be persuaded to go to this new paradise, then old England's own church and state might be kept "secure." Of course, when convicts could no longer be transported to the American colonies after 1776, Botany Bay in Australia filled the need for a place to send a "Wild Colonial Boy" inclined to go "Waltzing Matilda." By the middle of the eighteenth century, American colonists were protesting that continued efforts by the British to transport convicts to the New World were producing anything but paradise, but whether anyone ever protested in folk song is unknown.

In the nineteenth century, in the midst of mass migrations from Europe to the United States, and westward across the continent, the tradition of expressing disillusionment via song continued. "Oleana" was a Norwegian reaction to the story of Ole Bull.[16] About 1850 Bull, an internationally renowned violinist, decided to help his fellow Norwegians migrate to the United States by establishing an agricultural haven. Instead of picking flat, fertile soil on the plains, which might have made fjord-land people nervous anyhow, he acquired property in the Pennsylvania mountains. The land proved hard to farm, and questions arose about Bull's title, so the whole enterprise soon collapsed. Bull felt so embarrassed and guilt ridden that he spent a year giving concerts to raise the money to compensate his colonists. In 1853 a Norwegian newspaperman, Ditmar Meidell, published "In Oleana, That's Where It's Good to Be," satirizing the whole episode. The song begins with the call to head to Oleana to be free of the "chains of slavery" in Norway.[17] In Oleana farmers "get ground for nothing," while the grain grows "in a flash." A single potato is sufficient to brew a "pot of whiskey," while high-quality beer "runs in the creeks for the poor man's pleasure." Salmon jump willingly into frying pans, and roasted pigs roam the streets, searching out hungry immigrants. The cows not only milk themselves but also churn the butter and make the cheese. The pay is two dollars a day for "carousing" and four if "you're really lazy." With such blessings, it should come as no surprise that "the poorest wretch over there is a count." Other Danish songs made fun of the overblown hopes of migrants and promoters, but none quite so spectacularly as "Oleana."

Migrants within the United States also fell victim to unreasoning optimism, both their own and of others. They too responded with song. "The State of Arkansas" is a well-known ballad recounting the tale of a migrant who "never knew what misery was till [he] came to Arkansas."[18] Arriving in some likely town, sometimes identified as Little Rock or Hot Springs, the traveler takes shelter "behind the depot to dodge the blizzard wind," where he encounters a "walking skeleton" who claims to be the proprietor of the best hotel in the state. Accompanying this businessman to his establishment, the traveler observes "pity and starvation . . . in every face." Corn dodger is the staple food, for the meat he "[can] not chaw," even though the price is exorbitant. After a series of escapades, the unlucky migrant finally moves on, with no regrets. After bidding farewell to "swamp-angels, to canebrakes and to chills," the traveler remarks, "If I ever see that land again, I'll give to you my paw, [but] it will be through a telescope from here to Arkansas."

According to Texas tradition, a fork in the road west had a sign indicating the way to Texas; those who could read went on to the Lone Star state, while the others ended up in Arkansas.[19] Judging from some songs, however, Texas was not always the better choice. "Hell in Texas" has little good to say about the western parts of the state. It tells of a devil who, freed after being chained in hell for a thousand years, decides to "start up a hell of his own."[20] He goes to the Lord and asks if He has any land left over that might fit the purpose. The Lord replies He has some "down south on the Rio Grande" but doubts it is good enough to even "do for hell any more." On first sight, the devil is inclined to agree; but to "get the stuff off His hands," the Lord adds a few amenities. To water from a "bog hole that stunk like the deuce" is added "tarantulas over the roads, with thorns on the cactus and horns on the toads," along with "millions of ants," long-horned cattle, and rattlesnakes. If that were not enough:

He hung thorns and brambles on all of the trees,
He mixed up the dust with jiggers and fleas;
The rattlesnake bites you, the scorpion stings,
The mosquito delights you by buzzing his wings.
The heat in the summer's a hundred and ten,
Too hot for the Devil and too hot for men;
And all who remained in that climate soon bore
Cuts, bites, stings, and scratches, and blisters galore.

Should anyone chance to eat the red peppers from the area, he might well decide he had "hell on the inside as well as the out."

But there were worse places than Texas. According to the Lomax version of "Starving to Death on a Government Claim," a homesteader in Greer County, Oklahoma, finally gave up the struggle to claim his land and returned to Texas to marry and settle down.[21] In 1862, in the midst of the Civil War, Congress passed the Homestead Act, granting 160 acres to anyone who would settle on a claim for five years. By the time the act was passed, settlement had already extended into areas normally so dry that 160 acres were not enough to make a farm. The song, written in 1891, offers a powerful critique of the problems faced by a homesteader on a government claim and may explain why so much land was purchased from speculators rather than acquired in this way. The singer is a bachelor, perhaps like Joe Bowers, trying to establish his fortune before marrying. He begins by describing his dwelling, in this instance a sod house in which he "always get[s] wet when it happens to rain." Fortunately, or unfortunately, that is rarely a problem because "the winds never cease and the rains never fall." Instead of a home on the range where the deer and the antelope play, Lane County, or Greer County, or some similar place, are "the home of the grasshopper, bedbug, and flea."[22] After a hard day trying to extract crops from the unforgiving landscape, the weary homesteader crawls into bed, expecting a good night's rest. But that is not to be. Instead:

A rattlesnake rattles a tune at my head,
And the gay little centipede, void of all fear,
Crawls over my neck and down into my ear,
And the little bed bugs so cheerful and bright,
They keep me a-laughing two-thirds of the night,
And the gay little flea with sharp tacks in his toes
Plays "why don't you catch me" all over my nose.

Despite the lack of rain and the abundance of insects, what really drove men to despair was the harsh reality of economic failure. With "nothing to eat, and . . . nothing to wear," with "money . . . all gone and I can't get away," it is not surprising the homesteader concludes, "There is nothing that makes a man hard and profane like starving to death on a government claim." Having seen the elephant, the old bachelor heads back east to a wife and whatever fate waits there.

Not all chose to comment on overblown hopes as harshly as these few songs. Echoes of "Oleana" are evident in the utopian dreams of "The Big Rock Candy Mountain."[23] In this paean to a land that never was, a hobo—a migrant who never finds a home—describes his ultimate paradise. Among other attractions, the hobo hopes for handouts that grow on bushes, empty boxcars, and good weather every day. Cigarette trees and lakes of whiskey and stew, where "you can paddle all around in a big canoe," compete as lures, along with harmless bulldogs, blind railroad bulls (police), and jails easily escaped. Not only are there no tools for work on chain gangs, but the authorities have the sense to hang the "jerk who invented work in the Big Rock Candy Mountain."

The roots of this song run deep, and its meaning is open to interpretation beyond the obvious satire. "The Land of Cockaygne," probably written in Ireland in the 1330s, tells of a land far out to sea and west of Spain where work is scarce and material pleasures abound, including wine flowing in streams and roasted geese flying to hungry people. Monks and nuns take pleasure in each other's company in more than spiritual ways.[24] In the 1680s an "Invitation to Lubberland" echoed parts of "The Summons to Newe England" and anticipated "Oleana" when it promised rivers that "run with claret fine and brooks with rich canary."[25] "Hills [of] sugar candy" and the opportunity to "lead a lazy life" presage the Big Rock Candy Mountain. A song from the Ozarks in the twentieth century suggests the Big Rock Candy Mountain may be a metaphor for heaven, where all the hobos will "meet this fall." "The Dying Hobo" recounts the visions of paradise of a worn-out wanderer.[26] There he expects to find "handouts [that] grow on bushes" and "little streams of whiskey [that] come trickling down the rocks." No one will ever again make him change his socks, but even more delightful is the prospect of a "land where they hate the word called work." Harry "Mac" McClintock, an IWW songster and author of "The Big Rock Candy Mountain," provides a possible link to the Wobblies, suggesting this might also be a satire of the hopes of less radical laboring men and a warning not to heed their more conservative unions or prominent leaders. Alan Lomax may have recognized this, for he followed "The Big Rock Candy Mountain" in one collection of songs with Joe Hill's warning that those who listened to conservative preachers were condemned to accept the message, "You'll get pie in the sky when you die."[27]

Of course, in some instances the push to leave a place was sufficient to make any destination more agreeable. The great migration of African Americans out of the South in the early decades of the twentieth century was propelled by lynching; by legalized discrimination, made worse by the declaration of its constitutionality in *Plessy v. Ferguson* (1896); by the problems in the cotton fields associated with the arrival of the boll weevil from Mexico sometime in the 1890s; and later, by mechanization. The "Boll Weevil" is known widely across the South in varied forms but with the same basic message: the search for a home.[28] Striking differences in lyrics and melodies in the way this message was expressed across the South suggest the weevil spread so fast that the first songs could not keep up, inspiring constant composition in the face of this munching catastrophe.

At the start of the song, the boll weevil suddenly appears and is soon joined by his whole family "looking for a home." This "little black bug" is not welcomed by farmers, much as African Americans felt hostility from their white neighbors. Despite efforts to drive off the boll weevil by putting him on ice, burying him in sand, or feeding him Paris Green (an insecticide), the weevil perseveres and even prospers, commenting time and time again to his persecutors, "I can stand this like a man, I found me a home." At times the weevil settles down in the farmer's Stetson hat and his wife's raggedy dress, leaving both "full of holes." Although black farmers joined their white neighbors in trying to combat the pest, concluding verses occasionally draw an explicit bond between farmer and weevil in remarking that the man who sang the song is also looking for a home. Dorothy Scarborough, who reports the pleasure African Americans had in singing this song, remarks on the Robin Hood–like quality of the weevil, admired while hunted. He, like other bandits celebrated in song, was an outlaw endowed with superhuman powers to endure hardship and extraordinary cunning to outwit his oppressors.[29] But even black outcasts like the weevil had a limit to their endurance, and while that insect migrated across the South, African Americans fled social and political persecution and economic hardship to cities in the North, carrying with them the roots of jazz and the blues.

Other songs echo the sentiments of "Boll Weevil." Leadbelly's "Cotton Song," which achieved brief popularity in the late 1950s, reflects on the days when his mother would rock him "in the cradle in them old cotton fields back home."[30] He too recognized the problems caused by the weevil and a labor system that offered little room for negotiation to African Americans when he recalled, "You didn't make very much money" raising or picking cotton. Traveling within the South did not always improve prospects, since both racism and the weevil were ever present, so that when he moved to Arkansas to look for work his friends asked, "'What you come here for?'" Elizabeth Cotton's wonderfully plaintive and melodic "Freight Train" asks the listener not to tell "which train I'm on, so they don't know what route I've gone," alluding to the need for African Americans to disguise from their white employers their intent to leave the South until after they had escaped.

As African Americans moved into the cities of the North, they brought with them their old songs and invented new ones to fit the local conditions. The story of Frankie and Johnny (or Albert) could only have occurred in a city like St. Louis. Without the urban night life of the North (most Southern blacks lived in rural areas), Billy Lyons would not have had his fatal encounter with "Stack" Lee Shelton in 1895 over a Stetson hat.[31] Although the blues have rural Southern roots, this deeply personal music resonated in the highly impersonal cities of the North, where the old communal forms of African-American singing lingered on in the gospel music of the churchgoers.

♯ ♯ ♯

The American West has been a powerful force in the reality and imagination of the mobile American people. In 1893 Frederick Jackson Turner, then a professor at Wisconsin, identified the frontier, and especially the trans-Mississippi frontier, as one of the most significant forces in American history. Turner saw the frontier—the West—as offering free land and a chance to prove oneself on the basis of merit and ability rather than birth. Survival depended on how well one used an axe or rode a horse, not on who one's parents were. To Turner, this opportunity gave rise to democracy, the distinguishing characteristic of America. Turner has been severely criticized on many fronts, but few can find fault with his placing the West at the forefront of American imagination. American art, literature, film, and, of course, song would be much impoverished without the influence of the West.

One of the curious paradoxes of the West is that it was seen as both garden and desert, surely two quite opposite images.[32] There are a variety of explanations for this dichotomy, some related to short- and long-term climate cycles, others to overblown hopes. In one of the more optimistic predictions in American history, farmers moving into the normally drier lands west of the 100th meridian persuaded themselves that a fortuitous short-term cycle of wetter years as they began to farm there meant that "rain followed the plow," so that their very act of settling and turning the soil produced the rain needed for crops. Of course, their mistake became evident in the Dust Bowl of the 1930s and the ensuing emigration that gave rise not only to John Steinbeck's *The Grapes of Wrath* but also to Woody Guthrie's fifteen-verse summary of the book, "The Ballad of Tom Joad." Other than "Home on the Range," few folk songs endorsed the optimistic view of the West.

Cowboy songs have long held an interest for many Americans, despite the fact that the cowboys' time on the national stage lasted scarcely more than twenty years, from 1870 to 1890. The image and appeal of the cowboy as tough, independent, self-reliant, and free are rarely countered with the harsh realities of their daily lives: long days and nights herding stupid, uncooperative, and dangerous animals to their fate as supper on the tables of the East. After wintering over in Texas, cattle herds had to be driven north, either to railheads in Kansas, where they would be shipped to Chicago for slaughter, or on up to Montana for additional fattening during the summer months. Cowboys frequently made use of old tunes while composing new verses commenting on their hard lives. Curiously, a number of tunes connected to seafaring made their way into the cowboy repertoire, perhaps because the seemingly endless oceans of water and grass elicited similar feelings of isolation.

"I Ride an Old Paint," which makes use of the tune to "Blow the Man Down," is one of the songs of the cattlemen that found its way from the sea.[33] In several short verses it describes the rough life of a cowboy as he camps along the way on the road to Montana and his animals suffer from matted tails and sore feet. Whatever the problems of the trail, the cowboy could at least be glad he was not Bill Jones, whose family collapsed in his absence. According to one of the verses in "Old Paint," Bill Jones had either two daughters, or a daughter and a son. The two daughters left home, one for Denver and the other "went wrong." In the version with a child of each sex, the daughter still goes wrong, while the son shames his father almost as much as by going to college. In both instances, Bill's wife is killed "in a barroom fight." Faced with no home and no roots, Old Paint's cowboy, planning ahead for his death, requests, "Take my saddle off the wall, put it on my pony, lead him out of his stall, tie my bones on his back, turn our faces West, and we'll ride the prairie that we love the best." What the horse thought of this arrangement is unknown. Despite the dangers and hardships of the cattle trail, it was obviously where this cowboy felt most at peace.

This sentiment is echoed in "Bury Me out on the Prairie," in which a man is rejected by a woman after he loses his money gambling.[34] After Lou "laugh[ed] in his face at his fall," he begins to keep company "with evil companions" and eventually shoots a man who insults a picture of the girl in question. The rangers hunt the cowboy down and kill him while the singer reflects that if Lou had been a worthier mate, his friend "might have been raising a son," presumably for better things than college. As he lies dying, the cowboy's last request is to be buried out on the prairie, but sufficiently deep and covered with rocks so the coyotes cannot get at his bones.

A far more famous song expresses the opposite sentiment, calling on a song of the sea to do so. The mere title of "Bury Me Not on the Lone Prairie" makes clear that at least some shared the sentiment that a lonely death and isolated grave were not desired in the nineteenth century. "Bury Me Not" is a close adaptation of a sentimental song written in 1839 by the Reverend E. H. Chapin, "The Ocean Burial."[35] Many of the verses have been lifted directly from the minister's song, with a few obvious and even clumsy alterations to fit the change from the sea to oceans of grass.[36] Given the often crude and rough images from other songs of the West, the sentimentality in this song is striking, reflecting, perhaps, how short a time cowboys were part of the national experience, with little time to alter and refine the song through the normal workings of the folk process. The song begins with an evocation of the lonely and isolated prairie, "where the coyote howls and the wind blows free, and the old hoot owl cries mournfully." Just as burial at sea, away from family and friends, alarmed sailors, so did a lonely grave amidst waves of grass, for a young cowboy makes the following request:

Oh bury me not on the lone prairie,
These words came low and mournfully,
From the pale lips of a youth who lay,
On his dying bed at the end of day.

After thinking of "his home and his loved ones nigh," of "the scenes I loved in my childhood's hour," and of a "mother's prayer and a sister's tear," the dying cowboy murmurs, as sailors have before him:

I've often wished to be laid when I died,
In that old church yard on the green hill side,
Near my father's grave, oh, let mine be,
Oh bury me not on the lone prairie.

It matters not so I've been told,
Where the body lies, when the heart grows cold,
But grant, oh, grant this wish to me,
Oh bury me not on the lone prairie.

In a blunt reminder that death is demanding and bones could not practi-
cally be tied on the back of a pony to cart them home, the song concludes,
"We took no heed of his dying prayer, in a narrow grave just six by three,
we buried him there on the lone prairie."

As cowboys worked their herds north from Texas, either on the shorter
journeys to the Kansas railheads or on the longer trek to the Montana ranges,
they sang to amuse themselves, to alleviate boredom, and possibly to keep
the cattle from getting spooked into a terrifying and life-threatening stam-
pede. The actual work of herding cattle is probably not conducive to singing,
as the rhythm of a horse is rarely in keeping with the normal cadences of
cowboy songs, and few cowboys would be likely to burst into song while
dashing after wayward steers. But songs surely must have been shared around
the campfires at night before turning in to prepare for the next dawn; and
those who drew night watch no doubt hummed, whistled, and sang to stay
awake and pass the time, hoping perhaps that their music served to calm
the herd.[37]

Such songs, bluntly realistic about man and beast alike, varied widely
from the raucous and often obscene, like "The Old Chisholm Trail," to the
more plaintive, like "Git Along, Little Dogies." "The Old Chisholm Trail,"
with hundreds of verses, both decent and not, is probably the most widely
known of all the cowboy songs.[38] The song lends itself to the trail, with
numerous two-line couplets, often only loosely rhymed, commenting sa-
tirically and sardonically on the cowboy life. A sampling of verses from the
version in the Lomaxes' *Cowboy Songs and Other Frontier Ballads* ranges over
the quality of horses and food, to the length of the day, the conditions of
the work, and the limits of the appeal of the job:

Oh a ten dollar horse and a forty dollar saddle,
And I'm going to punch Texas cattle.

I'm up in the mornin' afore daylight,
And afore I sleep the moon shines bright.

My hoss threw me off at the creek called Mud,
My hoss threw me off round the 2–U herd.

It's cloudy in the west, a-looking like rain,
And my damned slicker's in the wagon again.

Saddle up, boys, and saddle up well,
For I think these cattle have scattered to hell.

Oh, it's bacon and beans most every day—
I'd as soon be a-eatin prairie hay.

I went to the boss to draw my roll,
He had it figured I was nine dollars in the hole.

Fare you well, old trail boss, I don't wish you any harm,
I'm quittin' this business to go on the farm.

"Git Along, Little Dogies" is a far more sophisticated song, both in structure and in meaning.[39] The verses offer a cohesive commentary on the whole experience, from the roundup in Texas in the early spring to the final fate of the cattle as "beef for Uncle Sam's Indians" on the reservations in the North. The chorus, with its wonderfully plaintive "whoopee ti yi yo," is nevertheless bluntly realistic, reminding the cattle, "It's your misfortune and none of my own." However much the wrangling of balky cattle was hard work and misery for the cowboys, they could comfort themselves with the thought of the fate that awaited their obstreperous charges.[40] After describing the preparations for heading out on the trail in the spring—including rounding up the dogies, branding them, bobbing their tails, and loading the chuck wagon—the song makes its first telling observation about the harsh reality behind the romantic image of life on the trail. Lest anyone be tempted to take up this life out of a false sense of adventure, the song warns:

Some folks go on the trail for pleasure,
That's where they're most terribly wrong,
You've got no idea the trouble they give us,
As we go herding them dogies along.

Whether from anger at the animals that were the cause of so much hardship or as simple means to distance themselves from the fate of the cattle, many of the remaining verses remind the dogies and their caretakers of the ultimate destination. Born to a mother "raised way down in Texas," the dogies are being fattened "till you're ready for the trail to Idaho," where they will be "beef steers some fine day," some for "Uncle Sam's Indians" and more for the slaughterhouses of Chicago.

Not all dangers in the West could be attributed to cattle or the natural environment. "The Cowboy's Lament" or "The Streets of Laredo" tells the story of a young man who "used to go dashing," until he got lured into the vices of the Western towns (what combination of women, drinking, and gambling is unspecified), finally to be "shot in the breast and . . . dying today."[41] It is at once a song of warning and a request for forgiveness, as the wounded cowboy not only seeks comfort from a comrade, recognizable from his "outfit" as a cowboy, but also wants to admit, "I know I've done wrong." As with "Bury Me Not," migration has taken the dying cowboy so far from home that his "friends and relations . . . know not where their poor boy has gone." A brief letter home to mother, sister, and "another far dearer" is asked of any of his literate comrades.

One of the more curious aspects of the song is the desire of the dying youth for a military-like funeral during which the mourners will "beat the drum slowly and play the fife lowly, and play the dead march as you carry me along." In fact, this request is rooted in an earlier version of the song known as "The Unfortunate Rake," popular in England in the 1790s. In the original, a soldier has been undone by syphilis, acquired in the urban dens of vice in the old country, but he wants his comrades to give him a proper funeral with military honors. The universal appeal of this story of sin and redemption, and the desire for a decent burial, is evident in other variants of the song, sometimes from the point of view of a girl, as in "The Bad Girl's Lament," and sometimes from an African-American perspective, as in "St. James Infirmary."

‡ ‡ ‡

Migration west often occurred individually or in temporary associations like wagon trains. But occasionally organized groups migrated together with the intent of settling in the same place. The Church of Jesus Christ of Latter-day Saints, commonly known as Mormons, was one such group. Joseph Smith, the founder of the church, had received his vision and prophecy in upstate New York, a region known as the burned-over district because of its frequent religious revivals and new sects. The Mormons placed a strong emphasis on community and first attempted to settle together in Ohio, before moving to Missouri in 1831. In 1838–39, about the time the Cherokee were being forced west on the Trail of Tears, the Mormons were expelled from Missouri by the governor after friction with their neighbors. They soon prospered in Nauvoo, Illinois, with converts coming from the United States and parts of Europe. Here too their distinctive ways and rapid expansion drew the anger of their neighbors, resulting in the arrest and lynching of Joseph Smith and his brother in 1844. Shortly thereafter, Brigham Young, the newly elected leader of the Mormons, led them to the Great Salt Lake in Utah, which he hoped would be far enough from other Americans and an unpromising enough environment to ensure they would be left alone. They arrived there in 1847, but soon hoards of migrants lured to California by gold needed to cross their territory on the way west, leading to further friction.

Although the Mormons had tried to escape the pressures of American society, their beliefs and practices continued to attract attention and produce conflict. Cohesiveness was easily interpreted as exclusiveness, not entirely without reason, but the belief that most intrigued and angered other Americans was polygamy. Brigham Young was known to have many wives and numerous children. One verse of "Sweet Betsy from Pike" relies upon this knowledge when it claims that when Ike and Betsy stopped in Salt Lake City "to inquire the way, . . . Brigham declared that Sweet Betsy should stay." When she became "frightened and ran like a deer, . . . Brigham stood pawing the ground like a steer."

Other songs also play upon this image, both as a comment on Mormon peculiarities and as a factor in the decision to migrate. Two versions of "Brigham Young," one sung to the same tune as "Sweet Betsy," remark on his many wives, often with wonder as to how he kept order at home.[42] According to one version, Young had forty-five wives ranging in age from sixteen to sixty-three. Since the singer believes "one wife at a time . . . is enough," he marvels over "how he keeps them quiet, . . . for they clatter and they chaw and jaw, jaw, jaw." Any store in town that could "supply them with half they desire" would be justly famous. The song claims Young became bald because "they have torn all the hair off his head" with their constant bickering. The singer of "I Wish I Was a Mormonite" thinks "fifty wives are just the thing the flesh to mortify," while reflecting that if he were to bring another home to his "Sarah Ann, there'd be the tallest kind of row that ever you heard tell."[43] The song concludes by speculating on the complexities of a will to divide property so many ways.

Mormon mission activity was strong in the Scandinavian countries. The musical tradition that produced "Oleana" also offered satire on the hopes of prospective Mormon migrants. In keeping with masculine amazement over how a man could keep many wives happy, "Ole Petersen and His Wife Dorthe's Journey to the Mormons" describes a rich farmer who was lured to Utah by the Oleanaish promise of living "on roasted goose that's filled with parsley."[44] Ole also thought well of the report that "each man gets to keep just as many wives as he likes." Dorthe was less certain about this, commencing to "bawl as if she'd been whipped," but she was persuaded to go with the promise of nothing to do but eat, sleep, and "drink good aged beer." Upon arriving in Utah and adding two more wives in a "ramshackle hut," the first wife's mood changed, so that Ole could only say, "God spare me, poor miserable wretch, for Dorthe got so furiously mad, she made a dreadful scene." Faced with hard work and simple food, including ample water but no beer, Ole and Dorthe soon returned to Denmark. Not all women were opposed to the prospect of polygamy, if "The Most Recent New Song about the Two Journeymen Masons from Copenhagen Who Sold Their Wives" is to be believed.[45] In this song, the wives of two masons who were attracted to the preaching of a Mormon missionary, and perhaps to the man himself, pestered their husbands to move to Utah. The men, however, preferred the taverns of Copenhagen to the rigors of life on the American frontier, and so finally decided to sell their wives to the missionary, which they did. As far as the masons were concerned, the women and the missionary deserved each other and the transaction "distribute[d] the suffering."

The Mormons themselves sang about their search for a secure home in Deseret, in songs clearly intended to recruit additional immigrants. This name was derived from a honeybee and gave rise to images of hives and bees swarming in songs like "In the Hive of Deseret."[46] Two songs from the Danish Mormon hymnal refer to the lure of Zion as "shelter against danger on the day of judgment."[47] As "God's children gather[ed] there," migrants could expect to find "joy," "peace," "salvation," "prophecy's true spirit," and "righteousness" amidst a "circle of friends." Many Mormons from Europe arrived in the United States via New Orleans and headed west from there. They often used large handcarts instead of covered wagons, a mode of transporting goods designed by Brigham Young and which he believed cut two weeks off the trip. Several songs celebrate the use of handcarts among migrants "free as a bee," urging them onward with advice many other migrants must have believed as well: "Even if it seems hard, it can be done."[48]

But few songs capture the hopes and expectations of this migrant stream as well as "Deseret."[49] This song is especially effective at combining the themes of religious sanctuary and the wondrous transformation wrought by hard work on men and land. Mormons were proud to have taken an unpromising environment and converted it into a home for many and a beacon for all, transforming Lane County into Oleana. The first lines make this abundantly clear:

Deseret, Deseret, 'tis the home of the free,
And dearer than all other land 'tis to me,
Where the Saints are secure from oppression and strife,
And enjoy to the full, the rich blessings of life.
'Tis a land which for ages has been lying waste,
Where the savage has wandered, by darkness debased,
Where the wolf and the bear unmolested did roam,
Away, far away! Deseret is my home.

Social perfection was readily available to all who would move to this new
paradise:

Deseret, Deseret, she's the pride of the world,
Where the banner of freedom is widely unfurled,
Where oppression is hated and liberty loved,
And truth and sincerity highly approved,
Where labor is honored, nor workmen oppresst,
Where youth is instructed and age finds a rest,
Where society frowns upon vice and deceit,
And adulterers find heaven's laws they must meet.

Not all agreed with this vision of perfection and honesty; opponents
often preferred blunt criticism to irony. "The Mormon Girl's Lament" tells of
the young Danish woman who found herself "lured and deceived . . . from
virtue and duty's true path."[50] Having given up sizeable property in Denmark
and been forced to become the eighth wife of a man she "abhorred," she
mourned, "Here I cannot live, here I cannot die." "The Mormon Bishop's
Lament" offers biting commentary, ostensibly through the ruminations of
a Mormon bishop, as statehood loomed in 1896 and the protections offered
by a relatively independent Deseret were soon to vanish.[51] As the Bishop
looks back over better days, he recalls the power he and other church leaders
shared and the lures they used to recruit converts. The Mountain Meadows
massacre of 1857, in which a wagon train of non-Mormons was almost entirely exterminated by a combined Mormon–Indian force, is celebrated, albeit
with the rueful remark, "What we did as deeds of glory are condemned as
bloody crime." At the end, the Bishop regretfully concludes he will soon join
Brigham Young in "the lowest pits of hell." Mormons refused to accept the
blame for the violence of 1857, in part because they were under the threat
of invasion by the U.S. Army in the same year; but others in the West were

certain the Mormon leadership was guilty and that the only acceptable response was to have "Utah, blush for shame."[52]

Not surprisingly, Mormons responded to these attacks, also in song. "Early This Spring We'll Leave Nauvoo," sung to the old banjo tune of "Old Dan Tucker," reminded Mormons and their neighbors of the violence and assassination of Joseph Smith that had sent them in search of Zion in the first place.[53] Aware of the critical comments in the form of song, Mormons replied, "They Cry 'Deluded Mormons,'" reminding their fellow believers that such remarks should not detract from the goal of making "this earth an Eden . . . [where] truth and virtue triumph, and peace and love abound."[54] Occasionally Mormon songs were moderately critical, especially about church-ordered efforts to settle farther south of Salt Lake City in the challenging environment that became known as Dixie. The work was hard and the climate unforgiving, but in the end the settlers transformed the land.[55] The remarkable story of the huge flock of sea gulls that arrived just in time to save their first crops from the ravages of a massive swarm of crickets was taken as a sign of God's favor in the aptly named song "Sea Gulls and Crickets."[56] But hard work and human effort also contributed to the hopes and success of the endeavor. "Home Manufactures" urges a curious mixture of environmental exploitation, utilization of natural geographic "tariffs" that protected Utah industry from competition, the Protestant work ethic, and technological adaptation to make Deseret both economically independent and a competitor of English factories and mills.[57] Despite the practical references to machines and hard work, this song recalls "Oleana" and "The Big Rock Candy Mountain" in its hopes for the future of the migrants engaged in "building up Zion."

♯ ♯ ♯

Most often rooted in the realties of time and place, and the hopes and fears of the people involved, folk songs about migration could also be used metaphorically and symbolically. In particular, songs that on the surface appear to be about migration bear strong religious meanings and often address the greatest trip of all—the trip to that "undiscovered country from whose bourn no traveler returns."[58] "When I'm on My Journey, Don't You Weep after Me" instructs those who remain behind to be content, if not joyous, for the traveler has gone to a better place.[59] There is no doubt that this song is about death, but the success of the metaphor draws on sorrow from separation from more worldly journeys. The song is the essence of simplicity, with one basic thought per stanza repeated three times and the admonition not to "weep after me" woven through the verse. The title comes from the opening lines:

> When I'm on my journey, don't you weep after me,
> When I'm on my journey, don't you weep after me,
> When I'm on my journey, don't you weep after me,
> I don't want you to weep after me.[60]

The theme of separation and return to the divine, to the life force that pervades us all, is recalled in the line, "Every lonely river must go home to the sea." To return to the place of origin, to the nurturing and welcoming sea, is hardly a source for grief and mourning. Likewise, as one ascends to heaven, rising above the problems of life, there is equal reason to celebrate: "High up on the mountain, leave my sorrows down below." When the final judgment comes, "when the stars are falling and the thunder starts to roll," there will be no need for pity or sorrow for those who have made the journey home.

Dorothy Scarborough recalled hearing an African-American woman who had cared for her when she was young make the situation clear with the words, "When I'm dead an' buried, don't you grieve atter me," though Scarborough understood the request as ironic, because the survivors were also expected to be "smitten with sorrow and remorse."[61] The admonition "Don't You Grieve After Me" was a migrant of sorts itself, appearing in at least one lighthearted song about a man on the move, escaping from stable owners, police, hotel managers, and restaurateurs to whom he owed money, or at least explanations. As the man flees one imminent disaster after another, he cries, "When I'm gone, don't you, don't you grieve after me," probably not the dominant emotion of most of those who wanted him to stay a little longer.[62]

Although many migrants moved in the company of family and friends, folk songs tend to stress the loneliness of the journey. One of the saddest, and shortest, songs is the fittingly titled "Lonesome Road."[63] The first of its two verses stresses both the inevitability and the sorrow of parting, as one friend sets off down that lonesome road:

> Look down, look down that lonesome road,
> Hang down your head and cry,
> The best of friends must part some day,
> And why not you and I?

But the parting is not entirely voluntary or without anger, as the second verse suggests. Whether the situation calls for the lament, "True love, true love, what have I done, that you should treat me so," or the harsher, "I wish to God that I had died . . . before I seen your smilin' face an' heard your lyin' tongue," the road is lonesome for more reasons than traveling alone.

Surely some who sang "You Got to Walk That Lonesome Valley" had in mind literal valleys, whether in the Appalachians, Ozarks, or Rockies, but others had more symbolic depressions in mind. Faced with a spiritual crisis or personal sin, the message is clear: "You got to walk it by yourself, ain't no one can go it with you, you got to walk it by yourself." Used in religious services, the congregation could easily substitute "mother," "father," "sister," or "brother" for "you," as a reminder that, in the end, we all stand before our maker alone. Of course, the lonesome valley could also be the psalmist's "valley of the shadow of death." When death was the intended reference, some chose to change the lyrics slightly to "you got to cross that River Jordan," where "you got to stand that test of judgment."[64] The lonesome valley carried powerful religious meanings among slaves who sang of the lonesome valley as the place "to meet my Jesus," or as a place to be marched through "in peace," with Jesus as guide.[65] Anticipating crossing the valley in peace, after being "dead and buried in the cold silent tomb," slaves might reassure each other, "I don't want you to grieve after me."[66]

For many mobile Americans who had crossed the Atlantic, the prairies, the rivers, the mountains, or even just moved down the road a piece, the last journey must have been anticipated as the most rewarding and satisfying of all. The nineteenth century brought social, cultural, and economic dislocation along with physical mobility. Harsh living conditions, dangerous work, and the necessity of family separation, while all difficult, might be endured, for Americans hoped they would finally be going to where the streets were truly paved with gold, work had in fact been abolished, and the family circle was once more unbroken.

CHAPTER 7

Nobody Knows the Trouble I've Seen

Hard Times and Hard Men

Famed Russian novelist Leo Tolstoy began *Anna Karenina* with the observation: "Happy families are all alike; every unhappy family is unhappy in its own way." Folk songs often express the same sentiment regarding the sorrows that have led so many individuals to sing some variation of the lament:

> Nobody knows the trouble I've had,
> Nobody knows but Jesus.
> Nobody knows the trouble I've had,
> Glory, hallelu.[1]

Joy and celebration are easily shared, but the ownership of sorrow and trouble is often private, at least in American culture. Surely the range of human experience is not so great as to make our problems truly unique, but when faced with faltering love, a sick child, unemployment, brutality, or isolation, it seems like nobody else "knows the trouble I've seen."

But trouble is also a great creative force, giving rise to any number of powerful folk songs that speak with familiar emotions to those in similar situations. The range of problems that have led sufferers to console themselves in song is endless, and some have already been encountered; here, however, the primary, though not exclusive focus is on songs of African Americans, who have certainly had more than their share of hard times in America. From the oppression of slavery, to their struggles after Emancipation with repressions both legal and violent, to the rural and urban origins of the blues, to celebrations and condemnations of hard men and women—African Americans have turned to songs to help them get through.

♯ ♮ ♯

Of all the hard times and sorrows any Americans have faced, slavery was among the worst. The first African colonists were sold into some type of bondage in Virginia in 1619, before the *Mayflower*. By 1660 a peculiar legal status known as chattel slavery had evolved for people of color. Unlike serfs on the manors of medieval Europe, who were attached to the land where their families lived with them, slaves were considered chattel, that is, personal property that could be bought and sold at the master's whim or to settle debts, with no regard to family attachments. Moreover, this lifetime status was soon made inheritable according to the status of the mother, so that the children of a slave mother would also be slaves for life, and so forth down through the generations. As personal property, slaves had no standing before the law except as property, so slave marriages were not legally recognized, and slave children belonged not to their parents but to the master or mistress. With no freedom to be restricted and no property to be taken, slaves could be punished only by beating, whipping, chains, or more extreme forms of physical torture. Many young white men and women arrived in the colonies as indentured servants, owing their masters four to seven years of service before regaining their freedom; but for Africans, after 1660 their bondage was permanent, with release coming only through death. No song from the days of enslavement expresses the misery of the system better than:

> Sometimes I feel like a motherless child,
> Sometimes I feel like a motherless child,
> Sometimes I feel like a motherless child,
> A long way from home.[2]

Sometime around 1785, Charles Ball had reason to sing this song. As he remembered later, "My mother had several children, . . . and we were all sold on the same day to different purchasers . . . and I never saw my mother, nor any of my brothers and sisters afterward." Years later Ball vividly recalled the trauma of the separation:

> My poor mother when she saw me leaving her for the last time, ran after me, took me down from the horse, clasped me in her arms, and wept

loudly and bitterly over me. My master seemed to pity her . . . telling her he would be a good master to me. . . . She then, still holding me in her arms, walked along the road beside the horse, and earnestly and imploringly besought my master to buy her and the rest of her children. . . . My mother then turned to him and cried, "Oh, master, do not take me from my child!" Without making any reply, he gave her two or three heavy blows on the shoulders with his raw hide. . . . My master then quickened the pace of his horse; and as we advanced, the cries of my poor parent became more and more indistinct . . . and I never again heard the voice of my mother. . . . Young as I was, the horrors of that day sank deeply into my heart, and even at this time, though half a century has elapsed, the terrors of the scene return with painful vividness upon my memory.[3]

Ball thought he was about four when this happened. He would be, for all practical purposes, a motherless child for the rest of his life.

Likewise, Frederick Douglass—who, though born a slave in Maryland about 1817, escaped as a teenager and went on to a distinguished public career as an abolitionist and American ambassador to Haiti (1889–91)—thought of himself as a "motherless child." In his autobiography Douglass recalled, "I never saw my mother, to know her as such, more than four or five times in my life." His mother lived on a different plantation and could come the twelve miles to see her child only after sundown, sacrificing her own brief hours of rest and risking capture by slave patrols. She would lie down with him to get him to sleep but was gone long before he awoke. As Douglass remembered, "Very little communication ever took place between us. Death soon ended what little we could have." Although he was about seven when his mother died, the boy was not allowed to be with her during her last hours or to attend her burial. "She was gone long before I knew anything about it."[4]

Without the reliable support of family, or perhaps even friends, while growing up, it is no wonder slaves' sense of isolation led them to sing, "Sometimes I feel like I have no friends," or to think, "Sometimes I feel like I'm almost gone." But the most powerful expression of rootlessness and isolation is in the image, "sometimes I feel like a feather in the air," drifting aimlessly, battered by unseen forces, with no sense of direction or usefulness. No wonder when the slaves sang their spirituals they often anticipated the release and possible reunion that came with death.

As Douglass recollected the songs of his fellow slaves, which he thought revealed "at once the highest joy and deepest sadness," he found himself "utterly astonished . . . to find persons who could speak of this singing, among slaves, as evidence of their contentment and happiness. It is impossible to conceive of a greater mistake. The songs of the slave represent the sorrows of his heart." With the sounds still fresh in his memory, Douglass believed, "The mere hearing of those songs would do more to impress some minds with the horrible character of slavery, than the reading of whole volumes of philosophy. . . . When [he was] a slave," Douglass, "did not . . . understand the deep meaning of those rude and apparently incoherent songs." But with freedom came the realization that "they told a tale of woe . . . of souls boiling over with the bitterest anguish." He believed the songs he heard as a boy provided him with his "first glimmering conception of the dehumanizing character, . . . with the soul-killing effects of slavery."[5]

A generation after the Thirteenth Amendment abolished slavery in 1865, Douglass's judgment was echoed by the great African-American scholar W. E. B. DuBois as he reflected on what he termed the "sorrow songs" of the slaves. DuBois was born and raised in the North, but he immediately recognized the songs for what they were when "they came out of the South unknown" to him. He believed the songs of the slaves were "the sole American music," born of a system unknown in Africa or Europe, making them "the singular spiritual heritage of the nation and the greatest gift of the Negro people."[6] Because slavery enmeshed all Americans in its pernicious net, the music that derived from it belonged to the whole nation, as both gift and condemnation—as an essential part of American history.

DuBois agreed with Douglass that this was not the music of a happy, carefree people, as white myth would have it, but was instead "the articulate message, . . . the heart-touching witness . . . of an unhappy people . . . tell[ing] of death and suffering and unvoiced longing." As "the slave[s] spoke to the world," their "message [was] naturally veiled and half articulate," with few songs of frolic, though the latter may simply have remained hidden. "The music is distinctly sorrowful," while the words "conceal much of real poetry and meaning." The meanings were hidden partly because slaves were using a "dimly understood theology" to express their sentiments but also because they were moved by "the shadow of fear" and the "limitations of allowable thought" to "eloquent omissions and silences."[7]

DuBois identified ten "master songs" that he thought expressed much of the black experience under slavery. The songs and their meanings include:

"The Coming of John"	the voice of exile
"Nobody Knows the Trouble I've Seen"	no promised land
"Swing Low, Sweet Chariot"	the cradle song of death
"Roll, Jordan, Roll"	the river of life and crossing over

"Wings of Atalanta"	fugitives
"Been a Listening"	attentiveness
"My Lord, What a Mourning"	end and beginning
"My Way Is Cloudy"	groping
"Wrestlin' Jacob"	hopeful strife
"Steal Away"	faith of the fathers

DuBois also singled out a number of recurring themes and images embedded in the master songs. The storms and trials of nature, as well as "monotonous toil and exposure," loom large. One might sing of being a "motherless child" or of bidding "farewell [to] my only child," but of fathers little is heard. Themes of friendlessness and homelessness are prevalent: "Fugitive and weary wanderer call for pity and affection, but there is little of wooing and wedding; the rocks and the mountains are well known, but the home is unknown." Perhaps the most damning condemnation of the system is in the brief observation, "Of deep successful love there is ominous silence," though the same might be said of all folk songs, whatever their origin. Faced with a life of toil and abuse, there can be little wonder that "of death the Negro showed little fear, but talked of it familiarly and even fondly, as a simple crossing of the waters, perhaps—who knows?—back to his ancient forests again."[8]

Among the most difficult relationships a slave could have was with his or her master or mistress. A mistress who recognized the humanity of her slaves, treated them like individuals, and provided sufficient food, clothing, and shelter was respected, for far too many did none of these things. A song from at least the start of the nineteenth century recalled "Hard Times in Old Virginia."[9] The slaves were aware that their "ol' mis'ess is a rich old lady" whose privileges depended on her slaves being faced with going to the well with a bucket to "draw some water," tending to the mistress's children, and, after parching corn, "lay[ing] by the fire" on the floor. Promises of freedom might keep slaves docile for a while, but such promises were not always fulfilled. For a fortunate few, freedom came with the death of both master and mistress, a stipulation George Washington made in his will before he left Martha a widow. But slaves frequently were disappointed. Even when "ole mistis dead an' gone," she often "lef' ole Sambo hoein' corn."[10] In other instances, the master or mistress survived for so long that their slaves despaired of ever being free. One rather sarcastic comment observed that a mistress lived for so long that her "teeth fell out and her head got bald, clean lost the notion of dyin' at all." Martha Washington was aware that her slaves knew they would be free upon her death, and so she decided to emancipate them ahead of time rather than risk someone giving freedom a helping hand.

Slaves understood they were vulnerable to the whims of their masters and had no recourse against even the most obvious cheating or physical abuse. Slaves also understood the economic inequities of the kleptocracy that was slavery when they sang:

> We raise de wheat,
> De gib us de corn;
> We bake de bread,
> De gib us de crust;
> We sif de meal,
> De gib us the huss;
> We peal de meat,
> De gib us de skin;
> And dat's de way
> Dey take us in.[11]

Frederick Douglass's mother was not the only slave who risked running into white patrols at night as she traveled from farm to farm on social errands without a pass from her master. The risks of escaping however briefly from their confinement were well known by slaves, who warned each other through the song "Run, Nigger Run":

> Run, nigger run, the patty-roller catch you,
> Run, nigger, run, for it's almost day;
> Massa was kind and Missus was true,
> But if you don't mind, the patty-roller catch you.[12]

Patrols occasionally interrupted slaves making music and punished them for violating restrictions on assembling, even if their master had signaled his approval by his presence.[13]

Resistance to the system might come by working slowly or singing of Paul and Silas being in jail for helping a slave, but it also came via satire and opaque messages. A Northern abolitionist may have written "The Blue-tailed Fly," but it expressed the sentiments of slaves well enough that they picked it up and made it one of their own, though possibly not until after they had become free.[14] The song alternates between an apparently sorrowful recounting of a slave's eventually futile efforts to keep the blue-tailed flies from biting the master's pony as he rode around the farm, which led to the master's untimely death when the pony bucked the master into a ditch, and the more honest and upbeat chorus, "Jimmy crack corn and I don't care, old master's gone away." In fact, the death of a master was often a time of great uncertainty because a new owner might be worse or debts could force the sale of slaves and lead to the separation of families. Escape was occasionally possible, especially for those who lived close to the North and freedom. "Follow the Drinking Gourd" was good advice for those seeking the way north, for the two stars on the front of the Big Dipper point the way to the North Star. Occasionally the Underground Railroad offered help, and if one was lucky, "when the sun comes back and the first quail calls, . . . the old man [would be] a waitin' for to carry you to freedom."[15] For those who could never escape the system while alive, there was always the time when the "sweet chariot" would "swing low, . . . coming for to carry me home."

"Roll, Jordan, Roll" was another of DuBois's master songs: the song of many waters.[16] At heart a religious song, with images of "brudder sittin' on de tree of life" and admonitions for children to "learn to fear de Lord" before being able to "march de angel march," the desire for the Jordan to roll had deep meaning. To cross that river, to meet the friends and family who had gone before, to lay one's burden down, and to have endured and conquered were goals of great merit. In terms of literal waters in the lives of slaves, the Atlantic separated them from their homeland, and many expected to return across that rolling water upon death. Frederick Douglass writes movingly of standing on the shores of the Chesapeake as a boy, watching the sails of the ships glide freely by and thinking of the day when he would join them. Many slaves found at least brief freedom when they were trusted by their masters to take crops to market aboard boats; the task of rowing was often arduous, but it offered a break from the monotony of chopping cotton or tending rice. The request, "Michael, Row the Boat Ashore," may well have originated among slaves hauling cargo to the Georgia sea islands, but it quickly acquired other messages. First there was the understanding that, although "Jordan stream is deep and wide, Jesus stand on t'oder side"; so it would be well to follow the advice, "Sinner row to save your soul."[17] Slaves may have been calling on the archangel Michael, protector of the poor and downtrodden, when they sang this song. Finally, the rolling river was a metaphor for long traditions of African and African-American culture kept alive in the New World through story and song. Alan Lomax recognized this tradition when he chose to title his series of folk song recordings from the 1930s *Deep River of Song.*

"Many Thousands Go" is one of the simplest, yet most powerful songs to come from the slave experience.[18] The white folks who wrote down this song as the Civil War came to a close were told the song was a product of the conflict, sung as the war made hopes of emancipation plausible. The song makes explicit mention of some of the pains and humiliations of slavery that would not be missed when the newly freed sang of "no more peck of corn" or "pint of salt," "no more driver's lash" or "mistress's call," and most important of all, "no more auction block for me." These verses offer a potent reminder that "many thousands" were indeed going from slavery into the uncertainties of freedom. But the song also demands recognition of the deep river of the lives of the many thousands who had been born, endured, and died in bondage, hoping for, but never attaining, freedom on this side of the Jordan. Bob Dylan's "Blowin' in the Wind" may have modified the tune and provided new words, but his debt to this song is obvious. African Americans had indeed walked down many roads and looked up many times before the mountain of prejudice eroded and they were called men and women.

♯ ♯ ♯

The hopes and expectations raised by the Emancipation Proclamation in 1863 and the Thirteenth Amendment, which abolished slavery in 1865, soon proved illusory. By 1876 white Northerners tired of the struggle to help the freed men and women, and abandoned them to the tender mercies of their white neighbors in the South. Reconstruction came to an end with a compromise over disputed Electoral College votes from Florida being awarded to the Republican candidate, who had lost the popular vote. White Southern Democrats gladly traded the presidency for freedom to reestablish the racial order they saw threatened by Emancipation. Over the course of the next generation, white Southerners repressed their black neighbors through intimidation by the Ku Klux Klan, widespread lynching, legal efforts to restrict rights by grandfather clauses and literacy tests for voting, and the Supreme Court case of *Plessy v. Ferguson* in 1896, which ruled that segregation was constitutional.

Economic repression was added to the mix via tenancy, sharecropping, and convict labor. Once this system was in place, it lasted well into the twentieth century. Tenants and sharecroppers, both white and black, who leased land from wealthy landlords faced numerous problems. Since the landlord kept the accounts of what the tenants owed and earned, it was rare for a tenant to come out ahead, unless the landlord was done with the tenants' services. "Down on Penny's Farm" makes it clear that George Penny's renters were no different.[19] To recruit renters, Penny promised them good living conditions; but when they got to the farm, they discovered hard work, poor housing, and starvation. Renters on Penny's farm were just like those elsewhere in the South, borrowing money for seeds, tools, and food, with the mortgages to be paid in the fall. But when fall came around and renters were short of cash, an offer of partial payment was met by both merchant and landlord with a phone call to "put you on the chain-gang, [where you] can't pay at all."

To be sentenced to the chain gang and fall victim of convict labor leasing was, in the words of one historian, "worse than slavery"; this is an apt judgment, for the system was labeled the "American Siberia" in 1891 by J. C. Powell, a man with direct experience running labor gangs.[20] Begun in Mississippi in the late 1860s and not abolished in Alabama until the late 1920s, convict leasing provided wealthy Southerners with cheap labor that they rented from the state at bargain prices. What made the system "worse than slavery" was that, while a slave owner had some incentive to protect his investment, the leasers of convicts provided little food, clothing, or shelter to their workers. Neither employer nor the judicial system cared if the convicts made it home alive, and many did not. In a 1947 interview, several blues musicians who had experienced the system recalled the general attitude among the white people was, "If you kill a nigger, I'll hire another nigger," an attitude parallel to "If you kill a mule, I'll buy another one."[21] When replacement workers were needed, word went out to local sheriffs and suddenly a "crime wave" produced numerous new convicts, the vast majority of whom were African American, to work at building railroads, cutting timber, mining coal, and, of course, tending crops.

The men, and occasionally women, who were caught up in this net of deceit and abuse reacted in many ways, including song. Three prominent song catchers of African-American songs from the 1920s included separate chapters of work songs, at least some of which came from convicts.[22] John and Alan Lomax recorded and then published a number of powerful, if indirect, critiques during their tours of Southern prison camps in the early 1930s, songs that were still in circulation on Southern prison farms in the 1960s.[23] A few songs comment on the way men fell into the system. "The Midnight Special," made famous by Leadbelly and widely known in Southern prisons, makes it clear that any questionable behavior in town, such as drinking or fighting, will lead to arrest and speedy conviction, so that one will soon be "Sugarland bound."[24] The "Joe Turner Blues" warns that when this brother of a Tennessee governor "come to town, he's [bringing] along one thousand links of chain; he's gwine to have one nigger for each link."[25]

Prisoners arrived at the state farms or work camps by trains or enclosed wagons whose names were commemorated in the names of songs. "Shorty George" was a small train that ran from Houston to the Central State Prison near Sugarland, Texas, and carried convicts to their fate. This, plus the fact that the same train occasionally brought women for brief visits before taking them home all too soon, had the convicts saying the train "ain't no friend of mine."[26] As late as the 1960s, the vehicle that carried men to prison was known as "Black Betty," though the same name may have also been used for the whip that so often was laid on the prisoners' backs, "bam-ba-lam."[27]

Once on the farm, the work was hard, unrelenting, and tedious. Guards drove the prisoners with little thought for their health or lives. "Ain't No More Cane on the Brazos" and "Go Down Old Hannah" offer insight into the convicts' lives.[28] Old Hannah was the convicts' name for the sun, which seemed to take forever to cross the sky and finally bring an end to another day's work. Working from sunup to sundown, the convicts begged Hannah, "Don't you rise no more" once she had set. If Hannah had to return, then she should "bring Judgment Day." However hard the times were by the 1930s, the song recognizes they had been worse in the past, when raising cane down on the Brazos "in 1910, they was drivin' the women just like the men," and visitors would have found "a dead man on every turn row." Or perhaps the singer felt that setting such abuses at an earlier date made criticism possible without inviting punishment. If prisoners could sing of the presence of bodies at the end of the row, of men who had succumbed to heat stroke and dehydration, or had possibly even been shot by a guard, one wonders what might have remained too sensitive for comment. Anyone who hears Leadbelly's poignant a cappella rendition of "Go Down Old Hannah" will understand how hard the life of a convict was.[29]

When convicts sang the plaintive lines to "Another Man Done Gone," they might have been referring to someone who had completed his sentence, but more likely they were singing about a prisoner who had died from overwork or violence.[30] Of course, he might have made good an escape, even though he was in chains. Recognizing that not all convicts were victims of a malicious judicial system, this song admits the absent man had "killed another man." Most convicts made at least a few friends, but in this case the singer confesses, "I didn't know his name." Perhaps he did not know the prisoner's name, perhaps he was covering up to the guards, or perhaps he was denying his emotions by distancing himself from his worst fears. In claiming, "I don't know where he's gone," the singer recognizes not only the uncertainty of the fate of the missing convict but also the ease with which he himself might disappear, leaving few to mourn and even fewer to investigate his fate.

Occasionally prisoners did escape from their living hell, especially if they could get to a river and thus lose the hounds on their trail. Those who succeeded were worthy of respect, if not necessarily emulation, for the odds were not good, and the guards were not overly concerned about bringing them back alive. Long John was "Long Gone," "like a turkey through the corn."[31] If "Old Riley" could not endure his treatment and made a run for it, walking "the water . . . on them long, hot summer days," the guards might turn out "Ol Rattler" to track him down.[32] If so, the convict's hopes were small, as this was an exceptional bloodhound, not easily fooled or distracted. Otherwise, all one could hope for was to have the Midnight Special shine its magical light into a cell, bringing the promise of release someday, perchance when Miss Rosie brought a longed-for pardon.

♯ ♯ ♯

The blues originated in the South in response to hard times in many forms. At the start of a recording session in 1947, Alan Lomax asked Big Bill Broonzy, Memphis Slim, and Sonny Boy Williamson an apparently innocent question: "Tell me what the blues are all about."[33] Two hours later they stopped talking, having made it clear that the blues were about far more than "a good man feeling bad."[34] These male blues artists started with the kind of superficial remarks they might have made to many white interviewers — that the blues were the result of woman problems (of course, female singers had their own view). As the conversation continued and the men either forgot about Lomax or decided they could trust him, they turned to problems with work and abusive bosses. To Memphis Slim, the blues were a way of "signifying and getting your revenge through songs." A comment to a mule to "get off my foot, goddam it," took on extra meaning with the boss nearby. Eventually the men began to reflect on the violence perpetrated on blacks by whites throughout the South. Big Bill Broonzy told of an uncle who was lynched for striking a white man. His uncle was trying to protect "his own wife, because he didn't want his wife to work out on the plantation," with one small child to care for and another on the way. Broonzy also recalled, with remarkable equanimity and deep resignation, the story of Andrew Belcher, who married his girl despite the fact that a white man "wanted her for hisself." This action so angered the white man and his friends that they killed not only Belcher but also eleven other members of the family. All this occurred in Arkansas in 1913.[35]

After descending into this hell of memory, the men finished the conversation with bizarre and possibly fictitious examples of racism in the South. One planter was reported to give any animal born on his farm that was not white to neighboring black farmers. A black man trying to get two mules, one gray and one black, to pull a load over an obstacle was supposedly forced by a passing white man to address the lighter-skinned mule as "Mister Mule." Rumor had it that in Louisiana, any African American who wanted to buy Prince Albert tobacco had to ask for a can of "*Mister* Prince Albert" because of the picture of the white man on the front.

When Lomax played the recording for the men, they were so frightened by the potential harm that could befall their families still in the South that they made Lomax promise not to reveal their names. He kept his promise for over a decade, until the South had become a marginally safer place. No wonder the South was "The Land Where the Blues Began."[36] Nor is it any wonder that in the 1920s, a song common among African Americans proclaimed, "Ain't It Hard to Be a Nigger," using the racial epithet to comment on the role forced upon them.[37] Little had changed from the days of slavery when slaves complained, "We sif de meal, de gib us the husk," as black Southerners working for wages now sang:

> Well, it makes no difference
> How you make out your time,
> White man sho' to bring a
> Nigger out behind.[38]

In a carryover from earlier days, they also commented:

> Little bees suck de blossoms,
> Big bees eats de honey.
> Niggers make de cotton an' corn,
> White folks 'ceive de money.[39]

Indeed, what is remarkable about this song, as Newman White observes, is that he was allowed to hear it, a "privilege" not many other whites had been given.

The blues, emerging out of field hollers in the rural South and giving rise to rock and roll in the urban North, were used to comment on many topics.[40] Although the blues were a new style of singing for African Americans, favoring the individual over the communal in form and content, the structure of an initial observation in each verse followed by a comment, often satirical, is reminiscent of the call-and-response form of many earlier songs.[41] Odum and Johnson cataloged some of the topics they had encountered in the blues over the first three decades of the twentieth century.[42] Places to leave or places as destination accounted for seventy songs. Memphis and Mississippi, Atlanta and Alabama, Tulsa and Texas: all produced the blues. Love, or the lack thereof, could make a man or woman wail in the night. One woman, worried about her "Changeable Daddy," might warn another to "Leave My Sweet Papa Alone." She longed to say, "My Man Rocks Me with One Steady Roll" and to ask her lover, "Do It a Long Time, Papa." But no one wanted a "Mistreatin' Daddy," lest one become a "Mistreated Woman." If "The Poor Man Blues" did not cause "The Crying Blues," they often led to "The Crazy Blues" or the "Don't Care Blues." Problems like "The House Rent Blues" might lead to "The Reckless Blues," which in turn could cause one to sing "The Going Away Blues" before landing in a new town, where the "Stranger Blues" would be appropriate. At their worst, a bad case of the blues must have felt, like Robert Johnson moaned, as if there was a "hell hound on my trail."[43]

As with the titles, the sentiments ranged widely, and many of the verses were frequently adapted.[44] The blues might be a general feeling of malaise, "nothing but a good man feeling bad" or "a poor man's heart disease." Or they might be more specific. Sometimes "a woman on a pore man's mind" was enough, or the blues were the uncertainty expressed in the question, "Honey, how long will I have to wait? Can I git you now or must I hesitate?" If the longing was great enough, one might sing, "Baby, I can't sleep, and neither can I eat; 'round your bedside I'm gwine to creep." But eventually the attraction could very well fade to the point where the singer states, "I'm tired of coffee and I'm tired of tea, I'm tired of you and you're tired of me." Sometimes white song catchers took obviously sexual songs literally, or at least they presented them that way, perhaps assuming that any readers who had encountered Freud would get the message. Although the offer, "I ain't no doctor, . . . [but] I can doctor you till de doctor come," or "I'll hold de congregation till the preacher comes" may be somewhat ambiguous, it is hard to believe the following is really about occupations:

My daddy was a miller,
And he taught me how to grind;
My daddy was a jockey,
And he taught me how to ride.[45]

The well-known "C. C. Rider" or "Easy Rider" has been claimed by some to refer to the easy fit of a guitar to a singer's body, but a woman seems more likely in view of the remark, "You're three times seven, and you know what you want to do."[46] In "Prison Cell Blues" Blind Lemon Jefferson leaves little doubt about the reference when he laments, "[Nell] used to be my rider but now she just won't treat me right."[47] When love goes bad a woman "tucks her head and cries," whereas her man is more likely to "catch a freight and ride." But sometimes all that is needed is the elusive "someone to call my own . . . someone to take my care."

Weariness with the world is evident in many blues lyrics. Inherited "bad luck in the family" might leave a man a "long ways from home," with "nowhar to lay my weary head." The unavoidable problems of life left many men and women feeling, "I'm tired of livin' and I don't want to die; I'm tired of workin', but I can't fly." For some there was a sense that, though "I'm weary now, I won't be weary long." The same was true for being "worried." Friends might try to help with the reassurance that "the four day blues ain't bad," but deep trouble felt like "it must not have been them four day blues I had." At their worst, the blues left a person feeling "too damn mean to cry" and swearing, "If de blues was whiskey, I'd stay drunk all the time." But sometimes the sense of loneliness and isolation was so great that even close friends or lovers could not help. This despair echoes through the lines, "You don't know my mind; when you see me laughin', I'm laughin' to keep from cryin'."

♯ ♯ ♯

For the women left behind when their men went to prison or caught the next train out of town, times could be hard regardless of race. "I Never Will Marry" does not explain why the woman in question intends to drown herself in the sea, except that she "expect[s] to live single all the days of my life." But the depth of her sorrow is evident. It has resonated so strongly with folks over the years as to make it from England in the eighteenth century to the Ozarks in the twentieth.[48] "The House of the Rising Sun" is less desperate, but the choices are not much better.[49] The House of the Rising Sun is clearly a brothel. It is here that the young woman singing the song is headed, having been betrayed by her husband, "a gambling man" or a "drunkard." All she can hope for now is to warn her sister not to "do like I have done," before boarding the train "back to New Orleans to wear that ball and chain." However long she survives, her "race is almost run," and she expects to "spend the rest of my days beneath the Rising Sun." One could always cry, "It's hard, ain't it hard . . . to love one who never does love you." Another option was to drown one's sorrows in drink, or even to "take a whiff on me" by using cocaine, which was more readily available at the start of the twentieth century, to mask the pain.[50]

‡ ‡ ‡

Hard times elicited a variety of responses—from endurance, through covert action, to outright rebellion. Reaction was occasionally collective, as when slaves rose to revolt or working men went out on strike. But when confronted with difficult situations, individual men, and a few women, fought back, resisting with actions the authorities would deem criminal. Both black and white Americans celebrated their criminals in song, though not always in the same way.

Lawrence Levine argues that black and white bandits were remarkably similar in reality, however much the legends and songs that grew up around them differ.[51] Regardless of race, the bad men who are celebrated in folk songs were often "solitary individuals" who asserted their "freedom from organized society." Living outside the law and the expectations of normal society, such men were "ruthless, destructive, selfish, asocial"—in other words, not ideal neighbors. According to Levine, when folk songs were composed about some of these bad men, African Americans tended toward a realism in which the very badness of the men was celebrated, with no hint of innocence and rare demonstrations of redeeming virtues. White Americans, on the other hand, often adopted some version of the Robin Hood myth, portraying their bandits as persecuted and decent at heart.

According to English social historian Eric Hobsbawm, Robin Hood is simply an English example of a more widely known social type he calls the "social bandit." Functioning in a rural setting, the social bandit engages in a "primitive form of organized social protest," generally striving to protect old ways and local customs against a new, modernizing social order being forced on the local population by outsiders. As a result, the bandit's neighbors see his actions as not really criminal, frequently offering aid in the form of supplies or at least protection via feigned ignorance of his whereabouts. Social bandits are almost always young, single males who retain local loyalties so long as they distribute some of their booty, but they lose their protection if they prey upon their neighbors. If the bandit lives long enough, a myth is likely to develop that he has supernatural powers that protect him from the law, so that when he falls it will be by betrayal or even magic, though the authorities will try to claim victory. What matters is not so much the reality of the bad man's story but how he comes to be known to the public.

Times that are rife with change and are unsettling to the social order are particularly prone to producing these men. The need is such that songs may ignore inconvenient realities about dangerous thugs or minor criminals to create useful myths.[52]

Historians have often described ballads about white bandits as fitting the social-bandit stereotype, claiming songs about black bad men are notably different. In fact, the distinction is not so clear, for African-American folk heroes like Railroad Bill fit the model well, however much Stagolee may not. Of all the bad-man ballads Americans have sung, those about Jesse James fit the social-bandit model best. Other ballads about white outlaws show some of the same tendencies, while some are better understood in other contexts.[53]

Jesse James was born in Missouri in 1847, four years after his brother Frank, with whom he would form a gang. His father was a Baptist minister who headed west for gold, perhaps in the same group as Sweet Betsy or Joe Bowers, and died in California. His mother soon married a local doctor who treated his stepsons well, depriving us of being able to blame Jesse's later life on a troubled childhood. He did, however, grow up in Missouri in the midst of the border warfare associated with Bleeding Kansas in the 1850s. The James family was pro-slavery, so when the Civil War broke out they sided with the Confederacy. William Quantrill, who had been active in Kansas, formed a guerilla band during the war, recruiting, among others, Frank James and Cole Younger, another noted bandit in later years.[54] Jesse was too young to ride with the gang at the start of the war but joined Quantrill in 1864. Because members of Quantrill's band were not a formal part of any Confederate army, their irregular status left them outside the law when peace returned. Faced with an uncertain future, Frank and Jesse began robbing banks and killing in February 1866, when they joined with Cole Younger and his brothers in a raid on a bank in Liberty, Missouri, supposedly the first peacetime bank robbery in the United States.

They remained contented with relieving banks of their cash until 1873, when they decided trains offered too good an opportunity to pass up. The Pinkerton Detective Agency, hired by corporate interests to look for the boys, ended up harming their kin in a raid on the family farm in 1875, when Frank and Jesse could not be found. A year later, the James and Younger gangs combined for a disastrous raid on a bank in Northfield, Minnesota, which led to the death of several gang members and the capture and imprisonment of Frank James and Cole, Jim, and Bob Younger. Frank and Cole were paroled shortly after 1900; Cole later joined a Wild West show sponsored by Frank, where he lectured on the perils of a life of crime.

Had Jesse been captured along with the rest of his gang and died of old age after outliving the age of the cowboys, he might not have been the subject of ballads; but he remained free for six years after the Northfield disaster, only to be shot in the back by his cousin, Robert Ford, in 1882, just before another bank robbery. As Jesse climbed on a chair to straighten a crooked picture, Ford saw an opportunity to collect a five-thousand-dollar reward on Jesse's head. Thus James was betrayed in the manner of any good social bandit. Before Jesse died, many newspapermen had already begun embellishing his career for myth-making purposes.[55] As Norm Cohen observes about this process and the songs that followed, "Much has been written, and some of that is accurate."[56]

The ballads of "Jesse James" are, in fact, a curious mixture of the social bandit and dangerous thug.[57] The songs admit that Jesse was involved in criminal action, albeit against the banks and railroads that seemed to intrude on and yet were beyond the control of most ordinary citizens. The opening stanzas of one version tell us, "Jesse James was a lad that killed many a man; he robbed that Danville train."[58] Elsewhere we learn "he robbed the Chicago bank, and stopped the Glendale train." Some verses refer to a stick-up of the bank in Glendale, during which the boys "shot Captain Sheets to the ground" for no obvious reason. Yet it is the Robin Hood, the social-bandit, part of the story that stands out. Despite Jesse's homicidal tendencies, the songs reassure us that Jesse was "a friend to the poor [who] never would see a man suffer pain," except, of course, poor Captain Sheets. Presumably his violent behavior could be excused by the fact that he "took from the rich and he gave it to the poor," targeting large corporations and their lackeys. Moreover, "Jesse had a wife to mourn for his life, three children they were brave," attaching him to the community and domesticating him.

As with all good social bandits, Jesse's end came by betrayal. According to myth, "the people held their breath when they heard of Jesse's death, wondered how he came to die." They knew the authorities "didn't have the sand to take Jesses James alive." The people would always know Robert Ford as "that dirty little coward who shot Mr. Howard [Jesse's alias], when he laid poor Jesse in his grave." Despite ridding the community of a robber and killer, Ford was disgraced because he shot Jesse "like a thief in the night," eager for the reward, even though he had "ate of Jesse's bread and slept in Jesse's bed." Thus it was the end of this man, who "came from a solitary race," that came to define the story in the ballads, despite, or perhaps because of the reiteration of numerous assaults on the emerging capitalist, industrialist economy and the occasional murder of men employed by remote corporations. A half century later Woody Guthrie used the familiar melody to "Jesse James" for his song "Jesus Christ," another man who opposed the authorities and came to his death by betrayal.

Long before Jesse James attracted the attention of American songsters, the notorious Captain William Kidd had been the subject of ballads on both sides of the Atlantic. His tale was used to promote morality through the lesson of a good man gone bad. Kidd started his fateful plunge into infamy in the latter part of the seventeenth century when he was raiding French shipping on behalf of the governor of the colony of New York. Soon his travels took him into the Indian Ocean, where he slipped over the line from privateering to piracy. He was captured and returned to England, where he was tried and hanged in 1701. The moral message of the long ballad associated with this wicked man may explain the song's enduring appeal, but the tune may also have contributed, living on not only in the ballad of the unrepentant "Samuel Hall" but later transformed into the sacred-harp hymn "Wondrous Love" and then into the children's song "She'll Be Coming Round the Mountain." Balladeers took no chances with the song's appeal, adding many lurid crimes to Kidd's list of actual sins, despite getting his name wrong.

The ballad of "Captain Robert Kidd" is indisputably moral, with Kidd narrating his sad decline and even sadder ending.[59] It begins with his fall from grace:

> My name is Captain Kidd, as I sailed, as I sailed,
> My name is Captain Kidd, as I sailed,
> My name is Captain Kidd, God's laws I did forbid,
> And most wickedly I did, as I sailed, as I sailed.
>
> Oh, my parents taught me well, as I sailed, as I sailed,
> My parents taught me well, as I sailed,
> My parents taught me well to shun the gates of Hell,
> But against them I rebelled, as I sailed, as I sailed.

Having "cursed [his] father dear" and sunk his Bible "in the sand," Kidd turned to murder, laying "William Moore . . . in his gore." The death of a sick mate caused him to realize "there comes a reckoning day," but soon the lure of wealth and the lack of social restraints led him astray once again. Unlike John Newton, who ultimately redeemed himself after his perception of "Amazing Grace" on board ship, Kidd only briefly tried to leave his sinful life, admitting, "My repentance lasted not, my vows I soon forgot," and recognizing that "damnation's my just lot, as I sailed." No betrayal and heroic ending awaited Kidd. Instead the message makes clear the fate of those who challenge the laws of God and man. From the nasty confines of Newgate prison, Kidd faced his fate: "To execution dock I must go, to execution dock, lay my head upon the block, and no more the laws I'll mock." There, in front of the "many thousands" who flocked to see the execution, Kidd, at least according to the ballad, offered the crowd his gold, acknowledging, "I've lost my soul, and must die." Lest any mistake the moral, the ballad concludes with Kidd saying, "Take warning now by me, and shun bad company, lest you come to Hell with me, for I must die."

Curiously, there are few surviving ballads of bad men from the seventeenth century until the end of the nineteenth century. Heroes of the normal ilk abounded, and comic characters provided relief from everyday strains; but it was not until after the Civil War, with the bitterness of racial repression and reaction against the emerging urban, industrial order that bad men once again attracted the attention of song makers. Most of the bad men memorialized in the songs that have endured did their nefarious deeds between 1865 and 1900.

Social bandits like Jesse James were largely rural in origin, though the James boys attacked the symbols of the urban, industrial order. But the prime African-American bad man, "Stagolee," was urban to the core. According to Lawrence Levine, Stagolee and other black bad men are more likely to fall under another of Hobsbawm's bandit types, "'the avengers'—bandits whose reputations are built not on justice but terror." For such men "to assert any power at all is a triumph," expressing by their actions "the profound anger festering and smoldering among the oppressed."[60] The true story of "Stack" Lee Shelton (the man behind "Stagolee") is not especially illuminating or different, but it served the ballad makers' purposes to express the anger and hostility of the urban black world as Jim Crow came to dominate American life.[61] Just as Pearl Bryan's death was adapted to the formulas of the murdered-girl ballads, so too the story of how Lee Shelton shot William Lyons was fitted to the needs and expectations about bad men.[62] Coincidently, Bryan's body was discovered scarcely more than a month after Stagolee shot Billy on December 25, 1895.[63] Much of the Shelton–Lyons story was reported in the St. Louis newspapers, along with the five other murders that happened on that Christmas Day; but unlike with the Bryan case, the newspapers do not seem to have indulged in myth making with their reporting of Shelton's crime. That was the work of the ballad makers.

Both Shelton and Lyons were accustomed to the St. Louis nightlife, and they were familiar sights in the saloons and brothels that catered to African

Americans and whites at this time. Both were also rivals in St. Louis politics. Appropriate to ballad tradition that nothing good ever happens in a tavern, Lyons was drinking with a friend when Shelton walked in and approached him. After some playful exchanges, Shelton seems to have damaged Lyons's hat, after which Lyons seized Shelton's white Stetson hat and would not return it until he was paid for his own hat. In a fit of anger, Shelton pulled out a pistol and shot Lyons, leaving him dying on the floor. Shelton took his Stetson, went home, or to a friend's house, and went to sleep, where he was arrested later that night, apparently undisturbed by the violent act he had just committed. After an initial trial produced a hung jury, Shelton was convicted in 1897 of the killing and sent to the Missouri State Penitentiary in Jefferson to serve a twenty-five-year sentence. He was paroled in 1909, but by early 1911 he was back in prison on an assault charge. He died there of tuberculosis early in 1912. His five-feet-seven-inch frame had shrunk to about 102 pounds shortly before his death at about the age of fifty.[64] So Lee Shelton was nothing more than a small man given courage by a pistol and possibly a drink.

But the songs tell another tale, producing a mythic bad man whose story has remained alive in the African-American community for a century and who, some have argued, served as a model for later songwriters and film-makers.[65] The core of most versions is clearly when Stagolee shoots Billy Lyons "'bout a five dollar Stetson hat." Stagolee's essential evil or cruelty is exemplified and amplified by verses reporting the famous exchange during which Lyons pleads for his life by appealing to his children and wife, to which Stagolee responds, "What do I care about your two little girls and your darling loving wife?" In one version, sexual insult is added to imminent injury when Stagolee tells him, "God bless your children, I'll take care of your wife."[66] After recounting this conversation, one singer asks the jury, "What do you think of that?" addressing the senselessness of killing a man over a "five dollar Stetson hat."[67]

What moved the Lee Shelton story into the realm of myth was the im-age that was created for Stagolee in addition to the songs. As Cecil Brown observes, the Stagolee "legend is not based on facts" but instead "exploits the facts according to the emotional and psychological needs of the teller and his or her audience."[68] In their 1947 recording-session discussion of the origins of the blues, Bill Broonzy and his friends made the distinction between a bad man who was at heart criminal, and a crazy man who had the temerity to "speak up for his rights," even in the face of almost certain death.[69] Stagolee seems to embody both. Although some early versions do report that Shelton was actually arrested in bed, it is common in ballads for the police chief to have trouble finding men willing to confront the bad man. And instead of dying quietly in prison of TB, Stagolee is generally hanged, with judge, jury, and citizens "all glad to see him die." Occasionally the judge is so fearful of Stagolee that he lets him go, either before trial or after efforts to hang him prove unsuccessful. In such cases, this black man is so bad that even the whites in charge of the legal system are intimidated. Mississippi John Hurt makes this same point in a more indirect fashion when he asks at the start and end of his song, "Police officer, how can it be, you can arrest everybody but cruel Stagolee?" Hurt may be reminding white authorities of their fears in the face of an unintimidated black man, but he may also be expressing anger at a system that put so many African-American men in jail for minor or nonexistent crimes, but only when they threatened whites. Since Stagolee murdered another black man, Hurt may be displaying contempt at the disinterest of the law in pursuing the case. Despite a certain pride in Stagolee's refusal to knuckle under, his neighbors must have wondered when they would fall victim to his rage. Lucious Curtis and Willie Ford warn their listeners that Stagolee will "get you where ever you may be," extending the threat of this bad man beyond the barroom. He certainly is no Robin Hood. Along with "The Farmer's Curst Wife," Stagolee occasionally shows up in hell, where he takes over from the devil. In an occasional reversal, based upon a mishearing of Lyons's first name, Stagolee becomes a more familiar hero, ridding the town of "Bully" Lyons.

Other black bad men fit at least part of the Stagolee mold.[70] "Duncan and Brady" came from St. Louis about the same time as "Stagolee" and is a response to police brutality toward African Americans.[71] Brady, an Irish-American police officer "with a shining star" on his chest, walked into the barroom to arrest Duncan, who was at work as a bartender. Duncan shot "King Brady" dead. Although the song does not often offer explicit praise of Duncan, its oblique and direct comments on Brady as a representative of the law cast the shooter in the light of a social bandit whose illegal action the community approves. Perhaps the most telling verse is one sung by Leadbelly, in which Brady is accused of doing wrong, "walkin' in the room when the game was goin' on, knockin' down windows, breakin' down doors." Since the police were not always as prompt to arrest killers as they were with Lee Shelton, it did not sit well when they were overly zealous about breaking up black amusements and intimidating residents. One satirical version begins, "Twinkle, twinkle little star," referring to the shiny badge on the chest of the not-so-shiny Brady, who "had not been sober in many a night."[72]

"Po' Lazarus" is almost as widely known and in as many variations as "Stagolee."[73] Technically, "Po' Lazarus" is about a bad man, and complex versions begin with him robbing the commissary of the company he worked for. But much of the song is, in fact, a protest against the law and its brutality. According to the story, the "high sheriff" or "judge" instructed his deputies to go out and "bring me Lazarus, dead or alive." With such permission, it is no wonder that when they "found him way out between two mountains" and Lazarus informed the deputies he "had never been arrested," they "blowed him down . . . with a great big .44." Lazarus was brought back to the commissary, placed on the counter from which he had seized the money, and left to die. His mother, in a gesture all too familiar among African Americans, cried out that they had killed her son. The poverty that may have driven Lazarus to act is evident when his mother and sister are portrayed as being unable to attend the funeral because they "had no shoes."

"Po' Lazarus" echoes both of the Lazarus stories in the Bible.[74] The ballad links to the story of the poor man, Lazarus, and the rich man, Dives, who offered no aid to his neighbor before the ailing man died, just as Po' Lazarus is left on the commissary table begging for a drink. Surely some African Americans who knew their scriptures must have hoped that, like Dives, the sheriff and his deputies would suffer in hell. Unfortunately, Jesus was not available to raise Po' Lazarus from the dead as he did Mary's and Martha's brother, the subject of the other Lazarus Bible story.

Of all the African-American bad men memorialized in song, "Railroad Bill" comes closest to being a social bandit. "Railroad Bill" has been linked to the life of Morris Slater, though some versions of the song may predate his story.[75] In a curious reversal of the folk process, the story of Slater's life and death is actually more suitable for myth than the ballads attached to him. According to the songs, Railroad Bill was not the kind of man anyone would want to meet on a dark night, or even in daylight. The fact that "Railroad Bill [was a] mighty bad man . . . always lookin' fer somebody's life" was ample reason for anyone to say, "I'm scared of Railroad Bill." As with any bad man worthy of being remembered in story and song, Railroad Bill killed his share of men, including law officers intent on his capture. But Bill was also a terror to his own community, and no Robin Hood. One version of the song begins with the blunt observation, "Railroad Bill ought to be killed, [he] never worked and he never will," before protesting, "Railroad Bill done took my wife, threatened me that he would take my life." Bill was such a bad neighbor that he "stole all the chickens the poor farmer had." In addition to violating the commandments against stealing, murder, and coveting a neighbor's wife, Bill showed little respect for his parents; he was "so mean and so bad, [he] whupped his mammy, shot a round at his dad, one morning just before day."

While Morris Slater did, in fact, kill Sheriff E. S. McMillen and several other law officers put on his trail, he does not seem to have been the evil man portrayed in the ballads. Slater lived in Alabama at the end of the nineteenth century, a hard time and place for any African American. He may have earned his living producing turpentine in the Southern forests. For some reason, the law went looking for him in 1894, and Slater did not wait to see if he would receive a fair trial. For the next several years he roamed up and down the backwoods rail lines of Alabama, holding up trains but more often throwing groceries and other goods out of boxcars and returning later to pick them up. According to legend, though not song, Slater shared his loot with poor black families in proper social-bandit style, and in return he may have been aided by them. Despite the efforts of numerous sheriffs and their deputies to capture him, Slater remained free until the day he was shot in 1897. So successful was he in eluding capture that legends grew that he was a conjurer, capable of shape shifting, sitting by the side of the road as a small animal and laughing at the futile efforts of his pursuers. Myth had it that he was invulnerable to normal bullets and could only be killed by a silver slug. Although his end was not as dramatic as that, it came as no surprise that he was ambushed in a small country store, shot from behind by the storekeeper while he fought off a constable. To dispel rumors of his prowess—and possibly to undercut his "folk memory as a black hero who held his white oppressors at bay and stole from them to aid his fellow blacks"—Slater's body was embalmed and exhibited in Montgomery, where three thousand people came to see the notorious outlaw/hero.[76] At least one man recalled hearing that Slater had not even killed McMillen but that the sheriff's gun had fatally misfired as he tried to shoot Railroad Bill.

It is ironic that Slater, who behaved like a true social bandit and an American Robin Hood, should have been immortalized in song as such a bad man, whereas someone like Jesse James, with far less to praise, should have become a folk hero. It may be that African-American bad men simply had to conform to certain stereotypes that were more Stagolee than Robin Hood. Or, as Norm Cohen suggests, Slater's story may have become attached to preexisting song of a suitable type to meet community needs. It is not surprising that men like Stagolee or Railroad Bill have been celebrated for their destructive behavior, for few African Americans in the 1890s had any fondly remembered social order to be preserved or restored.

A few black women joined their men in the annals of crime songs, though the women are not "bad" in the way the men are. When Frankie Baker shot Allen Britt in St. Louis in 1899, only four years after Lee Shelton began his march to fame as Stagolee, the ballad makers seized the story to tell the tale of "Frankie and Albert" or "Johnny."[77] While songsters soon created Frankie as a woman of action, refusing to put up with her man wandering around with other women, and they placed Albert's death in a hotel or brothel, she actually seems to have shot Allen when he roused her out of her own bed and threatened to cut her with a knife. She was acquitted on self-defense. Baker took no pleasure in her action or folk reputation, fleeing St. Louis and the people who sang the ballads when they saw her on the street. She is perhaps better understood in the context of the old English ballads about independent women than songs of bad men. The story of Delia Green, killed by Cooney Houston in Savannah, Georgia, on Christmas Eve in 1900, hints at a hard life but ultimately fails to depict her as a bad woman.[78] Delia is occasionally referred to as a "rounder" or "gambler" in the songs, but the focus of the songs is more on her death and how her killer will "wait in jail till Delia come back." There is more than a hint of tragedy here, as is appropriate for a case in which a fourteen-year-old girl has been killed for apparently hurting the feelings of a boy of the same age. Here it is the murdered-girl ballad that comes to mind, not "Stagolee" or "Jesse James."

The ballad of "John Hardy" is a widely known song about a murderer, with similar versions common among both black and white Americans.[79] Its crossover appeal was made possible by the fact that the story of this bad man does not seem to have been forced into moral service to fit the needs of any particular group. Hardy also accepts his death as just punishment for his actions, at least according to the ballads. Because of certain similarities, and perhaps some migrating verses, John Hardy has occasionally been confused with John Henry, though they clearly were not the same man nor the same tale.[80] Hardy was a real man who, like the fabled Henry, was both African American and a laborer on the railroads in West Virginia. According to the ballads, John Hardy "was a desperate little man" who "carried a gun every day." He shot a man in 1893 "on the West Virginia line" and tried to escape. Just as Hardy reached the "East Stone Bridge," which would take him beyond the immediate reach of the West Virginia law, "up stepped a man and took him by the arm, saying 'Johnny, come and walk along with me.'"

The remainder of the ballad discusses his trial and execution, with echoes of "The Gallis Pole." In that old Child ballad, the family of the young man to be hanged comes to watch the execution and refuses to provide bail; he is saved only by the timely arrival of his true love. John Hardy's family is more supportive and offers bail, but "money wouldn't do in a murdering case so they kept John Hardy locked in jail." The John Henry ballads occasionally refer to several women dressed in different colors coming to see their man in death. Similar verses are found in "John Hardy." One woman, "dressed in blue," tells him as he stands on the scaffold, "Daddy, I will always be true." Another, this time in a dress of red, follows "John Hardy to his hanging ground, saying, 'Daddy, I would rather be dead.'" His "loving little wife"— whether she is dressed in blue, red, or black is not made clear—whispers to him "on the scaffold high, . . . 'I'll meet you in the sweet bye and bye.'"

The songs actually say little explicitly about Hardy after the murder and his attempted escape, until the very end when he redeems himself by facing death with courage, apparently not "a desperate little man" in the face of the King of Terrors. In a form many Americans would have recognized from pamphlets published to accompany other public executions, Hardy addresses the audience, which was likely quite numerous:

> Now I've been to the East and I've been to the West,
> I've been this wide world 'round,
> I've been to the river and I've been baptized,
> And now I'm on my hanging ground.

White audiences who approved of the basic narrative and personal messages in "John Hardy" may also have found the story of "Cole Younger" appealing. The various ballads about Cole Younger, his brothers, and their intermittent alliances with the James boys are a cross between the social bandit and the criminal repenting of the sort of sinful life that is evident in "Captain Kidd."[81] Younger was born in Missouri in 1844 and joined Quantrill's raiders during the Civil War. From 1866 to 1876, Cole and his brothers robbed banks and trains, sometimes by themselves and sometimes with others, including the Jameses, whom they knew from their days with Quantrill.[82] After the disaster at Northfield, Minnesota, in 1876, which ended with the capture of all three Younger brothers, Cole seems to have reformed. He was a cooperative prisoner, which led to his parole in 1901; he lectured on the dangers of a life of crime during the rest of his life, dying in 1916.

In the ballads, always sung in the first person and by Cole himself, the tone oscillates between celebrating the life of crime and expressing regret for what he did, anticipating the change in his own life after prison. On the one hand he could brag, "I am a noted highway man, Cole Younger is my name," before admitting, "My crimes and depredations have brought my friends to shame." He could speak with apparent pride of "a bold, high robbery," before admitting that one such robbery of a solitary miner left him "sorry until [his] dying day." His decision to lead a life outside the law is explained in part by, he says, a need to "avenge our father's death" and to "fight those anti-guerillas until the day we die." On the other hand, he confesses, "Crimes done by our bloody hands bring tears into my eyes," especially the wrecking of a train in which the engineer was killed. As is common with ballads, the details of such crimes rarely match the actual facts, either regarding the rail line involved or the number of fatalities. But then, most stories worth telling are worth improving.

The centerpiece of most of the ballads is the Northfield robbery. As the stickup unfolds, Cole informs the teller, "Just hand us over the money and make no further delay, we are the famous Younger boys, we spare no time to play." But the cashier, "true as steel, refused [the] noted band," and so they kill him. Historians have argued over who pulled the trigger, but at least one song has Cole identifying Jesse James as the culprit, perhaps because Jesse escaped and so was not yet confronting trial. In true mythic tradition of fate anticipated and accepted, Bob Younger tells his brother as they plan the Northfield holdup, "Cole, if you undertake the job, you will surely curse the day." Bob later died in prison as the result of that "sad and fatal day" when they ventured into "the God-forsaken country called Minnesote-o." But what turns Younger from mere bandit into a man worthy of song is his personal integrity and willingness to accept his punishment when he stands up and declares, "The robbing of the Northfield bank is a deed I'll never deny, but which I will be sorry of until the day I die." In fact, Cole often denied involvement in various crimes, and his sorrow may have been more for the pain he caused his brothers than for the robbery itself. But the Cole Younger of legend and ballad stands out as a man of action, unafraid of institutions of power and wealth, but also a man who retains a spark of decency and regret about the life he chose.

Another bad man who accepts the consequences of his actions, at least according to ballad, is Charles Guiteau, the assassin who killed President Garfield in 1881 out of disappointment over being denied a job in Garfield's administration. The ballad is derived from a song about James Rodgers, who had been hanged for murder in 1858.[83] The chorus, which is in some ways the most important part of the ballad, echoes the courage and forthright character of Cole Younger when Guiteau declares, "My name I'll never deny," accepting responsibility for his actions. What he regrets, however, is leaving his "aged parents in sorrow for to die," saying, "Little did they think, when in my youthful bloom, I'd ever climb the gallows high to meet my fatal doom." Here is a song for every parent who has ever had hopes for a child but feared that child might do something irreparably foolish or worse. A loving sister comes, not to bring bail or pledge loyalty, but to "weep most bitterly" over a "darling brother" condemned to die for the murder of the nation's leader. Despite causing the death of the president, the song treats Guiteau with remarkable sympathy, not as a Jesse James or a Stagolee, but perhaps more as a Lazarus, involved with a system he did not really comprehend, or a Cole Younger, accepting the consequences of his actions.

One of the best known of the American outlaws was Billy the Kid, another young man who went astray and whose choices live on in ballad form.[84] By birth, Billy was more Stagolee than Jesse James, born in New York City in 1859 with the name of Henry McCarty. After his father's death during the Civil War, his mother moved the family west in a number of short hops, first to Indiana, then to Kansas, and finally on to New Mexico, where she died in 1874. Young Henry stayed with his mother until she died, waiting tables at times. In a story many Americans knew and more feared, he began to go astray after the loss of his mother's influence. Arrested for theft in 1875, Henry left town and turned to life as a cowboy, probably as Kid Antrim. He changed his work and name rapidly, participating in a range war in Lincoln County, New Mexico, as William Bonney, soon to be Billy the Kid. When the range war ended in March 1879, he hoped for amnesty for his actions, which included killing, but he was denied. He joined a gang in 1880, quite possibly for protection, and was arrested shortly thereafter for a barroom killing. He was tried and sentenced to be hanged, but he escaped. As he entered his dark bedroom in 1881, he was shot to death by Sheriff Pat Garrett, a onetime friend. Although the ballad claims Billy was hunting Garrett to make him his twenty-second victim, the Kid probably killed no more than four men, which one could argue is still enough to make him a dangerous psychopath.

The ballad of Billy the Kid makes no effort to create a hero of him, though recent historians have argued he was, then and now, a media creation, with a myth that far exceeds the sordid reality. The ballad maker was content to "sing of the desperate deeds that he did" in a violent, masculine world far from the city of his birth, where "a man's only chance was his own .44." Of course, the urban world of Stagolee offered a similar frontier, where guns and violence defined a man. According to the song, Billy had no characteristics of the social bandit, never helping the poor, nor, aside from Sheriff Garrett, confronting powerful, external authority. He is supposed to have killed his first man at the age of twelve, anticipating reality by six years. The ballad makes Billy acceptable to his new neighbors by having him adopt the racial prejudices of his new home, wooing "Mexican maidens" and "always [being] after the Greasers," keeping them "on the run." Far from righting wrongs and defending the oppressed, Billy is portrayed as being one of the oppressors.

Hard times, whether systemic or personal, often produced hard men. And some of those men had their lives memorialized and often improved in ballad and story. It was not necessary for a man's life to be truly inspirational or heroic, so long as there was a kernel of truth that could be used to build a tale and an image that were useful to his community. Nor was Robin Hood the only ideal to be held up as a model, positive or negative. Courage to resist a faceless or powerful enemy deserved respect, even when resistance meant almost certain annihilation. To be bad was acceptable if there were understandable reasons for wandering from the straight and narrow, and even more acceptable if repentance came at the end of a misspent life. Americans have always cherished the individual, even when, or perhaps especially when, that man (and almost all were men) expressed hidden urges to break the bonds of civilization. Ballads often had morals attached at the end to make them acceptable in polite company, but there must have been a thrill of vicarious wickedness that accompanied the singing of such songs. For many who could not or would not pick up a knife or a gun, a pointed song would serve as modest defiance against an all-too-imperfect world.

CHAPTER 8

How Can I Keep from Singing?

Huddie Ledbetter and Woody Guthrie

Over the centuries, folks have been busy creating music and composing lyrics to make their lives easier and more meaningful, and fortunately some have been preserved. The array of songs considered thus far is like the tip of an iceberg, so anyone who decides to learn some folk songs will have more than enough choices. The question is how to choose. For many, an engaging tune and/or a moving lyric that expresses some deeply held belief is enough to encourage the effort to commit a song to memory. Often the process of adding songs to a repertoire is eclectic and random, driven by the chance encounter of a new song while in a receptive frame of mind. At other times, learning new songs can be more purposeful, such as seeking out additional songs on a favorite topic, collecting songs as part of a scholarly project, or even finding songs for a book such as this. Personality and taste make some songs more appealing than others. The ups and downs, the joys and sorrows of life provoke or inspire some individuals to bring to life new verses and sometimes new melodies, which, if they are in harmony with the experience of others, may begin to circulate relatively unaltered or undergo the editing that is part of the folk process.

Singers of folk songs generally know comparatively few songs on a limited range of topics. But occasionally individuals will find folk songs so central to their whole existence that they become committed to learning, performing, and promoting the songs, earning a living that way if they can. A close examination of such a songster's repertoire is akin to reading that person's autobiography. Two of America's most talented and influential folk singers of the twentieth century, Huddie Ledbetter (Leadbelly) and Woodrow Wilson (Woody) Guthrie, told their personal stories in the songs they sang and wrote, though Guthrie actually wrote a conventional autobiography as well. Understanding the role music played in their lives may offer insight into the choices and preferences others of us have made. It is hard, if not impossible, to imagine the history of folk songs in America since 1950 without the influence of Leadbelly and Woody, not only for the specific songs they passed on, but also for the examples they set of how to use music to tell a personal story or comment on society. Since one of the main assumptions of this book is that folk songs speak directly to people's experiences and needs, it is appropriate to conclude with an examination of how the songs these two men knew and wrote defined and expressed their lives. Most singers of folk songs never acquire the range of songs or approach the creative abilities of these two men, but the songs we sing still speak to us in similar ways, however much more quietly and privately.

♯ ♯ ♯

On March 3, 1940, Will Geer, an actor and sometime folk singer, organized a concert in New York City to aid migrant workers in California. Alan Lomax ignored not only the work of his father but also the work of others, like Carl Sandburg and Dorothy Scarborough, when he later described this event as the start of the folk revival in America.[1] This concert was also notable for being the first time two of America's legends performed together: Leadbelly and Woody Guthrie. Both men were sons of Middle America, with a Southern flavor; both suffered enough hard times for several men, some of it of their own making; and both did more to preserve, promote, and expand folk songs in the twentieth century than any other singer–songwriters.

The lives of Guthrie and Ledbetter intersected and diverged in a true and somewhat improbable American story. Soon after the "Grapes of Wrath Evening," as the New York concert was called, Guthrie, recently arrived in New York, took up residence on the Ledbetters' couch and did not leave Huddie and his wife, Martha, for a year. The friendship of Ledbetter, a large, black, working man who had experienced the worst the segregated South could offer, and Guthrie, a skinny, white, middle-class man who rarely performed manual labor and who had accepted the racist attitudes of his parents and neighbors growing up in Oklahoma, is as remarkable as it was unlikely a decade and a half before the Supreme Court finally declared segregation unconstitutional. Even their attire set them apart, with the middle-class man regularly wearing work clothes, often none too clean, while the man who had spent long hours in the cotton fields was always impeccably dressed with a tie and jacket. Only the power of folk music could have brought them together.

Leadbelly (the name Ledbetter acquired in prison) and Guthrie both knew an impressive range of old music, from Child ballads and hymns, to cowboy songs, children's ditties, and the blues. Some they learned from their mothers, and some they learned during their frequent rambles. Both composed new songs with powerful lyrics that commented on current social conditions, and they often set their lyrics to old, familiar tunes. Even when they sang the old songs, they frequently added some new twist of melody or lyric that made the song distinctly theirs. Ledbetter loved popular music and incorporated it into his repertoire, while Guthrie was more inclined to labor union songs. By the standards of the modern, slick, overproduced music of today, in which singers sound like no one ever has sounded live, the recordings of Guthrie and Ledbetter are a bit rough around the edges. But there is power and conviction in the way each sang and played that will capture any listener who will pay attention. Of the two, there is no denying that Guthrie had the greater gift as a poet–lyricist, a talent he himself likened to that of Walt Whitman.[2] Nor can one deny Ledbetter's more accomplished skills as a musician or his claim to be "king of the twelve-string guitar." The man made his Stella ring with a confidence best expressed as he finished one lick, "It's so easy when you know how."[3]

For each man, his music was his life, not only in a professional sense, but also in how his songs told his biography. Carl Sandburg believed that "a song is a role" in which "a singer acts a part." He was convinced it was necessary for "all good artists [to] study a song and live with" it before their performances could be "authentic."[4] Ledbetter and Guthrie not only lived with their songs but also inhabited them. Their authenticity is undeniable. Nor could anyone doubt their "affinity with the moral and emotional message[s]" of the songs they sang, resonating as they did with the lives the two men lived.[5]

Both men pursued professional recognition for their music and sought to fashion self-images that would enhance their careers, sometimes transcending the dull facts of their real lives. But they did it differently. Guthrie saw himself as a champion of the people, describing problems in order to right wrongs. While seeking a certain amount of fame, with which he never seemed entirely comfortable, Guthrie regularly reminded his listeners that, despite the fact that most of us will always be anonymous Americans, our lives still matter. Ledbetter's choice of songs was often more personal, about the struggles he had faced, which were many. Even when his songs turned more explicitly to social issues, they tended to be framed around his own experience. Listening to Leadbelly sing, one can hear the conviction behind his vision as he testifies to what he has gone through and shares what he has learned. Guthrie, on the other hand, often seems to be performing self-consciously, even lecturing us about what he has seen and what he thinks about it. For him, the truth was in the words more than the melody.

♯ ♯ ♯

Huddie Ledbetter was born in 1888, probably on the Louisiana side of the border where Texas and Arkansas converge with the Bayou state. Along with most other African-American families in the South at the time, the Ledbetters made their living farming. Huddie attended school in Texas for about five years, learning to read and write, and picking up a little formal training in music.[6] He started school in 1896, the year the Supreme Court ruled segregated schools somehow provided equal and hence constitutional opportunities for black children.

Growing up, Huddie gradually acquired a wide variety of songs. As an adult, he clearly recalled with pleasure children's songs ranging from the conventional "Skip to My Lou" to ring songs like "Ha, Ha This A-Way" and "Sally Walker" that had possible roots in the African-derived ring shouts that were common in slave religious meetings.[7] "Grey Goose" is a children's tale with a satirical bite, telling the story of a preacher whose sin of hunting on a Sunday is rewarded when he catches the toughest goose in the world. Ledbetter's mother's influence led him to proper hymns, including "Let It Shine on Me," a song he linked back to the days of slavery and forward to the increasingly driving renditions of Baptists, Methodists, and Holy Ghost believers. Although Ledbetter rarely went to church, he attended the "Meeting at the Building" often enough to know that when the Baptists sang that old hymn, "they rock[ed] the church."[8] It is uncertain whether he learned the old Child ballad "The Gallis Pole" from his mother, but it was a favorite, and certainly the collectors of African-American songs in the 1920s found Child ballads among them.[9]

At the start of the twentieth century, African-American boys became men quickly. Perhaps the quality of his schooling was not appealing, perhaps the family needed money, or perhaps the young man was restless—whatever the reason, Huddie went to work fulltime in the cotton fields in 1902 when he was fourteen, early experience that continued in later years. However much he might enjoy boasting that he could "Pick a Bale of Cotton," he also recognized that "you don't make very much money" working in the "Cotton Fields," especially when the "Boll Weevil" showed up, like Huddie, "lookin' for a home." He was exposed to horse and cattle culture in Texarkana, learning and adopting cowboy songs like "Out on the Western Plains," a variation of the "Old Chisholm Trail" in which Huddie and "a bunch of cowboys" fight off Jesse James (though the outlaw was six-years dead when Huddie was born) and then have an even more unlikely encounter with Buffalo Bill at Bunker Hill.[10]

Huddie acquired his first guitar in 1903, which he soon took to local parties known as sukey jumps, adding dance music to the children's songs and hymns his mother taught him and the cowboy songs he had picked up. No doubt the backwoods parties on Saturday night contributed to the young man's education, but a trip to Shreveport, the local metropolis, when he was sixteen deserved a song. "Fannin Street" is an evocative story filled with tension between a young man lured by all the city has to offer and his mother anxious to keep him on the right path.[11] After Huddie's mother warned him, "[Those] women in Fannin Street gonna be the death of you," and he replied, "Why don't you let me go," she "commenced crying." She worried about women leading him astray, and perhaps rightly so, for it was on Fannin Street that he learned to sing of "Roberta." Between 1906 and 1908, Ledbetter lived in West Texas, picking cotton and making music on the weekends. He married in 1908 and returned to church briefly with his wife, but he soon left both to move to Dallas. There he teamed up in 1910 with Blind Lemon Jefferson, one of the creators of the blues. Huddie credited Jefferson with teaching him songs and playing techniques, though the latter must have learned a lot from the older Ledbetter as well.

About the time he took up with "Blind," as Huddie called him, he also discovered the twelve-string guitar, which soon became his signature instrument. He recalled "Irene" as the first song he learned on that booming guitar, claiming it as his own composition, though he probably learned it from an uncle who had somehow picked up the version written by Gussie Davis in 1886. Certainly Ledbetter made it his own. His song "Titanic" would have come from the time of this collaboration. Both men began to add songs from the emerging body of blues, including "Easy Rider," a male answer to the older "Careless Love," a song they also played. Whereas the woman whose apron strings no longer easily meet around her swelling belly laments of "Careless Love," Jefferson and Ledbetter answered, "See what you done done, you made me love you, now your man done come." The hard realism of the blues and men familiar with Fannin Street or the

Dallas nightlife is evident in the blunt reminder, "You're three times seven and you know what you want to do."[12]

Back in 1903, when Huddie bought his first guitar, he also acquired a pistol, another instrument that would shape his life. In 1915 he was arrested and sentenced to thirty days on the road gang for carrying the gun. He escaped after three days and disappeared into the cotton fields, living as Walter Boyd. In 1917 he was accused of killing Will Stafford in a fight and drew twenty years in the Texas prison system as a result. After an unsuccessful effort to escape, Leadbelly, as he had been newly named in prison, settled in as a model prisoner, perhaps understanding the fate of those who resisted too strenuously. In 1920 he was transferred to Sugarland, where he probably learned "The Midnight Special" as well as such songs from the convict-labor system as "Go Down Old Hannah" and "Old Riley."[13] Since the "Midnight Special" failed to shine its freedom-bearing light on him, Leadbelly was left regretting how "Shorty George" was always taking the women away and leaving the men behind. In 1925 Governor Pat Neff pardoned Leadbelly, who was eligible for release after seven years of good behavior. Later, the singer was fond of attributing his pardon to having performed for the governor in 1923.

When he was released, Ledbetter found a world in which his wife had left him and the blues was the dominant sound. After several years of a rough existence, he returned to prison in 1930, this time for stabbing a white man. He ended up in Angola, one of the worst spots in the Louisiana penal system. As his sentence wore on, two white men, John and Alan Lomax, showed up in 1933, recording songs sung by the prisoners. Leadbelly made an immediate impression on them by both the power of his singing and the range of his repertoire. Although the Lomaxes could not have known it, Leadbelly laid out his life for them in seven songs. He started with "The Western Cowboy," turned to the lures of urban life with "Honey, Take a Whiff on Me" (a song about cocaine), commented obliquely on his current condition with the "Angola Blues," turned to the violence of the African-American urban world with "Frankie and Albert," recalled the old dance tune "You Can't Lose Me Cholly," and offered up a bad-man ballad known as "Ella Speed." Leadbelly was calling upon his past and foreshadowing his future when he included the lovely "Irene."[14] Several songs clearly attributed to "Lead Belly" appeared the next year in *American Ballads and Folk Songs*. Shortly before Ledbetter was pardoned for good behavior in 1934, he wrote to John Lomax, offering to work for him as a driver and general handyman. Ledbetter, who was an ambitious musician, may have seen the elder Lomax as his ticket to a bigger stage. Lomax no doubt was glad to have the extra pair of hands and may have thought having a black ex-convict along would encourage other prisoners to open up. In the brief months between release and going to work for Lomax, Ledbetter returned to Shreveport, where he renewed acquaintances with Martha Promise, who became his second wife early in 1935.

The association proved fruitful for both men, though it soon ended in bitterness.[15] John Lomax was a son of the white South, born just after the Civil War. Although he had spent time in the North pursuing graduate work at the University of Chicago and Harvard, where George Kittredge, the leading disciple of Francis James Child, validated his interest in collecting cowboy songs, Lomax never entirely escaped the racial attitudes of his upbringing. He recognized the beauty and importance of African-American folk songs and did much to make them part of mainstream American culture, but his relationship with Ledbetter was always tinged with paternalism and an expectation of subordination. It was clear exploitation when Lomax published a book of Leadbelly's songs and kept the copyrights. He found Leadbelly often unreliable and at times threatening, impressions the singer sometimes fostered. Ledbetter's frustration may have been expressed best in the simple title "You Don't Know My Mind."

But Ledbetter would not have become Leadbelly without Lomax's promotional efforts. In December 1934, Lomax took his protégé/assistant north, stopping in Philadelphia to have him sing for the Modern Language Association. Remarkably, the good, gray professors responded with enthusiasm to the recently freed convict. By the start of 1935, they were in New York, where Lomax arranged concerts for Leadbelly, using his convict past to drum up interest via thinly veiled racial anxieties. Both men used newspaper interviews and radio programs to develop and embellish the myths of Leadbelly's past. But conflict soon emerged over money, lifestyle, control of the career, and even performance style. Ledbetter was a skilled musician who knew and enjoyed a wide range of American music, from old ballads to modern pop tunes. Lomax wanted him to stick to the folk and prison songs that had brought them to New York, while Leadbelly longed to display his full talents. Ironically, when he slipped up to Harlem to play for African-American audiences, they rejected him as too down-home and country to be appealing. By March, Huddie and Martha had left New York and John Lomax, returning South. Ledbetter found Alan Lomax much easier to deal with and so never lost contact with the family altogether.

In some ways it is remarkable that Leadbelly had any career at all. He was almost fifty when he arrived in New York, and the country was in the midst of the Depression, an economic disaster that ended numerous musical careers that had blossomed in the late 1920s. Although the Ledbetters returned to New York in 1936 with a new manager, Leadbelly never found a secure and profitable niche for himself. He and Martha lived in simple dignity on his earnings from concerts, modest record sales, and occasional radio work. Martha also contributed to the family income with various jobs. Still, they paid their rent and had enough to provide food and housing to homeless folk singers like Guthrie and Brownie McGee. Ledbetter moved to California in 1944–45, attempting, without success, to find roles in the movies, maybe assuming a real singing cowboy should have no trouble finding work. The experience left him bitter, as emerged in "4, 5, and 9," a song about a movie producer who told Huddie to call him at 8:15 in the morning, knowing full well no studio executive was ever in his office that early. The laughter of the telephone receptionist was humiliating.

Although Leadbelly frequently performed for labor and left-wing organizations, he seems to have been unmoved by most American politics, with the notable exception of race relations. His own experience in the South was reinforced in the North, where he found he could not get a meal in the nation's capital if he was with white friends. "Bourgeois Blues" was written in reaction to an argument between Alan Lomax and his landlord in Washington, D.C., in which the latter loudly objected to Huddie and Martha visiting Lomax's apartment as guests. Leadbelly also protested that in the nation's capital, as elsewhere, white folks knew all too well how to "throw a colored man a nickel just to see him bow." In a clever manipulation of the national anthem, Leadbelly declared that in the "land of the brave, home of the free, don't want to be mistreated by no bourgeois."[16] "We're in the Same Boat Brother" makes the telling point that "if you shake one end you're going to rock the other," adding that falling in the water leaves one wet, no matter which side of the boat one falls over. Few of his topical songs, however, had the power and lasting appeal of Guthrie's best verse.

In a tragic ending to his career, Leadbelly died of Lou Gehrig's disease in December 1949, six months before the Weavers went to the top of the popular charts with "Goodnight Irene," a slicked-up version, backed by a studio orchestra, of Leadbelly's signature song, one he had sung for the Lomaxes back in Angola in 1933. He recorded this song himself the year before he died, along with over ninety other songs in his *Last Sessions*, all on magnetic tape that not only produced better quality sound than previous recordings but also included his comments on his songs. During a brief trip to Paris in the spring of 1949, it became clear Huddie was not well, and the disease was diagnosed there. On his return, several concerts were organized, including one with Woody Guthrie and another at the University of Texas, John Lomax's home base, though the latter had recently died. Leadbelly performed many of his early songs in what was clearly a retelling of his life and his brief but critical collaboration with Lomax. Pete Seeger joined him for a few last concerts. After a funeral among friends and fellow musicians in New York City, his body was returned to Caddo Parish in Louisiana, where he had been born, to be interred at the Shiloh Baptist Church. The *New York Times* printed a major obituary, but in his home state only the Shreveport paper bothered even to note his passing.

♯ ♯ ♯

Woodrow Wilson Guthrie was born in Okemah, Oklahoma, on July 14, 1912, shortly after his namesake had been nominated for president.[17] His father, Charles, a local businessman and real estate speculator, was active in Democratic politics in the newly minted state. He both won and lost fixed elections. Although the Guthries were middle class and put on a fine display for their neighbors, they never quite made it into the upper echelons of Okemah society before their troubles started. Woody's mother, Nora, was close to her son and taught him many old songs, which she had learned from her own mother. But Nora was afflicted with Huntington's chorea, a genetic disorder that eventually renders its victims unstable, moody, and violent. When Woody was only seven, an older sister died from burns received when her dress caught fire. The girl claimed she set herself on fire to scare her mother, but the townspeople were unsure because Nora was already acting very strangely. She would eventually be committed to a state hospital in 1927, shortly after throwing a lit kerosene lamp on her husband while he was napping. Charles survived the ordeal but was unable to care for his family; so, at the age of fifteen, Woody was more or less on his own. Given the situation at home during the previous years, as his mother drifted "away over yonder in the minor keys" and his father struggled, increasingly unsuccessfully, with his speculations, Woody may have felt a certain relief to be free of the turmoil and tension.[18]

From an early age, Woody demonstrated remarkable creative talents. Although he was not particularly gifted in conversation, he could always write imaginatively and easily composed new verses to songs. He was at heart a poet who simply applied many of the old tunes he learned from his mother to his verses. Perhaps it was his way of honoring her. He was also a clever cartoonist, a talent he retained until Huntington's chorea cut him off from the rest of the world at about the age of forty. He loved to perform for people, singing, dancing, and generally mugging to whomever would watch and listen. Guthrie was able to do well in school if he was interested in the subjects; but he never graduated from high school, which was not surprising, given his unsettled home life. Throughout the rest of his life, until the disease stopped him, Woody readily added new songs to his repertoire, from family, friends, acquaintances, and the radio. Guthrie's family life collapsed around him in 1927, the year the Carter Family and Jimmy Rodgers were discovered at the famous recording session in Bristol, Virginia. It is clear that Guthrie heard Carter Family songs, for many of his most famous songs were set to tunes they made popular.

Once Woody had to start fending for himself, he never again truly settled down. He moved to Pampa, Texas, for a while to live with his father, who had recovered from his burns. Here Woody vibrated from one place to another, reading widely, getting religion briefly, working sporadically at sign painting and music, and acquiring a wife in 1933, and then children. By then, the nation's woes in the form of the Great Depression had been added to Woody's family problems. From Texas he was well situated to watch the dust storms roll in and the Okies roll out on their way west to California. In 1935 he wrote new lyrics to the tune of Carson Robison's "Billy the Kid," appropriately titled "Dusty Old Dust" and later to become famous as "So Long, It's Been Good to Know You."[19] This song, the first of his memorable lyrics, most of which were written between 1935 and 1941, was in many ways a testimony to his past and future life, for he admitted that, dust storm or not, "I've got to be drifting along."

Soon after, Woody began to do some "Hard Travelin'." He rambled across the country, hitching rides, caging a little cash by singing, and generally "going down the road feeling bad," determined, however, that he would not, or at least should not, "be treated this a-way." In 1937 he wrote the "Talking Dust Bowl Blues." In six verses he captured the hardship of the farmers forced off their land when the rains stopped and the dust clouds blew in. Never a farmer himself, Woody was remarkable at empathizing with his neighbors' plight, a trait he demonstrated many times over in his songs. Surprisingly, Woody's fortune looked up during a trip to California in 1937, when his cousin Jack recruited him to be part of a two-man singing cowboy act. Public performances with Woody on horseback were a bit dicey, as this son of the plains had a distinct aversion to his mounts, and they to him, but the duo soon found safer work in radio studios.

Through Jack, Woody was introduced to Maxine Crissman, who soon teamed up with Guthrie as Woody and Lefty Lou on KFVD in Los Angeles.

The two proved so popular they were given several shows a day and sold songbooks to their audience. The shows were pure Woody, unrehearsed, rambling, and engaging. One critical moment in his life came when an African-American listener wrote to protest a racial slur Woody had casually used. Woody's father had participated in efforts to deny black voters their rights in Oklahoma and had even joined the Ku Klux Klan for a time, so Woody had acquired his biases without thinking. When faced with this challenge to his attitudes, he quickly concluded he was wrong, apologized, and removed all such language from the songbook. He had come a long way from his roots when he became friends with Huddie and Martha Ledbetter. A contract and guaranteed salary from KFVD in the fall of 1937 led Woody to bring his wife, Mary, to California, after she had spent months at home in Texas with the children.

But Woody could not stand success. After a brief and contentious fling with XELO, one of the high-powered stations just over the border in Mexico, out of range of the limits placed on broadcast power by the U.S. government, Woody returned to KFVD, though not for long. Regular work and a family nearby sent him on the road early in 1938. As he roamed around the country, Woody became more involved in left-wing and labor politics. His songs soon reflected this.

For some reason, the story of Pretty Boy Floyd appealed to him, and in 1939 he wrote a ballad in Floyd's honor, depicting this unpleasant thug in true social-bandit terms. Instead of recognizing Floyd's robbery of a post office, netting three hundred fifty dollars in pennies (surely one of America's most awkward hauls), his thirty bank robberies, ten murders, or ignominious death in an Ohio corn field, Guthrie made Floyd into a folk hero. In the ballad "Pretty Boy Floyd," Floyd turns to a life of crime after killing a deputy sheriff who swore in his wife's presence. According to Guthrie, Floyd is soon blamed for every unsolved crime in Oklahoma, a nice trick since most of Pretty Boy's deeds were done back East. After verses recounting mythical stories of Pretty Boy paying mortgages and leaving one-thousand-dollar bills under napkins after he had begged a meal, Guthrie finishes with a memorable scene. He has Floyd send Christmas dinners to the poor in Oklahoma City. Moreover, as the Depression ground on and families lost their homes and livelihoods, Guthrie used the song to remind people that in this world some men would "rob you with a six gun and some with a fountain pen." Conveniently forgetting whatever happened to the families of the men Pretty Boy killed, Guthrie asserted, "You won't ever see an outlaw drive a family from their home."

186 • LIFE FLOWS ON IN ENDLESS SONG

About this time Woody encountered Will Geer, with whom he teamed up briefly. When they split, Geer asked Woody to come to New York sometime. After a quick and tension-filled visit to Pampa, where Mary had gone after Woody hit the road, he was on to New York, arriving there early in 1940, just in time for Geer's "Grapes of Wrath Evening" and a remarkable creative burst.

Woody had a lot on his mind from his travels around the country, much of which would come out in songs in the next two years. February 1940 started with "Slipknot," an angry attack on lynching set to the old children's song "She'll Be Coming 'Round the Mountain." Three weeks later, upset over the careless optimism he thought pervasive in Irving Berlin's popular "God Bless America," Guthrie penned a response, "This Land Is Your Land." Guthrie set the song to a familiar Carter Family song, "Little Darlin', Pal of Mine," but he may also have known the old Baptist hymn "Oh My Lovin' Brother," which the Carters borrowed. Although Guthrie would later cooperate in shortening this song to make it more acceptable to the American public, the original makes no bones about Guthrie's sense of outrage about what was happening to his fellow Americans. The familiar Whitmanesque celebrations of "sparkling sands" and "wheat fields waving" that he so loved about his country are all there, but so too are protests against signs declaring land to be private property and Woody's radical preference for the blank backs of the signs, which excluded no one. As Woody rambled around the country, he was not seeing the same America as Berlin. Encountering hungry people in food lines left him wondering "if God blessed America for me." At the bottom of the sheet on which he wrote the song, Guthrie added, "All you can write is what you see."[20]

In April, Woody was asked to write a ballad based on John Steinbeck's *The Grapes of Wrath*, which he did. According to Pete Seeger, he and Woody located a typewriter, paper, a half-gallon jug of wine, and a place to write. Woody set to work that evening. When Pete woke up the next morning, the wine was gone, Woody was asleep, and in the typewriter were seventeen verses to "Tom Joad," neatly summing up the novel. Woody used the familiar ballad of "John Hardy" for the tune, an appropriate choice because "Tom Joad" is clearly a story of a social bandit forced into activity the law viewed as criminal but his friends and neighbors saw as justified. The story and song finish with Tom reassuring his mother, "Wherever men are fightin' for their rights, that's where I'm gonna be."[21]

The next two years were, even for Woody Guthrie, tumultuous. New York responded well to his talents, and he soon had steady work writing and on the radio, making enough money to bring Mary and the kids East. Alan Lomax was active in fostering Woody's career, and Woody exchanged songs with numerous others, including Pete Seeger and Lee Hays. But Woody could not stand prosperity, especially if it came from working under discipline imposed by large institutions. Much to Mary's dismay, Woody abandoned his work and the city, loaded the family into a car, and headed for California, with no particular prospects there. Unfortunately for those around him who liked some stability, impulsiveness did have a way of paying off for Woody, even if only for a short time.

After several months with no work and little writing, Woody was hired by the Bonneville Power Administration as a temporary laborer to write songs promoting the project. In the month he worked for the BPA, he wrote twenty-six songs, which, given their overall quality, made that the most productive month of his life. "Roll On Columbia," set to the tune of Leadbelly's "Irene," captures the sense of the wilderness that gave rise to the Columbia River, before glorying in the work of men to subdue the mighty waters whose "power is turning our darkness to dawn." Guthrie links the project backwards to Thomas Jefferson's commission sending Lewis and Clark to explore the Louisiana Purchase, and to Phil Sheridan's efforts in the 1850s to fight off the Indians who were reluctant to give up their land. Woody may have had an awakening about the treatment of African Americans in the United States, but he does not seem to have shed his Western view of the Native Americans. The song admires the Grand Coulee Dam as "the mightiest thing ever built by a man" and celebrates the working men who tamed nature to the needs of civilization. In 1941 Guthrie was no environmentalist, but few were at that time. In the course of seven verses, Guthrie invokes and celebrates nature and technology, the past and the future, a president and working men, sweeping history and local places, conflict and triumph.

During the month, Woody adapted other tunes to the project. "Brown's Ferry Blues" became "Jackhammer John," a hammering man in the tradition of John Henry, and "The Wabash Cannonball" became "The Grand Coulee Dam." Although not directly related to the Bonneville project, Guthrie also wrote what many consider to be his most powerful song, "Pastures of Plenty," set to the old murdered-girl ballad "Pretty Polly." This song alone gives Guthrie the right to claim status as a poet of the first rank, an heir to Walt Whitman, whose works he knew and admired. The same love of the Western landscapes that pervades his other songs is evident here, as "green pastures of plenty [come] from dry desert ground" to produce peaches, prunes, and grapes. But the song truly belongs to the migrant workers whose voices are heard throughout. Guthrie sang on their behalf of long days tending and picking crops, and hard traveling from one field or orchard to another, always on the move to pick and load the crops from these "pastures of plenty." He knew how marginal the workers were in the eyes of many, momentarily visible as they passed by, but then quickly gone as "we come with the dust and go with the wind."

As World War II unfolded in Europe at the time, and the United States teetered on the edge of involvement, Guthrie recognized the patriotism in the hearts of the workers for whom it was uncertain if "God blessed America" when he had the migrants declare that the land "must always be free," though he may also have had in mind freedom from control by rich men or large corporations. This skinny little man with an artistic soul and a severe problem with authority later joined the Merchant Marine, along with his friend Cisco Houston, and survived three voyages across the Atlantic and two ships blown up under him, taking time out between voyages to record for Moe Asch. Woody's patriotism in shipping out was tempered by the fact that the army was threatening to draft him, and he wondered if he could survive that organization. It finally did in May 1945, and he did, as a thirty-three-year-old typist and sign painter.

While Woody was out West, several of his friends, including Pete Seeger and Lee Hays, formed a group known as the Almanac Singers. The group favored union and other left-wing causes and songs. In 1941 Woody finally decided the West was not where he wanted to be and dragged his family back to New York, where Mary finally decided she had had enough and headed back to Texas for good. He soon joined the Almanac Singers, with their floating and flexible membership. Although Guthrie did not found the group, he soon came to dominate it, setting a standard for lack of rehearsal and uncertain attendance at performances that eventually drove Seeger and Hays to form a more polished, professional group known as the Weavers. Back in New York by fall, Guthrie reacted to the news in October of the sinking of the *Reuben James,* an American destroyer escorting ships carrying war material to Great Britain, by writing "Reuben James," using the Carter Family's "Wildwood Flower" for the melody. At first a long and formless list of names, it was shaped, with help from the Almanac Singers, into a memorial for the "hard fighting men both of honor and of fame" who died two months before Pearl Harbor. Ever concerned with the common man, Guthrie asked, "What were their names?"

In 1942 Woody met the woman who would be his second wife and the mother of Arlo, the only child to follow his father into folk singing. Marjorie

Greenblatt was a dancer with the Martha Graham Company in 1942, and like Woody, she was married to someone else when they met. By 1943 their first child, Cathy Ann, was born. Woody settled into a reasonably happy life in New York, traveling some, performing, and writing. He was unable to persuade Uncle Sam that he had more value as an artist than as a sailor or soldier, but he returned safely to Marjorie and married her in the fall of 1945, after both were divorced. Marjorie was more in tune with the life of an artist than Mary had ever been, and so she survived Woody's peculiarities more readily. But the couple was sorely tried when an electrical short in a radio led to a fire that caused Cathy's death at the age of four, a tragic recurrence of the fires that had haunted Woody's early life.

In 1943 Guthrie published his autobiography, *Bound for Glory*, with some success. After the war, he turned more and more to writing, attempting plays and a novel. But in 1948 he wrote one last great song, "Deportee, or the Plane Wreck at Los Gatos Canyon." Inspired by a news account of a plane crash that had killed migrant workers being expelled from the country, Guthrie once again rallied to the cause of the working man and woman, insisting they be remembered as real people. Perhaps Huntington's chorea was already affecting his creative force, for he never found a tune for the verse, but he was able to summon the full power of his poetic imagination for the lyrics. He begins the song with a striking parallel between the waste of an over-productive agricultural system, in which peaches are left "rotting" and oranges thrown into dumps, and the loss of the lives of those who harvested the crops. Guthrie describes the frustration of migrant workers, who are accepted when needed and rejected when not, dying unknown and unmourned by most Americans. Guthrie uses the chorus to insist that these were real people, individuals with families and lives that deserved respect, however much the news media referred to them only as "deportees." He, however, insisted on saying goodbye to Juan and Rosalita, as well as, "Adiós mis amigos, Jesús y María." Ironically, Guthrie, a man who did relatively little physical labor in his life, was more prone to celebrating working men and women than Leadbelly, who had more than enough firsthand knowledge of the fields and farms.

Not long after, Guthrie began to behave more bizarrely as Huntington's chorea took control of his personality, sending him over to the "minor keys" to find his mother. By 1953 Woody was scaring Marjorie so badly that she left him. He encountered Anneke Van Kirk and soon lured her away from her husband, even though she was half Woody's age. They married, but the union did not last because the girl soon discovered she had taken on far more than she had bargained for. Woody was in and out of hospitals for the next several years, finally requiring permanent care in 1956. As his condition worsened, Marjorie stepped in to see that he was properly cared for. He died in 1967, his great gifts as a poet and musician cut short years before his body passed on. In assessing Woody's songs, Robert Cantwell points out the paradox of Guthrie's "imagery that loves, reveres and glorifies, [and] a language that points, exposes, rebukes."[22]

♯ ♯ ♯

It is hard to imagine American folk singing since 1950 without the influence of Huddie Ledbetter and Woody Guthrie. All four of the Weavers knew both men well and were active in promoting their legacy by singing their songs and honoring their memory. Young Bob Zimmerman, fresh out of Minnesota, visited Woody in the hospital and sang his songs to him in a remarkably similar style. Although the young acolyte later changed his last name to Dylan, he did not have to alter his appearance and wardrobe much to look like Guthrie. When Bruce Springsteen began to compose lyrics for social commentary, he modeled himself on Dylan, only later learning he was following in the footsteps of Guthrie. Tom Paxton may be the closest to Woody in terms of accessible lyrics and easy melodies. Odetta, glorious songster that she is, has relied on Leadbelly songs for many of her own standards.[23] To hear Little Richard's ecstatic and erotic rendition of Leadbelly's classic "Rock Island Line" or Taj Mahal engage with "Bourgeois Blues" is to appreciate how much Leadbelly's songs still mean today. A CD and video titled *A Vision Shared* includes many of America's best contemporary artists performing the songs of these two men. The Rock and Roll Hall of Fame inducted both singers early in its existence. All that is needed to recognize the folk roots of rock and roll is to listen to Leadbelly sing "Good Morning Blues." And who knows how many amateur musicians and living-room performers have at least one Guthrie or Leadbelly song among their favorites?

Despite the importance of these two men in helping folk songs live on, the music and lyrics themselves are what appeal. And themes of universal import. A semi-random list of modern songs in the folk style indicates that the daily lives of many Americans are still attached to those of their ancestors and with many of the same human concerns. Tom Paxton's "Lesson Too Late for the Learning" or Bob Dylan's "Don't Think Twice" demonstrate that the perils of courtship still can produce great songs. Likewise, children continue to need songs, which their parents are happy to sing when the songs are such gems as Paxton's "Marvelous Toy," Tom Glazer's "The Wheels on the

Bus," or the delightfully silly "On Top of Spaghetti," which metamorphosed from "On Top of Old Smokey." The Irish Rovers made the wonderful Shel Silverstein poem "The Unicorn" into an even more engaging song with their lilting melody.

Curiously, religion does not seem to have produced much modern music in the folk style, though moralizing is still evident. Perhaps Irving Berlin's "God Bless America" has crossed over into the oral tradition, but its roots connect as much with the national civic religion and its continuous evolution since the Revolution, as with the Great Awakenings and later revivals. Pete Seeger's gentle "Turn, Turn, Turn," from the book of Ecclesiastes—and a rare modern echo of the scriptures—reminds us that there is indeed "a time to every purpose under heaven." War, on the other hand, continues to bring forth creative efforts. In the 1950s and 1960s, recent memories of World War II and the emerging cold war produced not only Pete Seeger's classic "Where Have All the Flowers Gone?" with its rhetorical question "When will we ever learn?" but also Ed McCurdy's "Last Night I Had the Strangest Dream," in which the whole world "all agreed to put an end to war." Bob Dylan's "Blowin' in the Wind" adapted the melody from "Many Thousands Go" to lament the enduring power of both war and racial prejudice. During the Vietnam War, many learned at least a few lines and the tune of the patriotic "The Green Beret," though the song did not survive the conflict. In a transformation appropriate to folk song tradition, "Tie a Yellow Ribbon 'Round the Old Oak Tree" has been adapted to several recent conflicts in the Middle East, as families wait to welcome home their young men and women from war.

Popular songs like "Nine to Five," from the movie of the same name, remind us of the way work has changed in an economy that is increasingly office and service oriented, but few folk-style songs have found this new work regimen the stuff from which songs are made. The "Frozen Logger" is a wonderful, recent spoof of the Paul Bunyan myth, telling the story of a larger-than-life logger who "stirs coffee with his thumb." Since the waitress in the song is looking for another man as tough as her lost logger lover, this could also be about the perils of courtship. Woody Guthrie wrote many songs for and about the labor movement, but that tradition has not continued, perhaps reflecting the decline in union activity in the country. Merle Travis produced two memorable songs about life in the mines and the mining towns in the late 1940s, with "Sixteen Tons" becoming a national hit in 1955 after Tennessee Ernie Ford sang it on a Labor Day television broadcast. The chorus that remarks on both the situation of "another day older and deeper in debt" and the fear the miner has of being called by Saint Peter because, as he puts it, "I owe my soul to the company store," engaged and still engages America; many can relate to the demands of the remote and dehumanizing corporations that control their lives. "Dark as a Dungeon" is at least as good as "Sixteen Tons," though not as well known, possibly because it deals more directly with life in the mines, where it is indeed as "dark as a dungeon, . . . where the danger is double and the pleasures are few"; but few Americans can relate that to their lives, working as they do in secure, fluorescent environments.

Railroads and other forms of transportation continue to inspire folk-style songs. Elizabeth Cotton's lovely "Freight Train" may have been composed early in the twentieth century, but it became popular only after the Seeger family promoted her talents in the 1950s. Of course, few have learned this enchanting melody with a guitar played upside down as Cotton did to accommodate her left-handed playing.[24] Steve Goodman's "City of New Orleans" is a wonderful song about the "southbound odyssey" in search of the "disappearing railroad blues" that mourns the passing of the once mystical, magical iron horse. Goodman may not have been aware that he was recounting a trip back down the line, the Illinois Central, that many African Americans rode north to escape the "Boll Weevil" and the "Angola Blues." His regrets for a lost time harmonize with the need for "Casey Jones" to make up lost time on the way south on the same route.

Aside from Woody Guthrie's "Car Song," in which he made car sounds to amuse his children, the automobile has been more the subject of popular than folk music. But the aluminum bird has produced songs of farewell that are reminiscent of those sung about the iron horse. "In the Early Morning Rain" by Gordon Lightfoot and "Leaving on a Jet Plane" by John Denver both capture the ache of parting that is so vital to many railroad blues. Traveling farther, faster has done nothing to alleviate the pain of separation. Lightfoot also connected with seafaring songs and the dangers of the deep with his "Wreck of the Edmund Fitzgerald," based on the real wreck of an iron-ore ship on Lake Superior. In a less serious vein, "Monongahela Sal" reaches back to murdered-girl ballads like "Banks of the Ohio" and warnings about "Careless Love" to tell the tale of a more intrepid woman. When faced with betrayal and attempted murder by a steamboat captain who woos her and pushes her overboard, Sal swims ashore, hops a train headed down river, and shoots her false-hearted lover with a six-gun she seizes "from a yard bull who tried to molest her." No frail, fainting girls for the twentieth century!

As in earlier centuries, Americans continue to be a mobile people and continue to sing about their wandering. Tom Paxton recalled with fondness his friend the "Ramblin' Boy," while Richard Farina urged his listeners to "Pack Up Your Sorrows," most of which came from being on the road, where "nobody knows where you are." Farina summed up years of American wandering: "Too many highways, too many byways, and nobody's walking behind." Although Frederick Jackson Turner tried to foresee what the official closing of the frontier in 1890 meant, the West has kept its appeal to American dreams, as its well-populated states can attest. *Oklahoma*, one of Broadway's first great musicals, captures these dreams. *Paint Your Wagon* includes "They Call the Wind Maria," a sad and wistful song about being far from home, where there may be a name for the wind, but "there ain't no name for lonely." The gold miner who sings the song could have been another Joe Bowers. "Ghost Riders in the Sky," set to the old tune of "When Johnny Comes Marching Home," fits well with cowboy realism about the hard life following the herd, though in this case the life is made worse by having to chase the "devil's herd across that endless sky."

Despite rising standards of living and the triumphs of consumer capitalism, songs still protest the inequalities of American life and uncertainties of hard times. In the 1930s "Brother, Can You Spare a Dime" caught the despair of the Great Depression and the frustration of those who had built America but were now out of work. After World War II, another depression led Tom Paxton to write "Standing on the Edge of Town," about one more worker forced to leave home to find a way to support his family. The civil rights movement in the 1950s and 1960s reached back to old hymns, often reshaped by labor unions, to find songs to rally support and create unity, reminding the singers with optimism, not only that "We Shall Not Be Moved," but also that "We Shall Overcome." Of course, hard times have still called forth hard men, whether they be "Big, Bad John" or "Bad, Bad Leroy Brown." Such men live on in rap and hip-hop music, where most resemble Stagolee rather than Jesse James.

♯ ♯ ♯

The hymn asks, "How can I keep from singing?" How indeed, when there is so much that needs the comfort and release of song, that wants the safety of oblique and opaque satire, that requires the expression of joy and sorrow, hope and despair. From the social commentary embedded in "Froggy Went a Courtin'" and "The Fox," which hint at the discontent that sent migrants to the New World despite the dangers of the "Golden Vanity," to the question central to both "Where have all the flowers gone?" and "When will we ever learn?" Americans have relied on their songs to reassure themselves that because there is "a time to every purpose under heaven," if we can only hold on long enough, "we *shall* overcome."

Coda
Thinking about Folk Songs

The history of the collection and publication of folk songs in the United States begins in 1857–58, with Harvard professor Francis James Child's *English and Scottish Ballads*. Some of the most important contributions to this history to be discussed in the coda are summarized in table 1.

In both his initial work on English and Scottish ballads (1857–58) and his magnum opus of the 305 ballads he considered definitive (1882–98), Child was concerned solely with the texts and worked exclusively from manuscripts in libraries and published volumes. Child was interested only in certifiably old songs, with European origins, present in England and Scotland. He included numerous versions but believed there should be one prime text from which all others derived. His approach to songs as literary texts detached from the music dominated folk song scholarship until well into the twentieth century. Child's example need not have held such sway, for in 1867 the publication of *Slave Songs of the United States* offered a counterexample of living songs collected in the field from those who sang them, and it provided music along with the lyrics. William Allen, Charles Ware, and Lucy McKim Garrison did not indicate who sang the songs, but they did provide a general sense of where the songs were being sung.[1]

The tendency among historians of folk song scholarship is to start the story with Child's work, turn to the expansion of the canon to include songs other than English and Scottish ballads as part of America's heritage, and conclude with a shift in emphasis to songs as living entities with meaning

Table 1. Identifying, Expanding, and Promoting the Body of American Folk Songs

1857–58	Francis James Child, *English and Scottish Ballads.*
1867	William F. Allen, Charles P. Ware, and Lucy M. Garrison, *Slave Songs of the United States.*
1871	Fisk Jubilee Singers begins its tour presenting African-American songs.
1882–98	Francis James Child, *The English and Scottish Popular Ballads,* 305 ballads.
1888	American Folklore Society founded; begins publishing the *Journal of American Folklore,* including songs.
1888–1904	Early efforts to record folk songs on wax cylinders. 1900–1904: Charles Lummis recorded Spanish folk songs in California.
1910	John A. Lomax, *Cowboy Songs and Other Frontier Ballads.*
1917	Olive Dame Campbell and Cecil Sharp, *English Folk Songs from the Southern Appalachians,* revised in 1932 to 2 vols., edited by Maud Karpeles.
1920	OKeh Records issues Mamie Smith's "Crazy Blues"; the first "race" record.
1923	Ralph Peer of OKeh Records issues Fiddlin' John Carson's "hillbilly" music.
1923	Robert W. Gordon begins to edit "Old Songs That Men Have Sung" for *Adventure* magazine.
1924	Vernon Dalhart records "Wreck of Old '97," which sells several million copies.
1925–28	Dorothy Scarborough, Howard Odum and Guy Johnson, and Newman White publish books on African-American folk songs.
1927	Carl Sandburg, *The American Songbag.*
1927–28	Robert W. Gordon writes a fifteen-part series on American folk songs for *New York Times Magazine.*
1928	Robert W. Gordon becomes the first director of the Library of Congress Archive of American Folk Song.
1932	John and Alan Lomax embark on tour, recording mostly African-American songs in Southern prisons.
1933	The Lomaxes first record Huddie Ledbetter, known as "Leadbelly."
1934	John and Alan Lomax, *American Ballads and Folk Songs.*
1940	"Grapes of Wrath" concert at Carnegie Hall; first major folk song concert, with Leadbelly and Woody Guthrie, among others.
1940–41	Woody Guthrie writes "This Land Is Your Land," "Tom Joad," "Roll On Columbia," and "Pastures of Plenty," all to old folk tunes.
1948	Leadbelly records *Last Sessions* on high-fidelity tape; released in 1953.
1949	Stith Thompson establishes first Ph.D. in folklore at Indiana University.
1950	The Weavers top the charts with "Goodnight Irene," Leadbelly's signature song, six months after he died.
1952	Harry Smith, *Anthology of American Folk Music.*
Christmas 1955	The Weavers concert at Carnegie Hall signals their return to performing after blacklist.
1958	The Kingston Trio releases "Ballad of Tom Dooley."
1959–60	Alan Lomax again records in the South; issued on LPs by Atlantic and Prestige Records in 1960–65; thirteen CDs, remixed and expanded from the LPs, released by Rounder in 1997–98 as *Southern Journey.*
1999–2001	Alan Lomax releases *Deep River of Song,* a series made from field recordings of the 1930s.

to those who still sing and compose them. While Child clearly dominated early academic scholarship, with many collections into the twentieth century organized into a "Child and other" format, this focus ignores not only the collection of slave songs and the public acclaim of the Fisk Jubilee Singers as they brought slave songs to the wider world but also such pioneering efforts to expand the canon as John Lomax's 1910 book on cowboy songs. Lomax spent a year at Harvard, from 1906 to 1907, where he was encouraged to pursue cowboy songs by Child's most illustrious student, George L. Kittredge. Thus, when Olive Dame Campbell and Cecil Sharp collected many old British ballads from people living in the southern Appalachian Mountains between 1907 and 1916, which they published with the music included, they were adopting techniques already current in other parts of song catching.

One of the most important innovations in the collection and dissemination of folk songs was the application of recording technology and its steady improvement in quality. For the first time, strangers could hear how a singer actually sang or played a song, which led to recognition of the place of performance style in understanding a folk song. Likewise, collectors no longer had to ask singers to perform a song more than once while they transcribed the lyrics and music. Songs took on life as still current in someone's memory, moving out of the library or museum. From fragile wax cylinders before 1900, to bulky machines that cut metal disks in the 1930s, to magnetic tape after World War II—recording technology made rapid strides in ease of use, fidelity of sound, and lasting quality. With the advent first of LPs and then CDs, significant numbers of old recordings, including some field recordings, have become available to collectors, especially since 1990.

John and Alan Lomax have been justly celebrated for their fieldwork in the South from the 1930s to the 1960s, during which time they recorded thousands of songs and made a point of emphasizing the centrality of African-American folk songs to the country's national past. Here too others had already pioneered. Harry Smith noted that the first folk songs had been recorded by 1888, with others following in the closing years of the nineteenth century.[2] The 1920s were remarkable for commercial efforts to record and sell "race" and "hillbilly" music to niche markets of African Americans and Southern mountain folk, respectively. Although record companies like OKeh and acquisitions specialists like Ralph Peer had no academic interest in folk songs, they still contributed to the preservation of the past. In the same decade, radio stations played old-time music to appreciative audiences across the country. Interest in African-American songs was demonstrated in the 1920s when Howard Odum and Guy Johnson, Dorothy Scarborough, and Newman White published collections of "Negro folk songs," based on several decades of traditional song catching.[3] Even the Lomaxes' 1934 book of American folk songs intended for popular consumption had been anticipated by seven years by Carl Sandburg.

For almost a century and a half, folk songs have been collected and made available to the public, sometimes in scholarly form, sometimes via commercial promotions, and sometimes, as with the Lomaxes, where scholarship and promotion mix. The definition of folk songs worthy of inclusion has been extended to include lyrics and music in which Francis James Child would have had no interest. With recording technology, performance style has been incorporated into the understanding of folk songs. Listening to recorded songs, or even learning songs from books, may encourage us to imitate the songs as closely as possible; but the trend has also been to move folk songs away from some "pure" relic of the past, uncorrupted by modern life and in need of careful preservation, to recognizing them as an organic part of our lives. Folk songs continue to bring meaning as we sing them, and we have permission to fit and refit the music to our lives.

♯ ♯ ♯

Beyond the collection and publication of folk songs, scholarship in the field as it connects to history divides into three broad categories. Folklorists and musicologists have produced a number of excellent histories on songs or types of songs. A few examples follow. Norm Cohen's *Long Steel Rail: The Railroad in American Folksong* is a model of scholarship about the origins and history of many railroad songs.[4] Steve Turner's recent history of "Amazing Grace" not only connects the lyrics to the events of composer John Newton's life but also traces its emergence through creative misunderstanding as one of America's best-loved folk hymns.[5] Biographers Charles Wolfe and Kip Lornell, and Mark Zwonitzer give us important insights on writers/performers like Huddie Ledbetter and the Carter Family.[6] Robert Cantwell and Benjamin Filene provide histories on the folk revival(s) of the twentieth century, while general histories of American music, with their emphasis on composers and performers, recognize the place of folk songs in our musical past.[7]

Historians have had surprisingly little to say about or from folk songs. John Mack Faragher makes effective use of folk songs to uncover aspects of "the community of feeling" on the frontier in Sugar Creek, Illinois.[8] Jack Larkin reminds us that the "practice of music" played a central role in everyday life in the early nineteenth century.[9] Lawrence Levine mobilizes African-American folk songs to explore slave consciousness and the role of bad men like Stagolee and Railroad Bill in African-American culture.[10] Sean Wilentz and Greil Marcus make us aware of the enduring importance of both traditional and recent ballads in American culture.[11] But no one has systematically examined how folk songs fit into our past or what they can tell us about American history.[12]

One might think that any proper history should be organized chronologically, but in any work in which the primary focus is on the songs, a topical organization should prevail. A strict chronological organization is problematic. The very nature of folk songs is that we do not know precisely when or where many of them were first composed. We must infer a date from the content of the lyrics and/or the first record of the song's existence. Moreover, many songs that can be dated to the seventeenth century or earlier were still current and being collected in the twentieth century, suggesting deep meaning that transcends time and place. To limit discussion of "Barbara Allen" to the seventeenth century, when Samuel Pepys first mentioned it in his diary, seems unnecessarily time bound. "Froggy Went a Courtin'" remains a popular children's song, albeit with social lessons better fitted to an earlier era, even though scholars have traced it back to the 1580s. Of course "Yankee Doodle" and the "Battle Hymn of the Republic" can and will be connected to the Revolution and the Civil War, respectively, and certain labor songs arose from particular strikes that shaped their content; but on the whole, a topical organization with appropriate attention to chronology is best. Readers may find it instructive to compare the topical organization adopted here to the way the Lomaxes and Carl Sandburg arranged their material.

♯ ♯ ♯

Although, or perhaps because, I am by training and experience an historian, I want to offer a few brief suggestions about ways to think about folk songs that have proven useful to me. I am indebted to many of the authors listed in the bibliography for the compilation that follows. The order in no way expresses the relative importance of my observations, as particular perspectives may be more important for some songs than for others. In general, the first half of the suggestions deals with the songs themselves and their internal workings, while the second half is directed more to thinking about their meanings, though the two broad categories are not easily separated.

1. SONG TYPES. Songs can be thought of as fitting somewhere on several overlapping continuums. One common division places the European ballad, with its emphasis on a long, narrative story told by a single singer in an unvarying way, at one end of a continuum. At the opposite end is African group singing, which is characterized by general involvement with the song through call from a leader and response from the group, and a tendency to keep a song going for as long as anyone can think up a new verse. A second continuum places songs that stress action at one end and those that emphasize emotion at the other. Along these continuums, songs can address, among other themes, personal commentary or expression of emotion, religious sentiment (personal salvation or end of the world), social attitudes or relations, protest, work rhythms, criminal or other antisocial behavior (frequently without explicit moral comment), satire and parody, fooling around, children (via lullabies, games, or lessons), or folk lyric (assembled fragments).

2. PATTERNS OF RHYMES AND VERSES. Two questions to ask about a song are, What is the pattern of verse and chorus? and How does the rhyme scheme work? In a four-line verse, do all the lines rhyme, or do the rhymes occur with the first and third, second and fourth, only the second and fourth, etc.? This can be indicated schematically as aaaa, abab, or abcb, respectively. The rhyme scheme and relation of verse and chorus can influence how easy it is to remember a song.

3. MUSIC. In thinking about the music itself, the most important aspect involves the relation of music to the message or the purpose of the song. For example, songs in Western culture that express sorrow are often in a minor key, or, like the blues, use flatted or "bent" notes; some tasks (hammering or hauling) are best accompanied by two or four beats to a measure, while others use three; marching may require a moderate tempo or speed, while dancing can vary from rapid to slow. The internal workings of the tune can reinforce meaning, such as the three descending notes at end of the "Tom Dooley" chorus, wherein Dooley is informed he is "bound to die."

4. VOICE. Songs vary in the number of voices and in the consistency of voice throughout the song. The verses of "Tom Dooley" are singular while the chorus is plural. In the same song, direction of address shifts between the verse, in which Dooley seems to be speaking to us (or perhaps to himself), and the chorus, where he is on the receiving end of the comment. Dialogue is common in folk songs, with men and women, or authorities and subjects, speaking to each other. Attention to the gender, race, and class of the characters in the song can shed light on its meaning.

5. SETTING. Songs are often grounded in a specific and sometimes real time and place, though they may often be localized by singers, who prefer to give them a familiar context.

6. NARRATIVE STRUCTURE. In songs with definite narrative structures, such as ballads, it is worth paying attention to the way the story works. As with any good story, certain parts of a ballad deserve more attention than others; so there are frequently jumps in time from one important scene to another, with clusters of verses condensing and dramatizing parts of the story, and other verses providing contextual narration. This is sometimes referred to as "leap and linger." Frequently a narrator provides useful background to aid in the understanding of critical dialogue among the main characters. Other songs may assume a situation is so universal as to need no assistance to its being understood.

7. USE OF FAMILIAR/UNEXPECTED DEVICES. Folks songs commonly adopt familiar phrases, such as "lily white hand," "milk white steed," or "red, red rose." Listeners may be invited to "gather round" or "come all ye." While these clichés may seem repetitive or tiresome, they also establish a sense of comfort and connection. But occasionally a song will use an unexpected phrase or metaphor, and that is worth noting either for its artistic touch or as evidence of the evolution of a song.

8. UNFAMILIAR WORDS AND PHRASES. Old folk songs or songs from groups with a special vocabulary (whalers, miners, etc.) may include unfamiliar words or phrases that must be defined to enhance the understanding of the song. It is not always possible to determine the meaning of a word, especially when local dialect introduces a regionalism, but an effort should be made. Of course, many choruses contain nonsense syllables and words.

9. METAPHORS, FIGURES OF SPEECH, SYMBOLISM. Many folk songs are straightforward in meaning, but not all. Thus it is essential to be alert for symbolic language, especially when singers may be deliberately trying to obscure the meaning of a song from uninitiated listeners. It is a commonplace for many songs sung by slaves to contain meanings and references that could not be expressed directly to their masters. Symbolic language may be straightforward, as with the "little black train" representing death, which "ain't going to bring you back," or it may be more subtle, as with the complex social hierarchies that are implicit in "Froggy Went a Courtin'."

10. FOLK ART IS CONSERVATIVE. In general, folk songs, like all folk art, tend to stress familiar forms and express old values; fine arts stress virtuosity in form, content, and performance. Thus, while the meaning of a folk song may be embedded in symbolism, it is probably intended to speak to and resonate with an audience rather than to shock or amaze.

11. ORAL/AURAL TRANSMISSION. Transmission by voice and hearing is the most basic definition of a folk song. The absence of written texts and the need to hear and remember affect folk songs in several ways. Simplicity is the first quality, as it aids in remembering the words, tune, and basic meaning of the song. The latter is important, for if one forgets part of a verse, knowing the basic message may allow recovery of the missing part or the creation of an appropriate substitute. Memory aids in the form of rhyme schemes, repeated choruses, or musical reminders are common to folk songs.

Nonetheless, one of the inevitable results of oral transmission is variation. Anyone who has ever looked at the versions of the Child ballad known as "The Golden Vanity" (number 286) will recognize that the name has been altered greatly by mishearing or forgetting. Because the name does not matter beyond fitting the rhyme scheme, it is easy to see how singers have transformed the name into the "Green Willow Tree," the "Merry Golden Tree," the "Golden Silveree," or the "Golden Willow Tree," among others. Mishearing that produces a lack of understanding can lead to efforts to alter the text so that it makes sense, though alterations can do the opposite. Variations can also come from conscious editing. A singer may decide to eliminate what seem to be unnecessary frills or details to simply shorten the song or to highlight its perceived emotional core. Single words or whole verses may be changed or omitted if they make a singer uncomfortable psychologically. Such editing may be unconscious and permanent, or it may be conscious and temporary, as when a singer leaves out a verse that might offend a particular audience. Some scholars see editing and variation, at least after the initial composition of the song, as decay or corruption from an original pure text. Obviously some changes affect the meaning of a song more than others, sometimes even rendering it nonsensical; but other changes are only superficial, leaving the essential core intact. Some songs may be improved by the changes.

12. THERE IS NO ONE TRUE "VERSION" OF A SONG, ONLY ITS VARIATIONS. Based on the observations in the preceding section on transmission, we need to remember that we can never "know" a song completely. Nor is it necessary to do so. As long as a song satisfies its singers and listeners, then it is a good song. We may learn new verses or alter old ones as we encounter variations, but we need not do so.

13. FOLK MUSIC VERSUS FOLK SONG. It is important to distinguish between folk music and folk songs, with the latter referring to the lyrics. The two are intimately related, but not inevitably. Songs may be sung to quite different tunes, with remarkably different effects. The tune we commonly associate with "Amazing Grace" was first linked in print to that hymn over fifty years after it was written.[13] The same tune may be used for several songs. The old familiar "She'll Be Coming 'Round the Mountain" is derived from the tune to an old ballad about Captain Kidd, which itself was adopted as a hymn tune titled "Wondrous Love." It was later adapted to the labor song "Peg and Awl" and Woody Guthrie's anti-lynching song, "Slipknot."

14. SONG FAMILIES. As one listens to and sings folk songs, connections among them become apparent, whether from shared music, borrowed or migrating lyrics, or merely similar content. Thus song families exist that are worth noting. Sometimes the connections are easily discerned, as those between the "Butcher Boy" and "Tarrytown." But in other cases it takes a fine ear, and even suitable intervening songs, to hear the connections. It was only after many years of knowing both songs and hearing a number of different versions of each that I suddenly realized the musical link between "Coo Coo" and "Stewball."

15. PERFORMANCE STYLE. At the end of his career, Alan Lomax came to believe in the centrality of performance style in understanding folk songs, even developing a theory of performance styles around the world.[14] Although we may be familiar with a song as it is sung one way, it is worth asking how the song might affect and be affected if it were sung differently. "Bury Me Beneath the Willow" is a sorrowful song of forsaken love when sung slowly and mournfully, but its character becomes ironic when given a rapid and raucous rendering. In general, the British singing tradition emphasizes the song and not the performance, whereas the African tradition reverses those priorities, with the community drawing a powerful sense of itself from the collective performance. In neither case, however, is the individual, virtuoso performer to take precedence over the song.

16. INSTRUMENTS PROVIDE ACCOMPANIMENT. Many folk songs were originally sung unaccompanied, either because instruments were rare and expensive, or because they could not be readily used in many circumstances where music was desired. Although many modern performers have achieved remarkable levels of dexterity and speed in playing, that was not typical of the past. In general, voice(s) carried the melody and what instruments there were provided support.

17. AUDIENCE AND RECEPTION OF SONG. Folk songs were often sung alone, with the singer and audience as one. But they could also be sung in a communal setting, sometimes where the line between performer and audience blurred as the latter joined in. In other instances, the audience remained passive during the performance, expressing approval or disappointment only after the song was finished. We must be aware that the meaning of a song to a singer and how the audience receives it may be closely connected or widely divergent. The latter is especially true when songs derived from one culture are exported to another setting.

18. HOW AND WHY THE SONG WAS COMPOSED. To the extent that meaning is related to origins, we must consider, insofar as we can for a folk song, how and why the song was composed. It is worth asking what purpose it originally fulfilled and why it has proved enduring, since songs may survive in settings far removed from their origins.

19. THEMATIC CATEGORIES. Given the fact that we all think comparatively, organizing new experiences by how they fit in with the old, it is only natural that we categorize folk songs. Suffice it to say, categories are highly subjective, depending on the singer's/listener's own past. Moreover, most folk songs can easily fit into more than one category. Just because a song is treated under one heading, does not mean it could not just as easily and appropriately belong under another.

Notes

Chapter 1. Who Was Tom Dooley? History and Folk Songs

1. The story of Tom Dula has been told in West, *Lift Up Your Head*; for the history of the discovery and promotion of the ballad, see the prologue in Cantwell, *When We Were Good.*

2. West, *Lift Up Your Head,* 118–21.

3. Warner, ed., *Traditional American Folk Songs,* 5, 289–91.

4. Cantwell, *When We Were Good,* chapter 9, "Lady and the Tramp."

5. DuBois, *Souls of Black Folk,* 251, 257.

6. Sandburg, *American Songbag,* xii–xiii.

7. Lomax and Lomax, *American Ballads,* xxvi–xxviii.

8. A. Lomax, *Folk Songs,* xx–xxi.

9. *Anthology* was reissued by Folkway Records as a set of six CDs in 1997 along with Smith's original booklet and an additional booklet of essays and discussion. Two more CDs were issued in 2000, *Anthology of American Folk Music, Volume 4,* containing songs Smith intended to add but never finished.

10. From the foreword in Smith's booklet accompanying *Anthology.*

11. Marcus, *Invisible Republic,* chapter 4, "The Old Weird America." An adapted version of this chapter is included in the booklet accompanying Smith's *Anthology.*

12. Ibid., 113–15.

13. Ibid., 116–24.

14. Ibid., 124–25.

15. Rhys Isaac, *Landon Carter's Uneasy Kingdom: Revolution and Rebellion on a Virginia Plantation* (New York: Oxford University Press, 2004), 216.

16. Kristen Scheu, final exam in "American Folk Song/American History," Union College, June 2002.

17. Laws, *Native American Balladry,* 9.

18. N. Cohen, *Long Steel Rail,* 23.

19. Filene, *Romancing the Folk,* 4.

20. Jack Larkin, *The Reshaping of Everyday Life: 1790-1840* (New York: Harper and Row, 1988), 234.

21. Vic Gammon, *Desire, Drink and Death in English Folk and Vernacular Song, 1600-1900* (Aldershot, U.K.: Ashgate, 2008), 246.

Chapter 2. Careless Love: Courtship, Marriage, and Children

1. Robert V. Wells, *Revolutions in Americans' Lives: A Demographic Perspective on the History of Americans, Their Families, and Their Society* (Greenwich, Conn.: Greenwood Press, 1982).

2. Christopher Lasch, *Haven in a Heartless World: The Family Besieged* (New York: Basic Books, 1977).

3. Richard Godbeer, *Sexual Revolution in Early America* (Baltimore: Johns Hopkins University Press, 2002), chapter 8, "'Under the Watch': The Metamorphosis of Sexual Regulation in Eighteenth-Century New England." See also Daniel Cohen, "The Beautiful Female Murder Victim: Literary Genres and Courtship Practices in the Origins of a Cultural Motif, 1590–1850," *Journal of Social History* 31 (Winter 1997): 277–306.

4. Nancy Isenberg and Richard Burstein, eds., *Mortal Remains: Death in Early America* (Philadelphia: University of Pennsylvania Press, 2003), chapter 4, "Death and Satire: Dismembering the Body Politic," and chapter 6, "The Politics of Tears: Death in the Early American Novel."

5. Cray, ed., *Erotic Muse*; Logsdon, ed., *Whorehouse Bells*; Randolph, *Roll Me*.

6. Elizabeth Phelps, *The Gates Ajar*, ed. Helen S. Smith (Cambridge, Mass.: Harvard University Press, 1964). Originally published in 1860.

7. Child, ed., *English and Scottish Popular Ballads*, 10 vols.

8. Cazden et al., eds., *Folk Songs of the Catskills*; Flanders, *Ancient Ballads*, 4 vols.; Randolph, ed., *Ozark Folksongs*, vol. 1; Scarborough, *On the Trail*, chapter 2, "The Negro's Part in Transmitting the Traditional Songs and Ballads"; Sharp, ed., *English Folk Songs*, vol. 1.

9. Guthrie, *This Land Is Your Land*, track 12; Leadbelly, *Bourgeois Blues*, track 6.

10. Sandburg, *American Songbag*, 60–61. Sandburg labels this "Pretty Polly," confusing it with another old song. It is also known as "False Sir John" and "May Collean or Colvin in Scotland."

11. Sandburg, *American Songbag*, 156–57. Once again, Sandburg confuses the title of this song with another Child ballad, "The Brown Girl."

12. The recent film *O Brother, Where Art Thou?* is a retelling of the *Odyssey* in twentieth-century America and makes extensive and skillful use of many old folk songs.

13. Jean Ritchie, *Child Ballads in America*, 2:10.

14. Sharp, *English Folk Songs*, 1:161–82.

15. Smith, *Anthology*, 1:7; printed in A. Lomax, *Folk Songs*, 220. For other versions, see Randolph, *Ozark Folksongs*, 4:216 and Sharp, *English Folk Songs*, 2:123–27.

16. Lomax and Lomax, *Our Singing Country*, 126–27; recorded by Jennifer Rose on *Morning Will Come*, track 3. See also, Randolph, *Ozark Folksongs*, "Rolly Trudum," 3:77–79.

17. Ritchie and Watson, *Folk City*, track 9.

18. Sandburg, *American Songbag*, "The Roving Gambler," 312–13, "I Don't Like No Railroad Man," 326.

19. Lomax and Lomax, *American Ballads*, 446–47.

20. Randolph, *Ozark Folksongs*, 1:427–28.

21. Ritchie, *Folk Songs*, 71.

22. *Southern Journey*, 2:16.

23. Lomax and Lomax, *American Ballads*, 320–22.

24. Ibid., 323–24.

25. Ritchie and Watson, *Folk City*, track 14. Also printed in Ritchie, *Folk Songs*, 68.

26. A. Cohen, *Poor Pearl, Poor Girl!*

27. Laws, *Native American Balladry*, 193; see also part F, "Murder Ballads," in Laws; Friedman, ed., *Folk Ballads*, 202–3 and chapter 6, "Tabloid Crime." A recording of "Omie Wise" by G. B. Grayson, the grandson of the Grayson mentioned in "Tom Dooley," is in Smith, *Anthology*, 1:13.

28. Randolph, *Ozark Folksongs*, 2:112–14; Friedman, *Folk Ballads*, 203–5. Woody Guthrie would later use the tune for "Pretty Polly" for his great song "Pastures of Plenty." See Ritchie and Watson, *Folk City* for a recording of "Pretty Polly" (track 11), followed immediately by another in the genre, "Willie Moore" (track 12).

29. Laws, *Native American Balladry*, 62–65. Viers was killed in 1917.

30. Wilentz and Marcus, eds., *Rose and the Briar*, track 16.

31. Ibid., 211–17. This part of the book both reviews the history and includes several key variants.

32. Ritchie and Watson, *Folk City*, "Go Dig My Grave," track 2.

33. Sharp, *English Folk Songs*, 2:268.

34. Randolph, *Blow the Candle Out*, 2:647–49.

35. Friedman, *Folk Ballads*, 88–94; D'Avanzo, "Bobbie Allen," 22–29.

36. Sharp, *English Folk Songs*, 1:295–304; Child, *English and Scottish Popular Ballads*, number 295.

37. Child, *English and Scottish Popular Ballads*, number 200; Randolph, *Ozark Folksongs*, 1:152–60; Sharp, *English Folk Songs*, 1:233–39.

38. Known in Child as "James Harris, or the Daemon Lover," number 243. Sharp, *English Folk Songs*, 1:244–58.

39. Randolph, *Blow the Candle Out*, 1:53–57; Randolph, *Ozark Folksongs*, 1:181–85.

40. The Carter Family on Smith, *Anthology*, 3:11.

41. Sharp, *English Folk Songs*, 2:32–34.

42. Lomax and Lomax, *American Ballads*, 154–58.

43. Child, *English and Scottish Popular Ballads*, number 278; "The Old Lady and the Devil" recorded on Smith, *Anthology*, 1:5.

44. See for example, Sharp, *English Folk Songs*, 1:275–81.

45. A. Lomax, *Folk Songs*, 47–48.

46. Lomax and Lomax, *American Ballads*, 305–6.

47. Randolph, *Ozark Folksongs*, 2:347–49.

48. Child, *English and Scottish Popular Ballads*, number 46. The very first ballad listed in this collection, "Riddles Wisely Expounded," has the same motif.

49. A. Lomax, *Folk Songs*, xviii.

50. Toelken, *Morning Dew and Roses*. See 109–10 for a direct discussion of "The Riddle Song."

51. *Southern Journey*, 3:24; *Deep River of Song: Alabama*, track 15.

52. *Deep River of Song: Alabama*, "Hopali," track 20, and "Ain't Gonna Rain No More," track 21.

53. This song was based on a poem by Ruth Bonne and copyrighted in 1952 by Canadian folksinger Alan Mills. A Burl Ives recording in 1953 put it into oral circulation.

54. "A moste Strange Weddinge of the ffrogge and the mowse" was copyrighted in November 1580. Tolman and Eddy, "Traditional Texts and Tunes," 392–99. This article is often credited to George Kittredge.

55. Versions do vary regarding the ending, but the main point remains the same; see Sandburg, *American Songbag*, 143, or Lomax and Lomax, *American Ballads*, 310–13.

56. Lomax and Lomax, *American Ballads*, 307–8.

57. Ibid., 303–4.

58. Leadbelly, *Where Did You Sleep*, track 18.

59. Sandburg, *American Songbag*, 58–59; Laws, *Native American Balladry*, 221.

60. Child, *English and Scottish Popular Ballads*, number 95.

61. Scarborough, *On the Trail*, 35–43; Leadbelly gives a powerful rendition of "The Gallis Pole" on *Bourgeois Blues*, track 6.

62. Finson, *Voices That Are Gone*, chapter 3, "Familiar Journey: Protocols of Dying in the Nineteenth Century."

63. The Carter Family made this song famous, but it was first composed in 1907 by Ada Habershon.

Chapter 3. "Mine Eyes Have Seen the Glory": Of God and Country

1. The quote from Winthrop and those that follow are readily accessible both in published volumes and on the Internet.

2. David Stowe uses this phrase in *How Sweet the Sound* to discuss the central role of two hymns in American musical life: "Amazing Grace" and "We Shall Overcome." He notes the phrase was coined by G. K. Chesterton and used by Sidney Mead in a book on American ideology.

3. Sandburg, *American Songbag*, chapter 22, "Five Wars," and chapter 24, "White Spirituals"; Lomax and Lomax, *American Ballads*, chapter 23, "Wars and Soldiers," chapter 24, "White Spirituals," and chapter 25, "Negro Spirituals." See also Odum and Johnson, *Negro and His Songs*, chapter 2, "The Religious Songs of the Negro," chapter 3, "Examples of Religious Songs," and chapter 4, "Examples of Religious Songs, Concluded."

4. William McLoughlin, *Revivals, Awakenings, and Reform* (Chicago: University of Chicago Press, 1978), 140.

5. Ibid., 116.

6. Odum and Johnson, *Negro and His Songs*, 101; Sandburg, *American Songbag*, 480–81; Work, *American Negro Songs*, 202–3. Work was a musicologist affiliated with the Fisk Jubilee Singers.

7. Stowe, *How Sweet the Sound*, chapter 10, "The Nation with the Soul of a Church."

8. A number of excellent books examine the role of religious music and American musical history. Three basic texts deserve mention: Chase, *America's Music*; Crawford, *America's Musical Life*; Southern, *Music of Black Americans*. In addition to Stowe, *How Sweet the Sound*, already cited, three other more specialized studies worth noting include Epstein, *Sinful Tunes*; Marini, *Sacred Song*; and White and White, *Sounds of Slavery*.

9. A. Lomax, *Folk Songs*, 66–67, 71. See also Randolph, *Ozark Folksongs*, 4:16–20.

10. David Stannard, *Puritan Way of Death: A Study in Religion, Culture, and Social Change* (New York: Oxford University Press, 1977), chapter 3, "Death and Childhood."

11. For histories of "Amazing Grace" and its lyrics, see Stowe, *How Sweet the Sound*, chapter 10, and Turner, *Amazing Grace*.

12. For examples of sacred-harp singing, listen to Smith, *Anthology*, 4:4–5; *Southern Journey*, vols. 9 and 10; and Norumbega Harmony, *Sing and Joyful Be*. For examples of how the music looks, see Sandburg, *American Songbag*, 152–55.

13. Contemporary gospel music owes its origins to Thomas Dorsey in the 1930s; I have not included it in my discussion.

14. John L. O'Sullivan used these words in the *Democratic Review* in 1845 when defining manifest destiny.

15. Hinton, "Folk Songs of Faith," 31–37.

16. Patterson, *The Shaker Spiritual*.

17. Chase, *America's Music*, 205–6.

18. *The Cyber Hymnal*, http://www.cyberhymnal.org, and *Sing Out* 7, no. 1 (1957). For a lengthy discussion of the origins of the song, and for other lyrics, see *The Mudcat Café*, http://www.mudcat.org. It has been recorded by many different artists, including Pete Seeger (*I Can See a New Day*, 2:2) and Enya (*Shepherd Moons*, track 3).

19. The first two lines of the Lowry version of this verse begin, "What though my joys and comforts die? / The Lord my Savior Liveth."

20. Sanga Music, Inc. ©1957 (Renewed).

21. For a discussion of call-and-response music, see White and White, *Sounds of Slavery*, 20–71.

22. McLoughlin, *Revivals*, 138.

23. White and White, *Sounds of Slavery*, 115–16.

24. Southern, *Music of Black Americans*, 75–80.

25. Allen, Ware, and Garrison, comps., *Slave Songs*, iii–v.

26. Ibid., iv–v.

27. Odum and Johnson, *Negro and His Songs*, chapters 2–4; N. White, *American Negro Folk-Songs*, chapter 2, "Religious Songs."

28. DuBois, *Souls of Black Folk*, chapter 14, "The Sorrow Songs."

29. Smith, *Anthology*, 4:11.

30. See Odum and Johnson, *Negro and His Songs*, chapter 2.

31. Ibid., 126–7; Sandburg, *American Songbag*, 448; N. White, *American Negro Folk-Songs*, 91–92.

32. Leadbelly, *Where Did You Sleep*, track 22; also listen to Smith, *Anthology*, 4:13.

33. Stowe, *How Sweet the Sound,* 257–64.

34. Cleveland, *Dark Laughter.* Cleveland is a New Zealander, but his analysis easily crosses national borders.

35. The ballad is printed in Thompson, *Body, Boots and Britches,* 312–17. Thompson reports that the ballad was published in 1846 and recorded in the log of the whaling bark *Timor* following the entry for July 8, 1850. My copy was taken from a newspaper clipping in the files of the Schenectady City History Center. Marci Vail of the East Hampton Library verified my version with that in the log of the *Timor.*

36. For "Yankee Doodle," see Lemay, "Yankee Doodle," 435–64. It seems implausible Shuckburgh would write the "Ballad of Schenectady," for he was born in England and came to the colonies about 1735, almost half a century after the attack on Schenectady.

37. Crawford, *America's Musical Life,* 57–64.

38. Firth, ed., *American Garland,* 74–84.

39. A. Lomax, *Folk Songs,* 32, 42–43; Friedman, *Folk Ballads,* 288–90; Warner, *Traditional American Folk Songs,* 87–89.

40. Moore, *Songs and Ballads*; Scott, "Ballads and Broadsides," 18–23.

41. Ibid. See also, Hudson, "North Carolina Regulators," 470–85; and Schlesinger, "Patriot Propaganda," 78–88.

42. Lemay, "Yankee Doodle," is a thorough review.

43. Ibid., 436.

44. Moore, *Songs and Ballads,* passim.

45. Scott, "Ballads and Broadsides," 20.

46. Moore, *Songs and Ballads,* 1–17.

47. No account of the actual surrender mentions anything more than drums beating. The first link between this song and Yorktown occurred in the 1820s. The phrase was used in a song from the English Civil War in the 1640s.

48. Sandburg, *American Songbag,* 427–29.

49. A. Lomax, *Folk Songs,* 326, 332–33; Randolph, *Ozark Folksongs,* 1:272–75.

50. Sarah Vowell, "John Brown's Body," in Wilentz and Marcus, *Rose and the Briar,* 83–89.

51. Richard Schneider, *TAPS: Notes from a Nation's Heart* (New York: Morrow, 2002).

52. A. Lomax, *Folk Songs,* 84, 98.

53. Maris Vinovskis, "Have Social Historians Lost the Civil War? Some Preliminary Demographic Speculations," *Journal of American History* 76 (1989): 34–58.

54. Lomax and Lomax, *American Ballads,* 548–60; Sandburg, *American Songbag,* 435–44.

55. Randolph, *Roll Me,* 1:513–15; Sandburg, *American Songbag,* 440–42.

56. A more explicit version, provided to Vance Randolph by a man who sang it happily in the presence of women, observed, "The French they are a funny race, they fight with their feet and fuck with their face, hinky dinky, parlee-voo." During the war, the French introduced American soldiers not only to the horrors of modern warfare but also to the wonders of foot boxing and oral sex. The Lomaxes apparently knew this verse but cleaned it up by substituting "and save

their face" at the end (Lomax and Lomax, *American Ballads*, 557–60). They claim to have seen a private collection, not "mailable" (i.e., obscene), of six hundred verses about the mademoiselle.

57. Ibid., 548–51.

58. Ibid., 551–52; Sandburg, *American Songbag*, 435.

59. Lomax and Lomax, *American Ballads*, 552–54.

60. Ibid., 554–56; Sandburg, *American Songbag* titles this "Where They Were," 442–43.

61. Lomax and Lomax, *American Ballads*, 556–57; Sandburg, *American Songbag*, 444.

62. I remember such lines as, "It's not so bad for the first few weeks, but then when your coffin begins to leak, the worms crawl in and the worms crawl out, and the bugs play pinochle on your snout." A phrase I recall that would have pleased Renaissance sensibilities about the corruption of the corpse—and appalled twentieth-century American undertakers selling embalming—went, "Your stomach turns a nasty green, and pus comes out like whipping cream." Shortly after I wrote these lines in October 2004, Garrison Keillor and Prudence Johnson sang a variation of it on *A Prairie Home Companion*, testifying to the song's enduring nature.

Chapter 4. "Take This Hammer": Work and the Labor Movement

1. Odum and Johnson, *Negro Workaday Songs*, chapter 13, "John Henry: Epic of the Negro Workingman"; Lomax and Lomax, *American Ballads*, 3–10.

2. Nelson, "Who Was John Henry?" 53–79; Nelson, *Steel Drivin' Man*.

3. See Odum and Johnson, *Negro Workaday Songs*, 236; also listen to Mississippi John Hurt's wonderful rendition of "Spike Driver Blues" on Smith, *Anthology*, 6:10. Doc Watson and Jerry Garcia have used Hurt's version to good effect (Ritchie and Watson, *Folk City*, 3; The Jerry Garcia Acoustic Band, *Almost Acoustic*, 4). Variations on the theme can be found under "Take This Hammer."

4. Odum and Johnson, *Negro Workaday Songs*, chapter 13.

5. White and White, *Sounds of Slavery*, 180–82, describes how slaves in tobacco factories in Richmond, Virginia, used songs as weapons in their struggle to control their workplace.

6. Asch, *Leadbelly Songbook*, 56; Jackson, ed., *Wake Up Dead Man*, 99–101.

7. Asch, *Leadbelly Songbook*, 39; Leadbelly, *Where Did You Sleep* includes several work songs: tracks 2, 8, 9.

8. *Southern Journey*, 3:19.

9. Leadbelly, *Where Did You Sleep*, track 9. For other field hollers, listen to White and White, *Sounds of Slavery*, tracks 1–4.

10. Lemay, "Yankee Doodle," 435–64.

11. Ibid., 447–48.

12. Ibid., 450.

13. Lomax and Lomax, *American Ballads*, 446–47.

14. Rickaby, ed., *Shanty-Boy*.

15. Ibid., 3–10; Sandburg, *American Songbag*, 392–93.

16. Rickaby, *Shanty-Boy*, 41–42, 199–200; Friedman, *Folk Ballads*, 415–17.

17. Cazden et al., *Folk Songs of the Catskills*, 40–43; Flanders and Olney, comps., *Ballads Migrant*, 141–43.

18. Warner, *Traditional American Folk Songs*, 58–60.

19. Rickaby, *Shanty-Boy*, 11–24.

20. *Southern Journey*, 13:19.

21. Ibid., track 8.

22. Odum and Johnson, *Negro and His Songs*, 2–3.

23. Allen, Ware, and Garrison, *Slave Songs*, 23–24.

24. *Southern Journey*, 13:4.

25. A recent two weeks on the *Half Moon*, a replica of Henry Hudson's vessel from 1609, during which I worked the capstan and hauled lines to set and furl sails, impressed me with how often the work was not rhythmic or sustained enough to make shanties useful in those tasks.

26. Leadbelly, *Bourgeois Blues*, track 20.

27. Allen, Ware, and Garrison, *Slave Songs*, 61; Sandburg, *American Songbag*, 407.

28. Lomax and Lomax, *American Ballads*, 491–93.

29. Daniel Vickers, "Nantucket Whalemen in the Deep-Sea Fishery: The Changing Anatomy of an Early American Labor Force," *Journal of American History* 72 (1985–86): 277–96.

30. A. Lomax, *Folk Songs*, 40, 61; Friedman, *Folk Ballads*, 401–3. The Bodleian Library contains a broadside version from 1820–24.

31. "50, 100, and 150 Years Ago," *Scientific American* (October 2004): 18. See the column reprising studies from the past 50 to 150 years.

32. Green, *Only a Miner*, 50–51.

33. N. Cohen, *Long Steel Rail*, 553–56.

34. Green, *Only a Miner*, 63–111; for the quotation, see page 103.

35. Ibid., 77.

36. Ibid., 76.

37. For Crawford's poem, see ibid., 96.

38. For the song, see ibid., 66–67. Used by permission of Lars Edegran–GHB Records.

39. Ibid., 80.

40. N. White, *American Negro Folk-Songs*, chapter 7, "Gang Laborers."

41. Leadbelly, *Bourgeois Blues*, track 10.

42. Odum and Johnson, *Negro Workaday Songs*, 107.

43. N. Cohen, *Long Steel Rail*, 547–51; Lomax and Lomax, *American Ballads*, 20–22.

44. Over 550 songs from the nineteenth century have been printed in Foner, *American Labor Songs*. Foner includes at least brief discussions of the events associated with many of the songs.

45. Smith, *Anthology*, 1:12; A. Lomax, *Folk Songs*, 276, 283; for a brief history of shoe-making machinery, see John Chamberlain, *The Enterprising Americans: A Business History of the United States* (New York: Harper and Row, 1963).

46. For a description of life in the mills for a girl, see Lucy Larcom, *A New England Girlhood, Outlined from Memory* (New York: Houghton, Mifflin, 1889).

47. Thomas Dublin, *Women at Work: The Transformation of Work and Community in Lowell, Massachusetts, 1826–1860* (New York: Columbia University Press, 1979).

48. Foner, *American Labor Songs*, 40–45, but especially, 42–43.

49. Sandburg, *American Songbag*, 195.

50. Composed by Knowles Shaw no later than the 1870s; Sandburg, *American Songbag*, 282–83.

51. Foner, *American Labor Songs*, 49–50.

52. Smith, *Anthology*, 2:11.

53. Foner, *American Labor Songs*, 200–208; Green, *Only a Miner*, chapter 5, "Coal Creek Troubles," and chapter 6, "Roll Down the Line."

54. This system is well-described in Oshinsky, *Worse Than Slavery*, especially chapter 3, "American Siberia."

55. Smith, *Anthology*, 6:9.

56. Green, *Only a Miner*, 176–77, 208–9.

57. Foner, *American Labor Songs*, 208–10.

58. The Weavers sang a shortened version of this song on *Wasn't That a Time*, 4:18.

59. N. Cohen, *Long Steel Rail*, 611–15.

60. Green, *Only a Miner*, chapter 8, "Two by Travis."

61. Gerald N. Grob, *The Deadly Truth: A History of Disease in America* (Cambridge, Mass.: Harvard University Press, 2002), chapter 7, "Threats of Industry."

62. *The American Experience* has a Web page about a film it made on the Rockefeller family that includes commentary on Ludlow, http://www.pbs.org/wgbh/amex/rockefellers. The UMW has a separate Web page devoted to the massacre, http://www.umwa.org/index.php?q=content/ludlow-massacre.

Chapter 5. The Man Who Never Returned: Ships, Trains, and Other Transportation

1. For a brief history of the song and its roots, see N. Cohen, *Long Steel Rail*, 197–226, but especially 217–18.

2. The Kingston Trio, *Best of the Kingston Trio*, track 1.

3. George Rogers Taylor, *The Transportation Revolution, 1815–1860* (New York: Harper and Row, 1951).

4. Sandburg, *American Songbag*, 146–47.

5. N. Cohen, *Long Steel Rail*, 197–216. The song was made popular by Vernon Dalhart, *1981*, track 2.

6. Ibid., 200–201.

7. See Rod McDonald's Web site, http:// www.rodmacdonald.net/usa.htm. I am indebted to my brother-in-law, Keith Andersen, for this reference.

8. N. Cohen, *Long Steel Rail* offers over 700 pages of details about the origins and evolution of many favorites, as well as those of lesser-known folk songs.

9. Child, *English and Scottish Popular Ballads*, number 286.

10. Randolph, *Ozark Folksongs*, 1:195–201.

11. Miranda's speech, act 5, scene 1.

12. Firth, *American Garland*, 9–16.

13. Sandburg, *American Songbag*, 146–47; N. Cohen, *Long Steel Rail*, 199–200.

14. Leadbelly, *Last Sessions*, 2:15.

15. N. White, *American Negro Folk-Songs*, 347–49; Randolph, *Ozark Folksongs*, 4:144–45.

16. Smith, *Anthology*, 2:9. The Smiths' song is a slightly compressed version of the one printed in N. White, *American Negro Folk-Songs*, 347–48, which White dates from about 1915.

17. To fit the beat, the Smiths edited out some words but retained the meaning.

18. *Southern Journey*, 7:9, liner notes.

19. Lomax and Lomax, *Our Singing Country*, 220–22; Warner, *Traditional American Folk Songs*, 85–87.

20. Taylor, *Transportation Revolution*, chapter 3, "The Canal Era."

21. Lomax and Lomax, *American Ballads*, chapter 20, "The Erie Canal"; Sandburg, *American Songbag*, 180; Warner, *Traditional American Folk Songs*, 112–13. Several songs based on the Delaware and Hudson Canal, which ran from Pennsylvania across northern New Jersey to the Hudson River at Kingston, New York, are printed in Cazden et al., *Folk Songs of the Catskills*, 353–54, 622–27.

22. Lomax and Lomax, *American Ballads*, xxix. The Lomaxes' habit of improving songs by editing and combining offended many collectors, but their versions have had wide appeal.

23. Taylor, *Transportation Revolution*, chapter 4, "Steamboats on Rivers, Lakes, and Bays."

24. Wheeler, *Steamboatin' Days*. N. White, *American Negro Folk-Songs*, 307, has a verse or two that could have migrated from of one of the songs Wheeler took down.

25. Wheeler, *Steamboatin' Days*, 30, 17.

26. N. White, *American Negro Folk-Songs*, 307.

27. Wheeler, *Steamboatin' Days*, 38.

28. Ibid., 40–43.

29. Ibid., 55–56.

30. Taylor, *Transportation Revolution*, chapter 5, "Railroads."

31. N. Cohen, *Long Steel Rail*, chapter 1, "The Railway Cars Are Coming," is a brief history of railroads in the United States.

32. Ibid., 132–57. That the song continues to be of interest in American popular culture was proven by the appearance in my local newspaper, the *Gazette*, of a feature on the story on April 29, 2000, B7.

33. Hurt, *Satisfied*, track 9; Hurt, *Worried Blues*, track 6.

34. N. Cohen, *Long Steel Rail*, 132–34; Smith, *Anthology*, 2:10.

35. Dalhart, *1981*, track 6; The Jerry Garcia Acoustic Band, *Almost Acoustic*, track 11.

36. N. Cohen, *Long Steel Rail*, 197–226.

37. Dalhart, *1981*, track 2. "The Prisoner's Song," which was the front side of the record and has been recorded by many others.

38. N. Cohen, *Long Steel Rail*, 169–274.

39. N. Cohen, *Long Steel Rail*, 183–96. The Carter Family sold over ninety-three thousand copies of this song.

40. Ibid., 599, 608–9.

41. Ibid., 611–18.

42. Ibid., 625–28; Scarborough, *On the Trail*, 260–61. Perhaps no performance quite captures the anxiety and anguish of this song as the one by Boggs, *His Folkway Years*, 1:22; hear also the version by Guthrie, *Muleskinner Blues*, track 4.

43. Scarborough, *On the Trail*, 260.

44. N. Cohen, *Long Steel Rail*, 629–30.

45. Scarborough, *On the Trail*, 258.

46. Ibid., 253–55; N. Cohen, *Long Steel Rail*, 622.

47. Scarborough, *On the Trail*, 240–41.

48. N. Cohen, *Long Steel Rail*, 638–44.

49. Scarborough, *On the Trail*, 242; the Memphis Jug Band, "K.C. Moan" on Smith, *Anthology*, 6:11.

50. N. Cohen, *Long Steel Rail*, 503–18.

51. Odum and Johnson, *Negro and His Songs*, 169.

52. Ibid., 184.

53. Ibid., 222.

54. Scarborough, *On the Trail*, 242–43.

55. N. Cohen, *Long Steel Rail*, 491–517.

56. Boggs, *His Folkway Years*, 2:24; Guthrie, *Muleskinner Blues*, track 25; Houston, *Vanguard Years*, track 7.

57. N. Cohen, *Long Steel Rail*, chapter 9, "I've Got the Railroad Blues."

58. Ibid., 413–25. The "White House Blues" is on Smith, *Anthology*, 2:6; the Carter Family made a popular recording of the "Cannonball Blues" on *Wildwood Flower*, track 17.

59. N. Cohen, *Long Steel Rail*, 373–81.

60. Ibid.; chapter 8, "In a Boxcar Around the World."

61. Ibid., 374–75. The poem has no connection to "The Rock Island Line" later made popular by Leadbelly.

62. Leadbelly, *Bourgeois Blues*, track 4; Scarborough, *On the Trail*, 239; Wheeler, *Steamboatin' Days*, 54–55.

63. Scarborough, *On the Trail*, 43.

64. Ibid., 243–44.

65. Ibid., 246.

66. Leadbelly, *Where Did You Sleep*, track 32, liner notes.

67. N. Cohen, *Long Steel Rail*, 478–84; Leadbelly, *Bourgeois Blues*, track 8. Jackson collected a version of the song in 1964 in *Wake Up Dead Man*, 91–93.

68. Dalhart, *1981*, track 9.

69. Wolfe and Lornell, *Leadbelly*, 208.

70. Randolph, *Ozark Folksongs*, 4:95.

71. Guthrie, *Greatest Songs*, 1:7.

Chapter 6. Just Lookin' for a Home: Traveling On

1. Sandburg, *American Songbag*, 108–9; Lingenfelter and Dwyer, *American West*, 42–43. For several bawdy verses, see Randolph, *Roll Me*, 1:300–301.

2. See William A. Bowen, *The Willamette Valley: Migration and Settlement on the Oregon Frontier* (Seattle: University of Washington Press, 1978).

3. Stephen Thernstrom, *The Other Bostonians: Poverty and Progress in the American Metropolis, 1880–1970* (Cambridge, Mass.: Harvard University Press, 1973), chapter 9, "The Boston Case and the American Pattern."

4. For a good discussion of what Betsy and Ike might have experienced, see John Unruh, *The Plains Across: Overland Immigrants and the Trans-Mississippi West, 1840–60* (Urbana: University of Illinois Press, 1979) and John Mack Faragher, *Men and Women on the Overland Trail* (New Haven, Conn.: Yale University Press, 1979).

5. Lingenfelter and Dwyer, *American West*, devotes a whole chapter to "Seeing the Elephant," 85–105.

6. Sandburg, *American Songbag*, "What Was Your Name in the States?" 106.

7. Lingenfelter and Dwyer, *American West*, 39–40.

8. Lomax and Lomax, *American Ballads*, 429–30.

9. The phrase "overblown hopes" is used in Ronald Takaki, *A Different Mirror: A History of Multicultural America* (Boston: Little, Brown, 1993), 12.

10. This song, sung to a tune similar to "The Wagoner's Lad," may be found in Randolph, *Ozark Folksongs*, 4:222–24; Ritchie, *Folk Songs*, 68; and Dorothy Scarborough, *Song Catcher*, 327–28.

11. Sandburg, *American Songbag*, 130–31. The name and tune were adapted as a war song in Vietnam, referring to an air raid down the Red River of North Vietnam, http://ingeb.org/songs/redriver.html.

12. Lingenfelter and Dwyer, *American West*, 96–97.

13. Lomax and Lomax, comps., *Cowboy Songs*, 424–28; Gioia, "Big Roundup," 101–111.

14. Firth, *American Garland*, 51–53.

15. Ibid., xxv, 27–30. The reference in the final verse to "let Amsterdam send forth her Brats" suggests a link to the Pilgrims, who had moved to Holland before establishing the Plymouth Colony in 1620.

16. Wright and Wright, *Danish Emigrant Ballads*, 222–23. These and other lines from the same volume are reprinted with permission from the publisher.

17. Ibid. I am using the more literal translation by Rochelle Wright. The Wrights provide both the Danish original and an English translation. For a shorter version with rhymes in English, see A. Lomax, *Folk Songs*, 88–89.

18. A. Lomax, *Folk Songs*, 322–23. Lee Hays of the Weavers, a native of Arkansas, sings and speaks a wonderful version on *Wasn't That a Time*, 2:8. Harry Smith included a version, "My Name Is John Johanna," on Smith, *Anthology*, 1:14.

19. A. Lomax, *Folk Songs*, 308.

20. Lomax and Lomax, *American Ballads*, 398–401. Lomax and Lomax, *Cowboy Songs*, 317–19 has a slightly different version. Both come from a printed broadside given to John Lomax in 1909.

21. Lomax and Lomax, *Cowboy Songs*, 407–8; Lingenfelter and Dwyer, *American West*, 456–59. Sandburg, *American Songbag*, includes this as "The Lane County Bachelor," possibly from Kansas. Other versions of the song have the homesteader returning to Missouri or Topeka, Kansas.

22. Lingenfelter and Dwyer, *American West*, 448 has a song, also from 1891, promoting Lane County as an almost perfect place.

23. Lingenfelter and Dwyer, *American West*, 534–37; *O Brother*, track 2.

24. The University of Southampton has a fine version of this song at http://www.soton.ac.uk/~wpwt/trans/cockaygn/cockaygn.htm.

25. See the lyrics at *The Mudcat Café*, http://www.mudcat.org.

26. Randolph, *Ozark Folksongs*, 4:360–61.

27. A. Lomax, *Folk Songs*, 410–11, 423–24.

28. For print versions, see Sandburg, *American Songbag*, 8–10, and Scarborough, *On the Trail*, 76–79. For the variety in lyrics and tunes, listen to the Masked Marvel on Smith, *Anthology*, 2:12; Vera Ward Hall on *Deep River of Song: Alabama*, track 27; Willie McTell on *Deep River of Song: Georgia*, track 1; Willie Wilson on *Deep River of Song: Virginia*, track 7; Leadbelly on *Last Sessions*, 3:2.

29. Scarborough, *On the Trail*, 79.

30. Asch, *Leadbelly Songbook*, 39.

31. Brown, *Stagolee Shot Billy*.

32. Henry Nash Smith, *Virgin Land: The American West as Symbol and Myth* (Cambridge, Mass.: Harvard University Press, 1950), chapter 16, "The Garden and the Desert."

33. Sandburg, *American Songbag*, 12–13.

34. Lingenfelter and Dwyer, *American West*, 434–35.

35. For the connection between this song and "The Ocean Burial," see Friedman, *Folk Ballads*, 436–39. Lomax and Lomax, *Cowboy Songs*, includes "Bury Me Not" under the title of "The Dying Cowboy," 48–51.

36. Compare the verses in Friedman, *Folk Ballads*, 437–39, to Lomax and Lomax, *Cowboy Songs*, 49–51.

37. A few have doubted how much cowboys sang as part of their work; see Gioia, "Big Roundup," 108–11. But in *Cowboy Songs* the Lomaxes make a good case that songs were a central part of the cowboy life, xv–xx.

38. Lomax and Lomax, *Cowboy Songs*, 28–41, and Lomax and Lomax, *American Ballads*, 376–80, provide numerous presentable verses. For obscene versions, see Logsdon, *Whorehouse Bells*, 60–69, and Randolph, *Roll Me*, 1:199–205.

39. Lomax and Lomax, *Cowboy Songs*, 4–7.

40. Ibid., note on page 4. The term *dogie* may simply be a corruption of a Spanish word referring to the halter by which calves were kept from their mothers, or it may have originated from calling motherless calves, with extended bellies from eating grass too soon, dough-guts or doughgies.

41. Ibid., 417–22. The origins of the song are traced in Friedman, *Folk Ballads*, 424–29.

42. Ibid., 399–401; Lingenfelter and Dwyer, *American West*, 210–13. The latter has five sections of songs on the Mormons, covering seventy-six pages and thirty-eight songs.

43. Lingenfelter and Dwyer, *American West*, 209.

44. Wright and Wright, *Danish Emigrant Ballads*, 144–46.

45. Ibid., 147–48.

46. Lingenfelter and Dwyer, *American West*, 192–93

47. Wright and Wright, *Danish Emigrant Ballads*, 151–52.

48. Ibid., 153; Lingenfelter and Dwyer, *American West*, 196–201.

49. Lingenfelter and Dwyer, *American West*, 186–88.

50. Wright and Wright, *Danish Emigrant Ballads*, 142–44.

51. Lomax and Lomax, *Cowboy Songs*, 401–3.

52. Lingenfelter and Dwyer, *American West*, 234–35.

53. Ibid., 202–3.

54. Ibid., 189.

55. Ibid., 250–51; "Early Life in Dixie" starts as a lament but ends as a celebration. See also "Once I Lived in Cottonwood," 248–49, for a less optimistic conclusion.

56. Ibid., 245.

57. Ibid., 246–47.

58. Hamlet's soliloquy, act 3, scene 1.

59. Weavers, *Almanac*, track 1. This book owes its existence to this song, for it was the reaction to it by a friend, who had lost someone to death not too long before, that first alerted me to pay attention to the meanings behind the lyrics. Recently an elderly neighbor told my wife, "Don't weep after me," as death approached.

60. Sanga Music, Inc. © 1960 (Renewed).

61. Scarborough, *On the Trail*, 8–9.

62. Randolph, *Ozark Folksongs*, 2:331–32. Randolph noted the phrase was used by the Fisk Jubilee Singers in their version of "Jacob's Ladder."

63. Scarborough, *On the Trail*, 73–74; Sandburg, *American Songbag*, 322–23.

64. Sandburg, *American Songbag*, 486; Willie McTell on *Deep River of Song: Georgia*, track 11.

65. Allen, Ware, and Garrison, *Slave Songs*, 5, 73.

66. Ibid., 73.

Chapter 7. Nobody Knows the Trouble I've Seen: Hard Times and Hard Men

1. Allen, Ware, and Garrison, *Slave Songs*, 55.

2. Odetta, *Vanguard Years*, "Sometimes I Feel Like a Motherless Child," track 14.

3. Charles Ball, *Slavery in the United States: A Narrative of the Life and Adventures of Charles Ball* (New York: Negro Universities Press, 1969), 16–18.

4. Frederick Douglass, *Autobiography of Frederick Douglass* (New York: Bedford–St. Martins, 1993), 40.

5. Ibid., 46–47.

6. DuBois, *Souls of Black Folk*, chapter 14, "The Sorrow Songs." For a more recent academic analysis of slave songs, see Levine, *The Unpredictable Past: Explorations*

in American Cultural History, chapter 3, "Slave Songs and Slave Consciousness: Explorations in Neglected Sources."

7. DuBois, *Souls of Black Folk*, 253, 257.

8. Ibid., 259–60.

9. *Southern Journey*, 13:17.

10. Scarborough, *On the Trail*, 223–25.

11. Levine, "Slave Songs," 46; see also S. J. Celestine Edwards, *From Slavery to a Bishopric* (London: John Kensit, 1891), 38.

12. Southern, *Music of Black Americans*, 157.

13. Epstein, *Sinful Tunes*, 159.

14. A. Lomax, *Folk Songs*, 493, 505–6; Scarborough, *On the Trail*, 201–3.

15. Southern, *Music of Black Americans*, 144–45.

16. Allen, Ware, and Garrison, *Slave Songs*, 1; N. White, *American Negro Folk-Songs*, 87–88.

17. Allen, Ware, and Garrison, *Slave Songs*, 23–24.

18. Ibid., 48; Odetta, *Vanguard Years*, track 13.

19. Smith, *Anthology*, 2:11, as sung by the Bentley Boys; A. Lomax, *Folk Songs*, 286. See also chapter 4, "'Take This Hammer': Work and the Labor Movement," in this book, *Life Flows On in Endless Song*.

20. Oshinsky, *Worse Than Slavery*. See chapter 3, "American Siberia," for the background to the convict-leasing system.

21. A. Lomax, *Blues in the Mississippi Night*, track 16.

22. Odum and Johnson, *Negro Workaday Songs*, 71–117; Scarborough, *On the Trail*, 206–37; N. White, *American Negro Folk-Songs*, 250–80.

23. *Deep River of Song: Big Brazos*; Lomax and Lomax, *American Ballads*, chapter 3, "Songs from Southern Chain Gangs"; Jackson, *Wake Up Dead Man*.

24. Leadbelly, *Bourgeois Blues*, track 8.

25. Scarborough, *On the Trail*, 265.

26. Leadbelly, *Where Did You Sleep*, track 32; Lomax and Lomax, *American Ballads*, 199–201.

27. Jackson, *Wake Up Dead Man*, 194; Lomax and Lomax, *American Ballads*, 60–61; *Deep River of Song: Big Brazos*, track 2.

28. *Deep River of Song: Big Brazos*, tracks 1, 12; Lomax and Lomax, *American Ballads*, 58–59; A. Lomax, *Folk Songs*, 536–37.

29. Leadbelly, *Last Sessions*, 1:8.

30. A. Lomax, *Folk Songs*, 539; *Deep River of Song: Alabama*, track 1.

31. Lomax and Lomax, *American Ballads*, 75–79; *Deep River of Song: Big Brazos*, track 5.

32. Leadbelly, *Where Did You Sleep*, track 29; Lomax and Lomax, *American Ballads*, 66–67; *Deep River of Song: Big Brazos*, track 3; Jackson, *Wake Up Dead Man*, 290–96.

33. A. Lomax, *Blues in the Mississippi Night*. Alan Lomax made this recording in 1947 but it was not issued until 1959. The CD by Rounder Records (2003) comes with a booklet that offers an almost complete transcript of the conversation. Tracks 2, 6, 16, and 17 are especially informative.

34. N. White, *American Negro Folk-Songs*, 396.

35. A. Lomax, *Blues in the Mississippi Night*, transcript booklet.

36. A. Lomax, *Where the Blues Began*.

37. Odum and Johnson, *Negro and His Songs*, 254–55; Scarborough, *On the Trail*, 227–28.

38. Scarborough, *On the Trail*, 227.

39. Ibid., 228; N. White, *American Negro Folk-Songs*, 455.

40. As with prison songs, all three of the major collections from the 1920s have a special chapter devoted to the blues. See Odum and Johnson, *Negro Workaday Songs*, 17–34; Scarborough, *On the Trail*, 264–80; and N. White, *American Negro Folk-Songs*, 387–402. For examples of the field hollers, see White and White, *Sounds of Slavery* and the first four tracks on the book's accompanying CD.

41. Lawrence Levine, *Black Culture and Black Consciousness: African-American Folk Thought from Slavery to Freedom* (New York: Oxford University Press, 1977).

42. Odum and Johnson, *Negro Workaday Songs*, 29–33. Compare these titles to the range of topics on Jefferson, *Best of Blind Lemon Jefferson*.

43. Johnson, *Complete Recordings*, "Hellhound on My Trail," 2:6.

44. All of the following examples in the section on the blues are taken from Odum and Johnson, *Negro Workaday Songs*, 18–27; Scarborough, *On the Trail*, 265–79; and N. White, *American Negro Folk-Songs*, 391–99.

45. N. White, *American Negro Folk-Songs*, 399.

46. Leadbelly, *Bourgeois Blues*, track 3.

47. Smith, *Anthology*, 6:15.

48. A. Lomax, *Folk Songs*, 203, 222; Randolph, *Ozark Folksongs*, 1:341–43.

49. A. Lomax, *Folk Songs*, 280, 290. Men could also go astray at the House of the Rising Sun, as Doc Watson warns in "Rising Sun Blues" on *Essential Doc Watson*, track 9.

50. Lomax and Lomax, *American Ballads*, 186–88; Scarborough, *On the Trail*, 277.

51. Levine, *Black Culture*, 417–18.

52. Hobsbawm, *Primitive Rebels*, chapter 2, "The Social Bandit."

53. Richard White, "Outlaw Gangs of the Middle Border: American Social Bandits," *Western Historical Quarterly* 12 (October 1981): 387–408.

54. For a ballad about Quantrill, see Lomax and Lomax, *American Ballads*, 132–33.

55. N. Cohen, *Long Steel Rail*, 97–116.

56. Ibid., 99.

57. Ibid., 97–99; Lomax and Lomax, *American Ballads*, 128–31. Almeda Riddle sings a bit of the song for Alan Lomax, after informing him that Jesse was a cousin, of whom she was neither proud nor ashamed, *Southern Journey*, 5:1.

58. Lomax and Lomax, *American Ballads*, 128.

59. Ibid., 501–4. For the roots of this song and its tune, see Bronson, "Samuel Hall's Family Tree," 47–64. Samuel Hall may have been Jack Hall, hanged in 1707, six years after Kidd: *The Ex-Classics Web Site*, http://www.exclassics.com/newgate/ng110.htm.

60. Levine, *Black Culture*, 418.

61. The best study of the story and the myths is Brown, *Stagolee Shot Billy*. Odum and Johnson, *Negro and His Songs*, 196–98 recognizes the significance of Stagolee by placing his story first among black bad men. For versions that differ in story and tune, listen to Hurt, *Blues Collection*, 1:2; Frank Hutchison on Smith, *Anthology*, 2:5; and Lucious Curtis and Willie Ford on *Deep River of Song: Mississippi*, track 2.

62. A. Cohen, *Poor Pearl, Poor Girl!*

63. Bryan's body was discovered on February 1, 1896.

64. Brown, *Stagolee Shot Billy*, 35, 38.

65. Marcus, *Mystery Train*, chapter 3, "Sly Stone: The Myth of Staggerlee," 65–95.

66. Frank Hutchison on Smith, *Anthology*, 2:5.

67. Mississippi John Hurt on *The Blues: The Gold Collection*, 1:2.

68. Brown, *Stagolee Shot Billy*, 70.

69. A. Lomax, *Blues in the Mississippi Night*, track 16.

70. For a variety of songs about African-American bad men, see Odum and Johnson, *Negro Workaday Songs*, 47–70, and Lomax and Lomax, *American Ballads*, 89–120.

71. Brown, *Stagolee Shot Billy*, 131; Scarborough, *On the Trail*, 85–87; Leadbelly, *Where Did You Sleep*, tracks 12, 33.

72. Scarborough, *On the Trail*, 86.

73. Odum and Johnson, *Negro Workaday Songs*, 49–55; *Southern Journey*, vol. 5 has three versions, tracks 2, 10, and 17, the latter made famous as the opening to *O Brother, Where Art Thou?* Listen also to Vera Ward Hall on *Deep River of Song: Alabama*, track 3.

74. Luke 16:19–31; John 11–12.

75. N. Cohen, *Long Steel Rail*, 122–31; for recorded versions, listen to Hobart Smith on *Southern Journey*, 5:3, and Vera Ward Hall on *Deep River of Song: Alabama*, track 2.

76. N. Cohen, *Long Steel Rail*, 124–25.

77. Brown, chapter 9, "We Did Them Wrong," in Wilentz and Marcus, *Rose and the Briar*.

78. Wilentz, chapter 10, "Sad Song," in Wilentz and Marcus, *Rose and the Briar*; McTell, "Delia" on *Atlanta Twelve String*, track 3. For lyrics, see N. White, *American Negro Folk-Songs*, 215–16, and *The Mudcat Café*, http://www.mudcat.org.

79. For recordings, listen to Leadbelly, *Bourgeois Blues*, track 28; the Carter Family on Smith, *Anthology*, 2:3; Boggs, *His Folkway Years*, 2:15; Glenn Yarborough, *Come and Sit by My Side*, B:4. For lyrics, see Lomax and Lomax, *American Ballads*, 124–26; Randolph, *Ozark Folksongs*, 2:144–47; Sharp, *English Folk Songs*, 2:35–36.

80. N. Cohen, *Long Steel Rail*, 66–69; N. White, *American Negro Folk-Songs*, 189–90.

81. N. Cohen, *Long Steel Rail*, 117–21; Randolph, *Ozark Folksongs*, 2:12–16; Ed Crain on Smith, *Anthology*, 2:1; Boggs, *His Folkway Years*, 1:19; Oscar Gilbert on *Southern Journey*, 5:12.

82. N. Cohen, *Long Steel Rail*, 119, suggests the Younger–James alliance may have been exaggerated and that Cole and Jesse did not like each other.

83. A. Lomax, *Folk Songs*, 264–66, 273–74; Randolph, *Ozark Folksongs*, 2:29–32; Kelly Harrel on Smith, *Anthology*, 2:2. Lomax refers to *Rodgers* as *Rogers*.

84. Lomax and Lomax, *American Ballads*, 136–38.

Chapter 8. How Can I Keep from Singing?
Huddie Ledbetter and Woody Guthrie

1. Wolfe and Lornell, *Leadbelly*, 216.

2. Pascal, "Walt Whitman and Woody Guthrie," 41–59.

3. Leadbelly, *Last Sessions*, 2:6.

4. Sandburg, *American Songbag*, xiv.

5. Cantwell, *When We Were Good*, 328.

6. My comments on Leadbelly are taken from Wolfe and Lornell, *Leadbelly*, and liner notes from various recordings.

7. Leadbelly, *Where Did You Sleep*, tracks 18, 19; *Bourgeois Blues*, track 22.

8. Leadbelly, *Where Did You Sleep*, tracks 22, 23.

9. Leadbelly, *Bourgeois Blues*, track 8.

10. Ibid., track 24.

11. Ibid., track 1.

12. For a selection of Jefferson's songs, listen to *The Best of Blind Lemon Jefferson*.

13. Leadbelly, *Bourgeois Blues*, track 8.

14. For this encounter, see Wolfe and Lornell, *Leadbelly*, 114.

15. For the story from the Lomax perspective, see Porterfield, *Last Cavalier*.

16. Leadbelly, *Bourgeois Blues*, track 2.

17. The material for Guthrie's life has been taken from Klein, *Woody Guthrie*. See also Santelli and Davidson, eds., *Hard Travelin'* and Cray, *Ramblin' Man*.

18. Santelli and Davidson, *Hard Travelin'*, 4.

19. The four CDs of the *Asch Recordings* contain many of Guthrie's best-known songs. A fine collection of the best of Guthrie and Leadbelly, sung by many contemporary artists, is *A Vision Shared: A Tribute to Woody Guthrie and Leadbelly*, available on both CD and DVD.

20. Klein, *Woody Guthrie*, 140–41.

21. Ibid., 158–59.

22. Cantwell, "Fanfare," in Santelli and Davidson, *Hard Travelin'*, 160.

23. Odetta, *Lookin' for a Home* is a good place to start.

24. Cotton, *Elizabeth Cotton*.

Coda: Thinking about Folk Songs

1. Epstein, *Sinful Tunes*. Part 3 contains an excellent discussion of the origins of the work.

2. Introductory remarks in the booklet accompanying Smith, *Anthology*.

3. Odum and Johnson, *Negro and His Songs*; Odum and Johnson, *Negro Workaday Songs*; Scarborough, *On the Trail*; N. White, *American Negro Folk-Songs*.

4. N. Cohen, *Long Steel Rail*.

5. Turner, *Amazing Grace*.

6. Wolfe and Lornell, *Leadbelly*; Zwonitzer, *Will You Miss Me?*

7. Cantwell, *When We Were Good*, "Prologue: Tom Dooley"; Filene, *Romancing the Folk*; Chase, *America's Music*; Crawford, *America's Musical Life*; Southern, *Music of Black Americans: A History*.

8. John Mack Faragher, *Sugar Creek* (New Haven, Conn.: Yale University Press, 1986).

9. Jack Larkin, *Reshaping of Everyday Life*.

10. Levine, "Slave Songs," 99–130; Levine, *Black Culture*, 407–20. John Blassingame has also used folk songs in chapter 2, "Culture," of *The Slave Community: Plantation Life in the Antebellum South* (New York: Oxford University Press, 1972).

11. Wilentz and Marcus, *Rose and the Briar*.

12. Forcucci, *Folk Song History* attempts to do this but suffers from the musically trained author's relative lack of knowledge of the history.

13. Turner, *Amazing Grace*, chapter 7, "Meeting the Music."

14. A. Lomax, *Selected Writings*, chapter 18, "Folk Song Style."

Select Bibliography and Discography

General Books and Articles

Bronson, Bertrand. "Samuel Hall's Family Tree." *California Folklore Quarterly* 1 (January 1942): 47–64.

Brown, Cecil. *Stagolee Shot Billy.* Cambridge, Mass.: Harvard University Press, 2003.

Cantwell, Robert. *When We Were Good: The Folk Revival.* Cambridge, Mass.: Harvard University Press, 1996.

Chase, Gilbert. *America's Music: From the Pilgrims to the Present.* 3rd ed. Urbana: University of Illinois Press, 1987.

Cleveland, Les. *Dark Laughter: War in Song and Popular Culture.* Westport, Conn.: Praeger, 1994.

Cohen, Anne B. *Poor Pearl, Poor Girl! The Murdered Girl Stereotype in Ballad and Newspapers.* Austin: University of Texas Press, 1973.

Cohen, Norm. *Long Steel Rail: The Railroad in American Folksong.* 2nd ed. Urbana: University of Illinois Press, 2000.

Crawford, Richard. *America's Musical Life: A History.* New York: W. W. Norton, 2001.

Cray, Ed. *Ramblin' Man: The Life and Times of Woody Guthrie.* New York: W. W. Norton, 2004.

D'Avanzo, Mario. "Bobbie Allen and the Ballad Tradition in *Light in August.*" *South Carolina Review* 8 (1975–76): 22–29.

DuBois, W. E. B. *The Souls of Black Folk: Essays and Sketches.* Chicago: A. C. McClury, 1903.

Dylan, Bob. *Chronicles, Volume One.* New York: Simon and Schuster, 2004.

Epstein, Dena J. *Sinful Tunes and Spirituals: Black Folk Music to the Civil War.* Urbana: University of Illinois Press, 1977.

Filene, Benjamin. *Romancing the Folk: Public Memory and American Roots Music.* Chapel Hill: University of North Carolina Press, 2000.

Finson, Jon. *The Voices That Are Gone: Themes in Nineteenth-Century American Popular Song.* New York: Oxford University Press, 1994.

Foner, Philip S. *American Labor Songs of the Nineteenth Century.* Urbana: University of Illinois Press, 1975.

Forcucci, Samuel L. *A Folk Song History of America: America through Its Songs.* Englewood Cliffs, N.J.: Prentice Hall, 1984.

Gioia, Ted. "The Big Roundup." *American Scholar* 74 (Spring 2005): 101–11.

Green, Archie. *Only a Miner: Studies in Recorded Coal-Mining Songs.* Urbana: University of Illinois Press, 1972.

Hinton, Sam. "Folk Songs of Faith." *Sing Out* 16 (February/March 1966): 31–37.

Hobsbawm, Eric. "The Social Bandit." Chap. 2 in *Primitive Rebels.* New York: Praeger, 1959.

Hudson, Arthur P. "Songs of the North Carolina Regulators." *William and Mary Quarterly* 4 (1947): 470–85.

Klein, Joe. *Woody Guthrie: A Life.* New York: Knopf, 1980.

Koppelman, Robert, ed. *"Sing Out, Warning! Sing Out, Love!": The Writings of Lee Hays.* Amherst: University of Massachusetts Press, 2003.

Laws, G. Malcolm. *Native American Balladry: A Descriptive Study and a Bibliographical Syllabus.* Rev. ed. Philadelphia: The American Folklore Society, 1964.

Lemay, J. A. "The American Origins of 'Yankee Doodle.'" *William and Mary Quarterly* 33 (1976): 435–64.

Levine, Lawrence. "Slave Songs and Slave Consciousness: Explorations in Neglected Sources." Chap. 3 in *The Unpredictable Past: Explorations in American Cultural History.* New York: Oxford University Press, 1993.

Lomax, Alan. *Alan Lomax: Selected Writings, 1934–1997.* Edited by Ronald D. Cohen. New York: Routledge, 2003.

———. *The Land Where the Blues Began.* New York: Pantheon, 1993.

Marcus, Greil. *Invisible Republic: Bob Dylan's Basement Tapes.* New York: H. Holt, 1997.

———. *Mystery Train: Images of America in Rock 'n' Roll Music.* 3rd ed. London: Omnibus Press, 1990.

Marini, Stephen A. *Sacred Song in America: Religion, Music, and Public Culture.* Urbana: University of Illinois Press, 2003.

Nelson, Scott. *Steel Drivin' Man: John Henry—The Untold Story of an American Legend.* New York: Oxford University Press, 2006.

———. "Who Was John Henry? Railroad Construction, Southern Folklore, and the Birth of Rock and Roll." *Labor: Studies in Working Class History of the Americas* 2 (Summer 2005): 53–79.

Olmsted, Tony. *Folkway Records: Moses Asch and His Encyclopedia of Sound.* New York: Routledge, 2003.

Oshinsky, David M. *"Worse Than Slavery": Parchman Farmer and the Ordeal of Jim Crow Justice.* New York: Free Press, 1996.

Pascal, Richard. "Walt Whitman and Woody Guthrie: American Prophet-Singers and Their People." *Journal of American Studies* 24 (1990): 41–59.

Patterson, Daniel W. *The Shaker Spiritual.* Princeton, N.J.: Princeton University Press, 1979.

Pearson, Barry Lee, and Bill McCulloch. *Robert Johnson: Lost and Found.* Urbana: University of Illinois Press, 2003.

Porterfield, Nolan. *Last Cavalier: The Life and Times of John A. Lomax.* Urbana: University of Illinois Press, 1996.

Renwick, Roger. *Recentering Anglo/American Folksong: Sea Crabs and Wicked Youth.* Jackson: University of Mississippi Press, 2001.

Santelli, Robert, and Emily Davidson, eds. *Hard Travelin': The Life and Legacy of Woody Guthrie*. Hanover, N.H.: Wesleyan University Press, 1999.

Schlesinger, Arthur M. "A Note on Songs as Patriot Propaganda." *William and Mary Quarterly* 11 (1954): 78–88.

Southern, Eileen. *The Music of Black Americans: A History*. 3rd ed. New York: W. W. Norton, 1997.

Stowe, David. *How Sweet the Sound: Music in the Spiritual Lives of Americans*. Cambridge, Mass.: Harvard University Press, 2004.

Tawa, Nicholas. *High-Minded and Low-Down: Music in the Lives of Americans*. Boston: Northeastern University Press, 2000.

Thompson, Harold W. *Body, Boots and Britches*. Philadelphia: J. P. Lippincott, 1940.

Toelken, Barre. *Morning Dew and Roses: Nuance, Metaphor, and Meaning in Folksongs*. Urbana: University of Illinois Press, 1995.

Tolman, Albert H., and Mary O. Eddy. "Traditional Texts and Tunes." *Journal of American Folk Lore* 35 (1922): 335–432.

Turner, Steve. *Amazing Grace: The Story of America's Most Beloved Song*. New York: HarperCollins, 2002.

West, John Foster. *Lift Up Your Head, Tom Dooley: The True Story of the Appalachian Murder That Inspired One of America's Most Popular Ballads*. Asheboro, N.C.: Down Home Press, 1993.

White, John I. *Git Along, Little Dogies: Songs and Songmakers of the American West*. Urbana: University of Illinois Press, 1975.

White, Shane, and Graham White. *The Sounds of Slavery: Discovering African American History through Songs, Sermons, and Speech*. Boston: Beacon Press, 2005. Book and CD.

Wilentz, Sean, and Greil Marcus, eds. *The Rose and the Briar: Death, Love, and Liberty in the American Ballad*. New York: W. W. Norton, 2005. Book and CD.

Wilgus, D. K. *Anglo-American Folksong Scholarship since 1898*. New Brunswick, N.J.: Rutgers University Press, 1959.

Willens, Doris. *Lonesome Traveler: The Life of Lee Hays*. New York: W. W. Norton, 1988.

Wolfe, Charles, and Kip Lornell. *The Life and Legend of Leadbelly*. New York: HarperCollins, 1992.

Zwonitzer, Mark. *Will You Miss Me When I'm Gone? The Carter Family and Their Legacy in American Music*. With Charles Hirshberg. New York: Simon and Schuster, 2002.

Songbooks

Allen, William F., Charles P. Ware, and Lucy M. Garrison, comps. *Slave Songs of the United States*. 1867. Reprint, Bedford, Mass.: Applewood Books, 1995.

Asch, Moses, and Alan Lomax, eds. *The Leadbelly Songbook*. New York: Oak Publications, 1962.

Cazden, Norman, et al., eds. *Folk Songs of the Catskills*. Albany: State University of New York Press, 1982.

Child, Francis James, ed. *The English and Scottish Popular Ballads*. 10 vols. Boston: Houghton, Mifflin, 1882–98.

Cohen, Norm. *Long Steel Rail: The Railroad in American Folksong*. 2nd ed. Urbana: University of Illinois Press, 2000.

Cray, Ed, comp. *The Erotic Muse: American Bawdy Songs*. 2nd ed. Urbana: University of Illinois Press, 1992.

Firth, C. H., ed. *An American Garland, Being a Collection of Ballads Relating to America, 1563–1759*. Oxford: B. H. Blackwell, 1915.

Flanders, Helen H. *Ancient Ballads Traditionally Sung in New England*. 4 vols. Philadelphia: University of Pennsylvania Press, 1960.

Flanders, Helen H., and Marguerite Olney, comps. *Ballads Migrant in New England*. New York: Farrar, Straus and Young, 1953.

Foner, Philip S. *American Labor Songs of the Nineteenth Century*. Urbana: University of Illinois Press, 1975.

Friedman, Albert B., ed. *The Viking Book of Folk Ballads of the English-Speaking World*. New York: Viking Press, 1956.

Gordon, Robert W. *Folk-Songs of America*. Sponsored by the Joint Committee on Folk Arts, WPA. New York: National Services Bureau, 1938. Originally published in fifteen installments in the *New York Times Sunday Magazine* (January 1927–January 1928).

Green, Archie. *Only a Miner: Studies in Recorded Coal-Mining Songs*. Urbana: University of Illinois Press, 1972.

Jackson, Bruce, ed. *Wake Up Dead Man: Afro-American Worksongs from Texas Prisons*. Cambridge, Mass.: Harvard University Press, 1972.

Jackson, George S. *Early Songs of Uncle Sam*. Boston: Bruce Humphries, 1933.

Lingenfelter, Richard, and Richard Dwyer. *Songs of the American West*. Berkeley: University of California Press, 1968.

Logsdon, Guy, ed. *"The Whorehouse Bells Were Ringing" and Other Songs Cowboys Sing*. Urbana: University of Illinois Press, 1989.

Lomax, Alan. *The Folk Songs of North America in the English Language*. New York: Doubleday, 1960.

Lomax, John, and Alan Lomax. *American Ballads and Folk Songs*. 1934. Reprint, New York: Dover, 1994.

———. *Cowboy Songs and Other Frontier Ballads*. Rev. ed. New York: Macmillan, 1948.

———. *Our Singing Country: Folk Songs and Ballads*. 1941. Reprint, Mineola, N.Y.: Dover Press, 2000.

Moore, Frank. *Songs and Ballads of the American Revolution*. 1856. Reprint, New York: New York Times, 1969.

Odum, Howard, and Guy Johnson. *The Negro and His Songs: A Study of the Typical Negro Songs in the South*. Chapel Hill: University of North Carolina Press, 1925.

———. *Negro Workaday Songs*. Chapel Hill: University of North Carolina Press, 1926.

Randolph, Vance. *Blow the Candle Out: "Unprintable" Ozark Folksongs and Folklore*. Vol. 2, *Folk Rhymes and Other Lore*. Edited by G. Legman. Fayetteville: University of Arkansas Press, 1992.

————, ed. *Ozark Folksongs.* 4 vols. Rev. ed. Columbia: University of Missouri Press, 1980.

————. *Roll Me in Your Arms: "Unprintable" Ozark Folksongs and Folklore.* Vol. 1, *Folksongs and Music.* Edited by G. Legman. Fayetteville: University of Arkansas Press, 1992.

Rickaby, Franz, ed. *Ballads and Songs of the Shanty-Boy.* Cambridge, Mass.: Harvard University Press, 1926.

Ritchie, Jean. *Folk Songs of the Southern Appalachians.* 2nd ed. Lexington: University of Kentucky Press, 1997.

Sandburg, Carl. *The American Songbag.* 1927. Reprint, New York: Harcourt Brace, 1990.

Scarborough, Dorothy. *On the Trail of Negro Folk-Songs.* Cambridge, Mass.: Harvard University Press, 1925.

————. *A Song Catcher in Southern Mountains: American Folk Songs of British Ancestry.* New York: Columbia University Press, 1937.

Schinhan, Jan P., ed. *The Music of the Folk Songs.* Vol. 5, *The Frank C. Brown Collection in North Carolina Folklore.* Durham, N.C.: Duke University Press, 1962.

Scott, John Anthony. "Ballads and Broadsides of the American Revolution." *Sing Out!* 16 (April/May 1966): 18–23.

Seeger, Pete. *American Favorite Ballads.* New York: Oak Publications, 1961.

Sharp, Cecil, comp. *English Folk Songs from the Southern Appalachians.* Edited by Maude Karpeles. 2 vols. New York: Oxford University Press, 1932.

Warner, Anne, ed. *Traditional American Folk Songs from the Collection of Anne and Frank Warner.* Syracuse, N.Y.: Syracuse University Press, 1984.

Wheeler, Mary. *Steamboatin' Days: Folk Songs of the River Packet Era.* Baton Rouge: Louisiana State University Press, 1944.

White, Newman I. *American Negro Folk-Songs.* Cambridge, Mass.: Harvard University Press, 1928.

Work, John W. *American Negro Songs.* 1940. Reprint, Mineola, N.Y.: Dover Press, 1998.

Wright, Rochelle, and Robert L. Wright. *Danish Emigrant Ballads and Songs.* Carbondale: Southern Illinois University Press, 1983.

Recorded Music

The Almanac Singers. *Their Complete General Recordings.* CD. MCAD-11499.

American Roots Music. 4 DVDs. Palm Pictures DVD 3039-2.

America's Folk Heritage. Various artists. 6 records. Murray Hill S-4196.

Baez, Joan. *Classics.* Vol. 8. A and M CD 2506.

————. *Diamonds and Rust.* LP. A and M SP-3233.

————. *Farewell Angelina.* LP. Vanguard VSD 79200.

————. *The Joan Baez Ballad Book.* 2 records. Vanguard VSD 41/42.

————. *Lovesong Album.* 2 records. Vanguard VSD 79/80.

The Blues: The Gold Collection: 40 Classic Performances. Various artists. 2 CDs. Retro R2CD 40-08.

Boggs, Dock. *Dock Boggs: His Folkway Years.* 2 CDs. Smithsonian Folkways SF 40108.

The Carter Family. *The Carter Family, 1927–1934.* JSP Records CD JSPCD7701A-E.
———. *Wildwood Flower.* Living Era, ASV CD AJA 5323.
Cohen, John. *That High Lonesome Sound.* Videotape. Shanachie VHS 1404.
Cotton, Elizabeth. *Elizabeth Cotton.* Videotape. Vestapol 13019.
Dalhart, Vernon. *Inducted into the Hall of Fame: 1981.* King CD KSCD-3820.
Deep River of Song. Early Lomax field recordings. Rounder. 5 CDs.
   Alabama. CD 11661-1829-2.
   Georgia. CD 11661-1828-2.
   Mississippi. CD 11661-1824-2.
   Texas. CD 11661-1826-2.
   Virginia. CD 11661-1827-2.
Friends of Old Time Music: The Folk Arrival, 1961–1965. 3 CDs. Smithsonian Folk-
   ways SFW CD 40160.
Gladden, Texas. *Ballad Legacy.* Rounder CD 11661-1800-2.
The Great Blues Men. Various artists. 2 records. Vanguard VSD 25/26.
Greatest Folksingers of the Sixties. Vanguard VCD 17/18.
Guthrie, Woody. *The Asch Recordings.* 4 CDs. Smithsonian Folkways SFW CD
   40112. The four CDs in this set are titled *This Land Is Your Land, Muleskinner
   Blues, Hard Travelin',* and *Buffalo Skinners.*
———. *The Greatest Songs of Woody Guthrie.* Various artists. 2 records. Vanguard
   VSD 35/36.
———. *Hard Travelin'.* Arloco LP ARL-284.
———. *The Live Wire.* Woody Guthrie Foundation. CD.
———. *Woody Guthrie.* Archive of Folk Music LP FS-204.
Houston, Cisco. *The Best of the Vanguard Years.* Vanguard CD 79574-2.
Hurt, Mississippi John. *Avalon Blues: A Tribute to the Music of John Hurt.* Van-
   guard CD 79582-2.
———. *The Complete Studio Recordings.* 3 CDs. Vanguard CD 181/83-2.
———. *Satisfied . . . Live.* Boomerang CD BEA-51577.
———. *Worried Blues, 1963.* Rounder CD 1082.
Jefferson, Blind Lemon. *The Best of Blind Lemon Jefferson.* Yazoo CD 2057.
The Jerry Garcia Acoustic Band. *Almost Acoustic.* GDM GDCD4005.
Johnson, Robert. *The Complete Recordings.* 2 CDs. Columbia C2K 46222.
The Kingston Trio. *The Best of the Kinston Trio.* Capitol LP T 1705.
———. *College Concert.* Capitol LP T 1658.
———. *Greatest Hits.* Curb CD D2-77385.
———. *Here We Go Again!* Capitol LP T 1258.
———. *Sold Out.* Capitol LP ST 1352.
———. *Stringing Along with the Kingston Trio.* Capitol LP T 1407.
Ledbetter, Huddie (Leadbelly). *Bourgeois Blues.* Smithsonian Folkways SF CD
   40045.
———. *Last Sessions.* 4 CDs. Smithsonian Folkways SF CD 40068/71.
———. *Leadbelly.* Archive of Folk Music LP FS-202.
———. *The Legendary Leadbelly.* Olympic LP 7103.
———. *Where Did You Sleep Last Night.* Smithsonian Folkways SF CD 40044.
Lomax, Alan. *Blues in the Mississippi Night.* Rounder CD 82161-1860-2.

———. *Blues Songbook.* Rounder CD 82161-1866-2.

———. *Collection Sampler.* Rounder CD 1700.

———. *The Land Where the Blues Began.* Rounder CD 82161-1861-2.

Lunsford, Bascum Lamar. *Ballads, Banjo Tunes, and Sacred Songs of Western North Carolina.* Smithsonian Folkways SF CD 40082.

Makeba, Miriam (for African roots). *Africa.* Novus CD 3155-2-N.

———. *Miriam Makeba.* RCA Victor LP LPM-2267.

———. *Pata Pata.* Reprise/Warner LP 6274.

McTell, Willie. *Atlanta Twelve String.* Atlantic CD 82366-2.

Monroe, Bill. *The Best of Bill Monroe.* MCA CD 088 170 190-2.

Norumbega Harmony. *Sing and Joyful Be.* Norumbega Harmony CD NBH-0001.

O Brother, Where Art Thou? CD, Mercury 088 170-069-2; Videotape, Touchstone VHS 24194. See also *Down from the Mountain* (Artisan VHS 12225), a videotape of the music from the film performed in concert.

Odetta. *Best of the Vanguard Years.* Vanguard CD 79522-2.

———. *Lookin' for a Home: Thanks to Leadbelly.* M.C. Records CD MC-0044.

Ritchie, Jean. *Child Ballads in America.* 2 CDs. Folkways F-2301/2302.

Ritchie, Jean, and Doc Watson. *Jean Ritchie and Doc Watson at Folk City.* Smithsonian Folkways SF CD 40005.

Rodgers, Jimmie. *The Singing Brakeman.* IMC CD CTS 55459.

Rose, Jennifer. *Kentucky Home Tonight.* Jennifer Rose Music CD JR-395.

———. *Morning Will Come.* Jennifer Rose Music CD JRM799.

Seeger, Mike. *Southern Banjo Sounds.* CD. Smithsonian Folkways SFW CS 40107.

Seeger, Pete. *The Bitter and the Sweet.* Columbia LP CL 1916.

———. *Darling Corey and Goofing-Off Suite.* Smithsonian Folkways CD SF 40018.

———. *I Can See a New Day.* Columbia LP CL 2257.

———. *Pete Seeger.* Archive of Folk Music LP FS-201.

———. *Pete Seeger and Friends.* Earth Music CD LMUS 0032.

———. *Story Songs.* Columbia LP CL 1668.

———. *Waist Deep in the Big Muddy and Other Love Songs.* Columbia LP CS 9505.

———. *We Shall Overcome.* Columbia LP CL 2101.

———. *Young vs. Old.* Columbia LP CS 9873.

Seeger, Pete, and Arlo Guthrie. *Together in Concert.* 2 records. Warner Brothers 2R2214.

Smith, Harry. *Anthology of American Folk Music.* 6 CDs. Smithsonian Folkways CD FP 251/252/253.

———. *Anthology of American Folk Music Volume 4.* 2 CDs. Revenant/Harry Smith Archives 211.

———. *The Harry Smith Project: Anthology of American Folk Music Revisited.* 2 CDs and 2 DVDs. Shout 826663-10041.

Smith, Hobart. *Blue Ridge Legacy.* Rounder CD 1799.

Songcatcher. Videotape. Lion's Gate VM 7541.

Southern Journey. Field recordings by Alan Lomax in the 1950s and 1960s. Rounder.

Vol. 1. *Voices from the American South.* CD 1701.

Vol. 2. *Ballads and Breakdowns.* CD 1702.

Vol. 3. *61 Highway Mississippi.* CD 1703.
Vol. 4. *Brethren, We Meet Again.* CD 1704.
Vol. 5. *Bad Man Ballads.* CD 1705.
Vol. 6. *Sheep, Sheep Don'tcha Know the Road.* CD 1706.
Vol. 7. *Ozark Frontier.* CD 1707.
Vol. 8. *Velvet Voices.* CD 1708.
Vol. 9. *Harp of a Thousand Strings.* CD 1709.
Vol. 10. *And Glory Shone Around.* CD 1710.
Vol. 11. *Honor the Lamb.* CD 1711.
Vol. 12. *Georgia Sea Islands.* CD 1712.
Vol. 13. *Earliest Times.* CD 1713.
A Vision Shared: A Tribute to Woody Guthrie and Leadbelly. Various artists. CD, Columbia CD 44034; DVD, Columbia 49006.
Watson, Doc. *Doc Watson on Stage.* Vanguard CD VCD 9/10.
———. *Elementary Doc Watson / Then and Now.* Collectables CD COL-5839.
———. *The Essential Doc Watson.* Vanguard CD VCD-45/46.
———. *Rare Performances, 1963–1981.* Videotape. Vestapol 13023.
———. *Third Generation Blues.* With Richard Watson. Sugar Hill CD SUG-CD 3893.
Watson, Doc, and Clarence Ashley. *The Original Folkways Recordings, 1960–62.* 2 CDs. Smithsonian Folkways SF 40029/30.
The Weavers. *Almanac.* Vanguard LP VRS 9100.
———. *At Carnegie Hall.* Vanguard LP VRS 9010.
———. *At Home.* Vanguard LP VRS 9024.
———. *On Tour.* Vanguard LP VSD 6537.
———. *Together Again.* Loom Records LP 1681.
———. *Wasn't That a Time.* 4 CDs, Vanguard VCD4-147/50.
———. *Wasn't That a Time.* Videotape. Warner 38304-3.
———. *The Weavers Reunion at Carnegie Hall—1963.* Vanguard LP VSD 2150.
———. *The Weavers Reunion at Carnegie Hall, Part 2.* Vanguard LP VSD 79161.
White, Josh. *The House I Live In.* Elektra LP EKL-203.
———. *In Memoriam.* Everest LP 2094.
Wilentz, Sean, and Greil Marcus, eds. *The Rose and the Briar: Death, Love and Liberty in the American Ballad.* Columbia Legacy CD CK 92866.
Yarborough, Glen. *Come and Sit by My Side.* LP. Tradition Records TLP 1019.

Index

ROBERT V. WELLS is the Chauncey H. Winters Professor of History and Social Sciences at Union College in Schenectady, New York. He is the author of *Revolutions in Americans' Lives: A Demographic Perspective on the History of Americans, Their Families, and Their Society; Facing the "King of Terrors": Death and Society in an American Community, 1750–1990*; and *Uncle Sam's Family: Issues in and Perspectives on American Demographic History.* He has enjoyed singing folk songs for half a century.

MUSIC IN AMERICAN LIFE

America's Music: From the Pilgrims to the Present (rev. 3d ed.)   *Gilbert Chase*

Secular Music in Colonial Annapolis: The Tuesday Club, 1745–56
   John Barry Talley

Bibliographical Handbook of American Music   *D. W. Krummel*

Goin' to Kansas City   *Nathan W. Pearson, Jr.*

"Susanna," "Jeanie," and "The Old Folks at Home": The Songs of Stephen C.
   Foster from His Time to Ours (2d ed.)   *William W. Austin*

Songprints: The Musical Experience of Five Shoshone Women   *Judith Vander*

"Happy in the Service of the Lord": Afro-American Gospel Quartets
   in Memphis   *Kip Lornell*

Paul Hindemith in the United States   *Luther Noss*

"My Song Is My Weapon": People's Songs, American Communism, and the
   Politics of Culture, 1930–50   *Robbie Lieberman*

Chosen Voices: The Story of the American Cantorate   *Mark Slobin*

Theodore Thomas: America's Conductor and Builder of Orchestras, 1835–1905
   Ezra Schabas

"The Whorehouse Bells Were Ringing" and Other Songs Cowboys Sing
   Collected and Edited by Guy Logsdon

Crazeology: The Autobiography of a Chicago Jazzman   *Bud Freeman,
   as Told to Robert Wolf*

Discoursing Sweet Music: Brass Bands and Community Life in Turn-of-the-
   Century Pennsylvania   *Kenneth Kreitner*

Mormonism and Music: A History   *Michael Hicks*

Voices of the Jazz Age: Profiles of Eight Vintage Jazzmen   *Chip Deffaa*

Pickin' on Peachtree: A History of Country Music in Atlanta, Georgia
   Wayne W. Daniel

Bitter Music: Collected Journals, Essays, Introductions, and Librettos
   Harry Partch; edited by Thomas McGeary

Ethnic Music on Records: A Discography of Ethnic Recordings Produced in
   the United States, 1893 to 1942   *Richard K. Spottswood*

Downhome Blues Lyrics: An Anthology from the Post–World War II Era
   Jeff Todd Titon

Ellington: The Early Years   *Mark Tucker*

Chicago Soul   *Robert Pruter*

That Half-Barbaric Twang: The Banjo in American Popular Culture
   Karen Linn

Hot Man: The Life of Art Hodes   *Art Hodes and Chadwick Hansen*

The Erotic Muse: American Bawdy Songs (2d ed.)   *Ed Cray*

Barrio Rhythm: Mexican American Music in Los Angeles   *Steven Loza*

The Creation of Jazz: Music, Race, and Culture in Urban America
   Burton W. Peretti

Charles Martin Loeffler: A Life Apart in Music   *Ellen Knight*

The University of Illinois Press
is a founding member of the
Association of American University Presses.

Composed in 9/13 ITC Stone Serif
with ITC Stone Sans display
by Jim Proefrock
at the University of Illinois Press
Manufactured by Cushing-Malloy, Inc.

University of Illinois Press
1325 South Oak Street
Champaign, IL 61820-6903
www.press.uillinois.edu